Dewey Decimal Classification

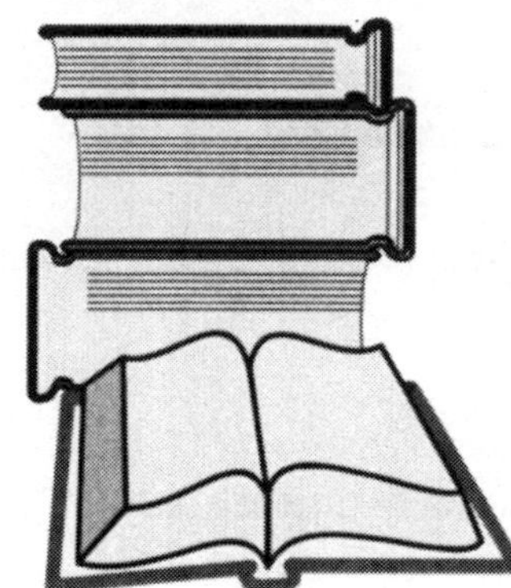

22nd Edition

A Study Manual and Number Building Guide

Mona L. Scott

Westport, Connecticut • London

Library of Congress Cataloging-in-Publication Data

Scott, Mona L.
Dewey Decimal classification, 22nd edition : a study manual and number building guide / by Mona L. Scott.
p. cm.
Includes bibliographical references and index.
ISBN 1-59158-210-5 (alk. paper)
1. Classification, Dewey decimal—Handbooks, manuals, etc. I. Title.
Z696.D7S36 2005
025.4'31—dc22 2004063829

British Library Cataloguing in Publication Data is available.

Library of Congress Catalog Card Number: 2004063829
ISBN: 1-59158-210-5

First published in 2005

Libraries Unlimited, 88 Post Road West, Westport, CT 06881
A Member of the Greenwood Publishing Group, Inc.
www.lu.com

Printed in the United States of America

The paper used in this book complies with the Permanent Paper Standard issued by the National Information Standards Organization (Z39.48–1984).

10 9 8 7 6 5 4 3 2 1

Contents

Preface xi

1—DDC History and Current Status 1
The Modern History of DDC 3
OCLC Forest Press and the Editorial Policy Committee 8
DDC Activities at the Library of Congress 8
DDC's International Presence 10
The DDC Today 11
Literature Cited 12

2—General Aspects of the Dewey Decimal Classification 15
DDC's Theory of Knowledge 15
DDC's Structure (the Schedules) 17
Hierarchical Order 17
Centered Entries 18
Broad and Close Classification 19
Relative Index 19
The Manual 22
Types of Changes Found in *DDC* 22 23
Expansions 23
Discontinuations 24
Relocations 24
Overview of *DDC* 22 Revisions 25
Literature Cited 26

3—Principles of Number Building 27
Principles of Book Classification 27
The Theory of Number Building 29
Notes 29
Tables 31
Options 33
Classifying and Building Numbers 33
Literature Cited 34

4—The Tables 35
Table 1. Standard Subdivisions 36
Table 1 Summary and Applications 37
Citation Order 37

DDC 22 Table 1 Revisions 39
Table 2. Geographic Areas, Historical Periods, Persons 41
Table 2 Summary and Applications. 41
DDC 22 Table 2 Revisions 43
Table 3. Subdivisions for the Arts, for Individual Literatures, for Specific Literary Forms 85
Table 3A 85
Table 3B. 86
Table 3C. 86
DDC 22 Table 3 Revisions 87
Table 4. Subdivisions of Individual Languages and Language Families. . 88
Table 4 Summary and Applications. 89
DDC 22 Table 4 Revisions 89
Table 5. Ethnic and National Groups. 92
Table 5 Summary and Applications. 92
DDC 22 Table 5 Revisions 93
Table 6. Languages 95
Table 6 Summary and Applications. 95
DDC 22 Table 6 Revisions 96
Literature Cited 104

5—Class 000: Generalities 105
Summary and Details of Class 000 108
The Number Building Process 110
DDC 22 Class 000 Revisions. 111
004–006 Computers Revisions 111
010 Bibliographies Revisions 113
020 Library Sciences Revisions. 114
030–060 Serials and Museums Revisions 116
070–080 Journalism and General Collections Revisions. 117
Exercises in the Use of Class 000 119
Literature Cited 119

6—Class 100: Philosophy, Parapsychology and Occultism, Psychology. . . . 121
Summary and Details of Class 100 122
The Number Building Process 124
DDC 22 Class 100 Revisions. 125
130–150 Parapsychology and Psychology Revisions 125
170–190 Ethics and Philosophy Revisions 126
Exercises in the Use of Class 100 127
Literature Cited 128

7—Class 200: Religion 129
Summary and Details of Class 200 130
The Number Building Process 132
DDC 22 Class 200 Revisions 133
Exercises in the Use of Class 200 144
Literature Cited 145

8—Class 300: Social Sciences 147
Summary and Details of Class 300 148
The Number Building Process 152
DDC 22 Class 300 Revisions 152
300 Social Sciences Revisions 153
320 Political Science Revisions 162
330 Economics Revisions 166
340 Law Revisions 176
350 Public Administration and Military Science Revisions 186
360 Social Problems, Services, and Associations Revisions 187
370 Education Revisions 188
380 Commerce, Communications, Transportation Revisions 188
390 Customs, Etiquette, Folklore Revisions 192
Exercises in the Use of Class 300 194
Literature Cited 195

9—Class 400: Language 197
Summary and Details of Class 400 197
The Number Building Process 198
DDC 22 Class 400 Revisions 199
Exercises in the Use of Class 400 207
Literature Cited 208

10—Class 500: Natural Sciences and Mathematics 209
Summary and Details of Class 500 209
The Number Building Process 213
DDC 22 Class 500 Revisions 213
510 Mathematics Revisions 213
520–530 Astronomy and Physics Revisions 220
540 Chemistry and Allied Sciences Revisions 221
550 Earth Sciences Revisions 227
560–590 Life Sciences Revisions 229
Exercises in the Use of Class 500 235
Literature Cited 235

11—Class 600: Technology (Applied Sciences) 237
Summary and Details of Class 600 238
The Number Building Process 241
DDC 22 class 600 Revisions 242
610 Medicine Revisions. 242
620–630 Engineering and Agriculture Revisions 246
640 Home and Family Management Revisions 249
650 Management and Auxiliary Services 252
660 Chemical Engineering Revisions 257
Exercises in the Use of Class 600 258
Literature Cited 259

12—Class 700: The Arts; Fine and Decorative Arts 261
Summary and Details of Class 700 262
The Number Building Process 265
DDC 22 Class 700 Revisions 266
700–776 Fine and Decorative Arts Revisions 266
780 Music Revisions 269
790 Recreation and Performing Arts Revisions. 270
Exercises in the Use of Class 700 271
Literature Cited 272

13—Class 800: Literature (Belles-Lettres) and Rhetoric 273
Summary and Details of Class 800 275
The Number Building Process 276
DDC 22 Class 800 Revisions 276
Exercises in the Use of Class 800 279
Literature Cited 279

14—Class 900: History, Geography, and Auxiliary Disciplines 281
Summary and Details of Class 900 281
The Number Building Process 283
DDC 22 Class 900 Revisions 283
910–920 Geography, Travel, and Biography Revisions 283
930 History of Ancient World 286
940 History of Europe 288
950 History of Asia 299
960 History of Africa 304
970 History of North America 310
980 History of South America 315
990 History of Other Parts of Our and Other Worlds 317
Exercises in the Use of Class 900 318
Literature Cited 318

15—Book Numbers 319
The Functions of Book Numbers 319
Book Number Schemes 320
Cutter Tables 320
Library of Congress Author Numbers 322
Practical Use of Book Numbers 323
Literature Cited 324

Select Bibliography 325
Appendix: Answers to the Exercises 329
Index 337

Preface

This work is a comprehensive guide to 22nd edition of the Dewey Decimal Classification (*DDC* 22). As in the previous edition of this study manual, it begins with a brief history of its development up to this edition and the impact of DDC internationally. It continues on to a review of the general structure of DDC, and the 22nd edition in particular, with emphasis on the framework (hierarchical order, centered entries), which aids the classifier in its use.

An extensive part of this manual is an in-depth review of how DDC is updated with each edition, such as relocations, discontinuations, and expansions, and detailed lists of such changes in each Table and Class. Each citation of a change will indicate the new number at the left followed by the current name or topic heading. Where appropriate, the previous topic, name, or a comment, such as "New Number" will be in the third column with the old number in the right column.

Besides these lists of changes, each Table and Class is introduced with a brief background discussion about its development and structure to familiarize the user with it.

As in the previous edition, this DDC study manual combines information from Bloomberg and Weber's *Introduction to Classification and Number Building in Dewey* (Libraries Unlimited, 1976) to provide a complete reference for the application of DDC. Detailed examples of number building for each Class and Table will guide the classifier through the process, which will result in notations for particular works within that Class. In addition, lists of book summaries are provided as exercises in number building with Library of Congress (LC) classifications provided in the Appendix as benchmarks.

The last chapter is concerned with book or author numbers, which, combined with the classification and often the date, provide unique call numbers for circulation and shelf arrangement. Guidelines in the application of cutter tables and Library of Congress author numbers complete this comprehensive reference to the use of *DDC* 22.

1

DDC History and Current Status

Edition 22 of the Dewey Decimal Classification (DDC) displays the continuous revitalization efforts that have kept it contemporary throughout the twentieth, and now into the twenty-first, century. Progress made in science, technology, and even thought and culture is consistently reflected within the classification. For this reason, its use by catalogers continues to grow nationally and internationally.

The late nineteenth century in which the DDC was devised and developed was a time not quite of isolation, but one of looking inward. The United States was still building and recovering in the east following the cataclysmic devastation of the war between the northern and southern states. At the same time, it was expanding rapidly into the west, as settlers pushed the Native Americans aside and began farming, ranching, and mining the land. Transportation was evolving as the first transcontinental railway line was completed in 1869, and ships were moving from wind power and sails to steam.

This was the era and climate in which Melvil Dewey existed as he began his work on the DDC. Neither he nor any of his contemporaries could have foreseen today's easy movement of people, materials, and information from continent to continent in hours rather than days, or our reach into space with men walking on the moon and the robotic exploration of Mars. Nor could he have anticipated that his classification system would eventually be used in many languages and libraries around the world. His parochial view of its use and his concept of knowledge perfectly reflected his world.

Table 1.1.
Growth of the Unabridged DDC's Elements

Edition	Date	Table Pages	Schedule Pages	Index Pages	Total Pages	Editor
1	1876		10	18	42	M. Dewey
2	1885		176	86	314	M. Dewey
3	1888		215	185	416	M. Dewey
4	1891		222	186	471	M. Seymour
5	1894		222	186	471	M. Seymour
6	1899		255	241	612	M. Seymour
7	1911		408	315	779	M. Seymour
8	1913		419	332	850	M. Seymour
9	1915		452	334	856	M. Seymour
10	1919		504	358	940	M. Seymour
11	1922		539	366	990	D. Fellows
12	1927		670	477	1243	D. Fellows
13	1932	4	890	653	1647	D. Fellows
14	1942	4	1044	749	1927	C. Mazney
15	1951	1	467	191	716	M. Ferguson
15r	1952	1	457	400	927	G. Dewey
16	1958	5	1313	1003	2439	B. Custer
17	1965	249	1132	633	2153	B. Custer
17r	1967	249	1132	940	2439	B. Custer
18	1971	325	1165	1033	2718	B. Custer
19	1979	452	1574	1217	3385	B. Custer
20	1989	476	1804	726	3388	J. Comaromi
21	1996	515	2205	899	4037	J. Mitchell
22	2003	530	2318	923	3983	J. Mitchell

Note: Although the table is helpful in seeing the progression of DDC, explanations are necessary to understand the figures completely. For example, the amount of information per page has not been consistent; edition 15's pages were spare, whereas edition 14's were full and even compact at times. Edition 14 also was outsized on purpose to allow for the distillation of it for the Standard Edition. The elimination of "see references" considerably reduced the index pages in edition 20. The inclusion of longer introductions and more and fuller tables, the incorporation of a manual, and other changes resulted in only three additional pages because it was far more compact than its predecessor.

In the twentieth century, DDC's success in the United States was easily transmitted abroad as the United States was looked up to as the leader in all things. It was only then, and as more and varied cultures began to immigrate to the United States, that Dewey's white Anglo-Saxon Protestant (WASP) bias became a real issue. The DDC's success generated its own need to evolve with the worldwide culture. Its focus on the Christian religion had to be lessened, and aspects of race needed to be replaced with a focus on other cultures. Each decade the DDC rejuvenates itself with changes that reflect not only new ideas and technologies but also the evolution of thought and concepts of human inter-relatedness. The vitality of the classification system is reflected in its ability to adjust and grow as humankind itself evolves.

The Modern History of DDC

Dewey's loyal editorial team dissolved almost simultaneously with publication of *DDC* 13 (1932) after sixty years of close and personal interaction. That edition continued the trend toward enumerative expansion upon existing number assignments. Nearly one-third larger than its predecessor, it still missed the equitable growth of all sections that many users wanted.

After considerable jockeying for control, a new editor took charge halfway through preparations for *DDC* 14 (1942), but he lasted only until it was published. Questions of copyright, spelling, schedule proliferation, and cooperation with the International Institute of Bibliography shadowed that work. Its express goal was to develop all as yet unexpanded portions. Demand was growing for a "standard" edition that could serve the needs of an average-sized library of fewer than 200,000 volumes. It would bridge the gap between an intricately detailed bibliographic edition for large institutions, or for indexing purposes, and an abridged edition for school and small public libraries. *DDC* 14 was intended to provide a comprehensive support for the controlled reductions anticipated in the forthcoming standard edition. It missed its publication deadline by a year, still failing to provide complete and uniform expansion. Nevertheless, it was a popular, unexpectedly long-lived edition.

However, what *DDC* 17 called "slot-ification," or "classification by attraction," reached its zenith in *DDC* 14 (Butcher 1979, 8). Subsequent editions increased synthetic modular devices such as auxiliary and precedence tables. Simple enumeration could not satisfy the requirements, in part because of the enormous growth of factual knowledge (Matthews 1971, 572–77).

When the Standard Edition appeared in 1951 it was, at best, a qualified success. Theorists said it abandoned or obscured the logical principle of development from the general to the specific. Its index was drastically reduced. It had less in common with *DDC* 14 than was predicted. On the other hand, it cut out much deadwood, curtailed the troublesome simplified spelling, and introduced modern terminology. A revised *DDC* 15 appeared in 1953 with expanded form divisions, a considerable lengthened index, and other modifications. But irreversible antipathy curtailed sales and accelerated the trend to reclassify from DDC to the Library of Congress scheme.

Caught in acute financial distress, the Lake Placid Club Education Foundation appealed to "outsiders" to help its programs. For instance, it solicited both the American Library Association and the Library of Congress for professional input. In later 1953, the Forest Press, its operational branch, contracted with the

Library of Congress to do the editorial work on schedule and according to predetermined criteria.

The result led to putting DDC numbers from both editions on Library of Congress printed cards and set a more or less consistent policy for future development (Library of Congress 1951, 1). The resuscitation was partly the work of new editor Ben Custer, although most basic policy decisions had been made when he assumed charge in September 1956.

The modern history of DDC is generally dated from 1958, with publication of a refocused Edition 16 that emphasized continuity and disciplinary integrity. Changes were kept to a minimum, reflecting only those most urgently needed to accommodate existing knowledge. Wherever possible, specific numbers were left vacant when discontinued. Only the 546–547 (Inorganic and Organic chemistry) sections were fully recast, inaugurating the overhaul in each successive edition of limited portions that were especially inadequate or unpopular (Dewey 1958, 23). Dewey's idiosyncratic spelling almost disappeared. Instructional notes were polished and multiplied.

Critics, especially in foreign countries, still found fault. The American Protestant bias remained although the editors had worked to reduce it. Enumeration prevailed over rudimentary faceting for composite subjects. Users had trouble classing comprehensive works, especially where the decimal notation no longer reflected hierarchical subdivision. *DDC* 16 may not have been a classifier's nirvana, but it sold well, assuring the solvency of Forest Press and ensuring a systematic production schedule for later editions. A seven- to eight-year revision cycle was established. *DDC* 17 came out in 1965. Its editor's introduction emphasized:

> new or renewed emphasis on subject integrity and subject relationships, on the fundamental process of classification as distinct from what has been called "slot-ification."
>
> Encouraged by Melvil Dewey's notable preference for practicality over theory in all activities, misled by the common American view of classification as little more than a system for assigning each book a convenient address or "slot" at which it can be stored and from which it can be retrieved, influenst [sic] by the failure of earlier editions of the DDC to provide under every discipline an expansion as full as was warranted by the literature acquired by libraries, classifiers of the past many times unwittingly abandoned the most fundamental feature of the system. (Dewey 1965, 43, 46)

While continuing to call its approach enumerative, *DDC* 17 took a long step toward faceted number synthesis by expanding the table of form divisions, renaming it the "Table of Standard Subdivisions," and adding an "Area Table" that freed class 900 from its burden of enumerative detail and liberated geographic and political specifications from their tradition American distortion.

"Divide like" and "Add area notation" instructions directed users to number sequences where established patterns of subdivision could be applied to different but related disciplines. The number of relocations was again reduced, although it still exceeded the announced limitation of 500. As for "completely remodeled schedules," the only explicit one was 150 (Psychology), which incorporated much of the material formerly located in class 130. Incidentally, the editor elsewhere cited Sections 614 (Public health) and 616 (Medicine) as areas of major relocation activity (Custer 1965, 557).

The Index gave trouble. It represented a 40-percent reduction of class number entries, but an enormous increase in cross-references. The editor later said of it:

> Previous indexes had contained entries chiefly for those topics that were named in the schedules, plus significant synonyms and subtopics, but had supplied numbers only for those aspects where the topics were named, making no effort to guide the classifier to the vast hidden resources of the system. . . . The new seventeenth index provided full information for only a limited number of broad core concepts, referred to these from more specific topics, and made many "scatter" references to remind the classifier of other aspects. . . . This procedure called attention to many possibilities often previously overlooked, but frequently it did not supply a precise number that could be used without close scrutiny of the schedules. Because of the scarcity of exact numbers this index proved to be difficult and time consuming to use, and was replaced in 1967 by a conventional index. (Custer 1972, 135)

Reminiscent of efforts to salvage the old Standard Edition, the new index was sent free with an apology to purchasers of the original *DDC* 17. Even so, *DDC* 17 was thought difficult to use. The editor's introduction, designed to replace the *Guide to Use of Dewey Decimal Classification* that accompanied *DDC* 16, was murky (Guide 1962). Instruction notes within the schedules were inadequate. Centered headings that were meant to show the hierarchy were confusing. Yet with all its shortcomings, real or imagined, sales topped those of DDC 16 by 23 percent.

Problems of precedence, sequence, and relationship among topics represented by the notation are inevitable in a linear classification. Benjamin A. Custer's reemphasis on hierarchical development brought renewed concern for consistent handling of nuclear topics or their facets with respect to their disciplines or subjects. The editor's introduction in *DDC* 17 carried a new section, "Priorities of Arrangement." Its corresponding section in *DDC* 18 adopted the more current name "Citation order" and carried a whole sequence of hints on modes of choice. The generalized instructions carried over into section of *DDC* 19 with only minor revisions and expansions. They start with a reminder to check specific schedule tables and notes.

DDC 17 took a long step toward solutions at specific schedule points by introducing Tables of Precedence. They were infrequent and experimental but proved successful. *DDC* 19 converted some minor tables into "order of precedence" notes. The number of such instructions has steadily increased, with elaborate schema now appearing in the Schedules proper, in auxiliary tables, and in the Manual. They are distinctively formatted with class numbers to the right of the headings.

The provisions of options in DDC is a long-standing tradition. Dewey's introduction to *DDC* 12 (1927), which was reprinted in later editions through *DDC* 18, carried some suggested variations that could be applied to conform to local needs.

DDC 18, published in 1971 with an improved three-volume format, introduced the term "phoenix schedule" for its fully revised classes 340 (Law) and 510 (Mathematics). For ready reference, a reworked editor's introduction got its own index, and all relocations and discontinued numbers were tabulated. Five more auxiliary tables materialized. The older "Divide like" and "Add" notes were consolidated and simplified by listing a "base number" to which the extension could be added. Tables of Precedence helped users determine citation order when building numbers. The Index curtailed its entries with class numbers, and increased in cross-references, but it was better received than the *DDC* 17 Index.

Foreign sales and translations steadily increased, while the flight from DDC to LC moderated. Already in 1973, two years after publication, more copies of *DDC* 18 had been sold than of any previous edition. Edition 20's early sales surpassed even those of Edition 18.

DDC 19 continued the structure, style and goals of *DDC* 18. The Index was difficult to use and usually unproductive. The revision of 301–307 (Sociology) was met by a storm of criticism, and Forest Press brought out a revised and expanded version of 301–307 in 1982 to placate the critics. At the same time the press published the *Manual on the Use of the Dewey Decimal Classification:* Edition 19, which was highly praised by the few who read it, and it would later become a part of Edition 20.

DDC 20 continued the structure and goals of *DDC* 19. The Index was not as difficult to use as its predecessor, but was usually as unproductive. The revision of 780 (Music) was met by discordant murmurs and widespread rejection. Teachers and trainers appreciated the completely revised introduction. This edition was the first to be edited and available electronically.

The appearance of *DDC* 20 differed from that of immediately preceding editions chiefly in the number of volumes (4) and its compressed layout. Increasing costs of paper and binding, together with a gradual but significant growth in the total number of entries, stimulated the search for a more compact product.

DDC 21 continued to reflect the needs of its users, especially those in foreign countries where criticism of the Protestant, Christian bias spurred major revisions in Religion. Tremendous strides were made in this direction by the consolidation of Christian aspects, thus bringing the classification more in line with that of other religions. The edition also continued the movement toward the structural emphasis on topics, such as Public Administration, which was revised to reflect the emphasis of first the topic, then on the domain, rather than the previous emphasis where the domain was the structural emphasis under which the topics were found. The same is found in Life Sciences, where the movement was from "organism/process to process/organism." Also in Life Sciences, notations were simplified with "more specific and shorter numbers for fishes and mammals" (Dewey 1996, 1:xxiii).

An increase in cultural and social sensitivity resulted in changes in the language used to describe various peoples, such as with disabilities. The person precedes the affliction, where "physically handicapped persons" is replaced by "persons with physical disabilities" (Dewey 1996, 1:xx). A new number for "Collected persons treatment of members of specific racial, ethnic, national groups" (Dewey 1996, 1:32) was assigned, and areas in which changes take place rapidly, such as computer science and country tables, were revised and expanded to reflect the differences.

Lastly, *DDC* 21 continued to become more "user-friendly," with strategically placed information, headings that were both more succinct and helpful, and the enlarged and enhanced Relative Index and Manual more easily used to assist in the selection of appropriate notations.

DDC 22 continues in the same evolutionary direction as its predecessors. The edition completes the process of diminishing the Christian bias found in 200 (Religion), reflects changes requested by classifiers in travel-related topics, and continues to reflect increased sensitivity to differences in race and culture. New aspects in technology and science are reflected in the many new numbers in the schedules.

Major changes in the structure of the edition are the elimination of Table 7 and the reorganization of the Manual. Notations found in the schedules and –08 in Table 1 replace Table 7. Directions and suggestions on the use of the schedules and tables were moved from the Manual to those locations where possible, resulting in greater ease and efficiency in the application of the schedules to the organization of knowledge.

This evolution of the schedules has allowed the system to be as current today as at the time of its creation. At its 125th anniversary in August 2001, representatives from six continents attended the ceremonies (Library of Congress 2001, 1).

The DDC's vitality is evident in its use on the World Wide Web. Because of the its easy application to knowledge and familiarity to users, librarians have used the classification in efforts to bring order to that unorganized warehouse of knowledge called the Internet, creating portals to direct researchers to legitimate information on almost anything. Public, school, and academic libraries have Web pages describing the DDC and how to use it in research. And finally, the DDC itself is found on the Web as WebDewey (http://www.oclc.org/dewey/versions/webdewey/).

OCLC Forest Press and the Editorial Policy Committee

As in the past, the Decimal Classification Editorial Policy Committee (EPC) directed the course, while under contract the Decimal Classification Division of the Library of Congress completed the actual revisions of the classification. The committee, composed of leaders in the field of classification from various backgrounds as well as from several countries, provided the experience and wisdom that propelled the innovations found in major sections, such as religion, law, the social sciences, mathematics, data processing, and computer science.

The committee's commitment to listen to DDC users' concerns and respond to their needs is evident in the survey of users conducted in preparation for this new edition. EPC members, users, educators, and others reviewed various parts of the schedules to ascertain the changes that should be made to maintain the schedule's currency, which are reflected in *DDC* 22 (Dewey 2003, 1:xv).

The day-to-day editing continues to be done on contract in the Decimal Classification Division of the Library of Congress. Benjamin A. Custer, chief of the division and editor of editions 16 through 19, and abridged editions 8 through 11, was a strong force in the revitalization of DDC. His successor and editor of Edition 20, John Phillip Comaromi, continued the process of "de-slot-ification" that he had begun, repudiating Dewey's cynicism regarding logical structure and its dependence on verbal indexing. This concept supplements enumeration with structured citation orders and facet analysis (Custer 1980, 102), techniques that had developed chiefly in India and the United Kingdom. Joan S. Mitchell has continued these efforts to keep the DDC abreast of knowledge and change as editor of editions 21 and 22.

DDC Activities at the Library of Congress

The Library of Congress decision in the 1890s not to use the Dewey Decimal System in organizing its collection has been well documented. Whether Dewey, through his refusal to permit modifications, surrendered the balance of influence to Cutter's Expansive Classification is still being debated. However, the shrewd Dewey decided that his classification scheme should have its numbers on LC cards, and early in 1925 he started a campaign to have DDC classifications printed on LC card sets. At first, the officials dragged their feet, partly because of financial hurdles. However, Dewey's aversion to "no" and "impossible" finally found the American Library Association, the Carnegie Corporation, and even the Library of Congress helping to finance the project.

> The work of assigning class numbers began on April 1, 1930, and cards with numbers on them began to appear by the end of the second week in April. By Aug. 1 a staff of three began carrying out a program even broader than anticipated . . .
>
> The following classes of books currently cataloged by the Library of Congress are being assigned Decimal Classification numbers:
>
> (a) All books in English, with the exception of city directories, telephone directories, and nearly all current fiction.
>
> (b) Some foreign books, as many as the time of the present staff will permit.
>
> (c) Nearly all serial publications (D.C. Numbers 1930, 786)

But the Federal Connection was still a long way from satisfactory. After Constantin Mazney was dismissed in 1942, the editorship fell between the Decimal Classification Section of LC's Subject Cataloging Division and the Editorial Office, now also located in Washington, D.C. Weak financial support was probably a result, rather than a cause, of differences over developing the scheme as a whole, and over the kinds and quantity of materials for which LC would supply DDC numbers. At long last, in 1958, the two units merged (Library of Congress 1958, 1). Still, the relatively low percentage of catalog cards carrying DDC numbers decreased further during the early 1960s, when book publishing and library budgets accelerated more exuberantly than did the personnel available for processing. A second major influence in the flight from Dewey was the cost of determining DDC class and book numbers locally, as compared to adopting LC's ready-made call numbers. In 1967, an LC Processing Department reorganization elevated the Decimal Classification Office to division status, with a corresponding increase in staff and production.

> Adding spectacularly to its direct service to libraries as a central source of DDC numbers for specific works, the Division classed 74,335 titles, compared with 59,799 in 1967 and 35,000 in 1966. The 1968 coverage included all titles cataloged for the MARC program, all current (1966–1968) titles cataloged in English, and the more important and difficult current titles cataloged in the other major western European languages, and received through the National Program for Acquisitions and Cataloging. (Welsh 1969, 189)

LC assigned 110,290 DDC numbers in 2002 (Library of Congress 2002, 1), and at a fiftieth anniversary party in May 1980, it was announced that 2,253,731 titles had "received DDC numbers for use by libraries everywhere and of every kind and size" (Library of Congress 1980, 243). Records with DDC numbers now run consistently over 100,000 per year.

The editing of all DDC editions after the 15th has been contracted to the Library of Congress, and a copy of the agreement for producing DDC 16 was published in Cataloging Service to make users aware of developments (Library of

Congress 1954, 1–10). The Library's record of its Dewey classifications is the closest thing to a working shelflist that DDC editors have.

DDC's International Presence

Functioning as a national library, LC can exchange information and enter into mutually beneficial agreements with foreign DDC users, as the following report shows:

> Because thousands of users from Japan to Israel and Brazil to Mauritius utilize the Dewey decimal classification there is wide interest in its editorial development and in standardizing its application. Since 1969 the Decimal Classification Division has engaged in a lively exchange of information with the British National Bibliography, not only through transatlantic mail, which often moves weekly in each direction, but also through a six-week interchange of decimal classification specialists in 1972 as well as others with the Australian National Bibliography and Canadiana, the national bibliography of Canada. The result has been a common understanding of editorial policy, progress toward standardized interpretation of the schedules, and a vigorous expression of opinion and much give-and-take among four of the most important users of Dewey.
>
> Recently the interchange with Great Britain entered a new dimension when British librarians, including the staff of BNB, undertook development of new schedules, subject to the guidance and review of the Decimal Classification Divisions. The first undertaking was the schedule for the new local administrative divisions of the United Kingdom that went into effect in April 1974. It will be followed by a revision of the Dewey decimal scheme for music. This type of dialogue has proved most useful and should be extended since through it overseas user obtain a more complete understanding of official Dewey policy and practice. In turn, they provide expertise in the development and application of the classification in fields of major concern to them. (Library of Congress 1975, 23)

The early WASP bias in Dewey classification is well known; it was more or less inevitable, and even justifiable as discussed earlier. Social change and the growing use of the system abroad sparked efforts to broaden its outlook. The decade of the mid-1960s to mid-1970s saw three major surveys of the impact of DDC outside North America, plus one on its use in the United States and Canada. These surveys were variously encouraged and partially financed by the Forest Press, the International Relations Office of ALA, the Library Association, the Asia Foundation, and the Council on Library Resources. Among other things they found:

1. Approval of techniques to give preferred treatment to local/national materials

2. Lack of enthusiasm for mixed notation

3. Concern over DDCs indifference to the "cuttering concept" or the use of book numbers

4. Some dissatisfaction with the order of the main classes

5. Criticism of numbers (usually synthetic) supplied in the index though not in the schedules

6. Lack of familiarity of DC& and consequent ignorance of schedule revisions prior to publication of each new edition

7. Desire for more information on DDC policies and revision plans

Concern for the non-English-speaking user dealt the coup de grace to simplified spelling. *DDC* 19 announced "a return to conventional American spelling from the residual simpler spellings of Editions 16–18 (e.g., divorst, publisht) which greatly frustrated those whose native tongue is not English" (Dewey 1979, 1:xxiii).

Celebration of the Dewey centennial in 1976 stimulated a variety of cross-cultural activities such as the European Centenary Seminar at Banbury, England. British classificationists, who have long been interested in American schemes, have contributed penetrating commentary. The British serial *Catalogue & Index*, the English-language *International Classification* (published in Germany), and various foreign library association journals, particularly those in Canada, Australia, India, and South Africa, carry articles from time to time on DDC. Western European writers are particularly fond of comparing it to its Fédération Internationale d'Information et de Documentation (FID)-sponsored offspring, the Universal Decimal Classification (UDC). The studies do not usually resonate to the praise of DDC, but they show more respect than they once did.

The appearance of DDC translations, sometimes abridged, or just as often locally expanded, is further evidence of DDC's international headway. With or without authorization, editions are available in such non-European languages as Hebrew, Thai, and Vietnamese.

The DDC Today

The Dewey Decimal Classification is the product of a series of strong personalities who successively poured their energies into its infancy, development, maturity, and perpetuation. Melvil Dewey, Evelyn (May) Seymour, Dorkas Fellows, Milton Ferguson, David Haykin, and Ben Custer cast shadows over DDC, shaping its inner consciousness and its outer presence. The advisor activities of the Editorial Policy Committee and the contractual service of LC's Decimal Classification Division have not essentially altered this paternalistic aspect.

The LC classification seldom inspires the enthusiastic personal commitment that is frequently accorded DDC. Proponents of the latter absorbed its rudiments in their school libraries, exploring its idiosyncrasies and learning to live with them as public or college library patrons. They are conditioned to its mnemonic, practical comprehensibility and its broad comprehensiveness. As the present work will show, Edition 22 stands in the same tradition that has kept DDC functioning for thousands of libraries for more than a century and continues the pattern of development set by Custer with Edition 17.

Literature Cited

Butcher, Peter. 1979. Dewey? We sure do! *Catalogue & Index* 55:8.

Custer, Benjamin A. 1965. Dewey 17: A Preview and Report to the Profession. *Wilson Library Bulletin* 39 (7): 557.

———. 1972. Dewey Decimal Classification. In *Encyclopedia of Library and Information Science*. Vol. 7. New York: Marcel Dekker.

———. 1980. The View from the Editor's Chair. *Library Resources & Technical Services* 24 (2):102.

D.C. numbers on LC cards. 1930. *Library Journal* 50 (17):786.

Dewey, Melvil. 1958. *Dewey Decimal Classification and Relative Index*. 16th ed. Lake Placid Club, NY: Forest Press.

———. 1965. *Dewey Decimal Classification and Relative Index*. 17th ed. Lake Placid Club, NY: Forest Press.

———. 1979. *Dewey Decimal Classification and Relative Index*. 19th ed. Vol. 1. Albany, NY: Forest Press.

———. 1996. *Dewey Decimal Classification and Relative Index*. 21st ed. Vol. 1. Albany, NY: Forest Press.

———. 2003. *Dewey Decimal Classification and Relative Index*. 22nd ed. Vol. 1. Dublin, Ohio: OCLC Online Computer Library Center.

Guide to Use of Dewey Decimal Classification, Based on the Practice of the Decimal Classification Office at the Library of Congress. 1962. Lake Placid Club, NY: Forest Press.

Library of Congress. 1975. Annual Report of the Librarian of Congress for the fiscal year ending June 30, 1974. Washington, DC: Library of Congress.

———. 1951. *Cataloging Service Bulletin* 25:1. Washington, DC: Library of Congress.

———. 1954. *Cataloging Service Bulletin* 32:1–10. Washington, DC: Library of Congress.

———. 1958. *Cataloging Service Bulletin* 51:1. Washington, DC: Library of Congress.

———. 1980. *Library of Congress Information Bulletin* 39 (28): 243. Washington, DC: Library of Congress.

———. 2001. *LC Cataloging Newsline* 9, no. 11. Washington, DC: Library of Congress.

———. 2002. *LC Cataloging Newsline* 10, no 11. Washington, DC: Library of Congress.

Matthews, W. E. 1971. Dewey 18: A Preview and Report. *Wilson Library Bulletin*, 45 (6):572–7.

Welsh, William J. 1969. The Processing Department of the Library of Congress in 1968. *Library Resources & Technical Services* 13 (2):189.

2

General Aspects of the Dewey Decimal Classification

A discussion of DDC must be from two points of view. One is *pure theory*, and is how DDC looks at the world (knowledge) and then arranges it into a logical organization. The second is the *physical structure* of the classification that supports the theory behind the organization of knowledge.

DDC's Theory of Knowledge

The theory behind the Dewey Decimal Classification is divided into four parts:

The realm of reason (wherein the mind attempts to understand itself and the spiritual and physical world outside itself): the sciences and the arts

The realm of imagination (wherein the mind produces literary inventions regarding life, no matter how much based in fact): belletristic literature, imaginative literature

The realm of memory (wherein the mind records events and conditions regarding the life of the planet and of humanity): geography, biography, history

Generalia (all other topics not included in the three "realms")

It is generally the case that the 800s take precedence over the rest of the Classification; that is, a novel about conditions in the meat packing industry of Chicago (e.g., *The Jungle,* by Upton Sinclair) is classed in the 800s, not in meat packing in the 660s. *King Henry V* goes in English drama, not in English history.

But a dialogue by Plato is classed in philosophy in the 100s; an expository poem on the circulation of the blood, in human physiology; a counting book in rhyme, in arithmetic. It is important to be careful in this first sorting of the nature of a work, especially when dealing with works for children.

The first realm, the realm of reason (science) unfolds into philosophy, the source of systems for all other fields and the most general field of study. Theology, the science of the absolute and the ultimate field of philosophy, comes next. Religion, which is not scientific but is tributary to theology, is included in theology.

As human kind achieves its most spiritual role within society and in relation to the state, the social and political sciences are logically the next fields of study. The political sciences are jurisprudence, in which society puts constraints on the individual. The social sciences are political economy, whereby in combination human kind gains ascendancy over nature and uses it for personal ends. Education is the method by which human kind is initiated into the society's structure and rules. Placed at the end of the social and political sciences is philology, as it is the result of self-conscience thought, a society's best record of itself, and the connecting link between the spiritual and the natural.

The natural sciences follow, and these are followed by the useful and fine arts. The first unfold the laws of nature; the next apply them to social uses. The point of transition between them is medicine, which is part science and part art. This brings to an end the subjects whose major mode of treatment is the scientific.

The second realm collects works of the imagination: poetry, prose fiction, and so on.

The last realm is the historical. History comprises geography and travels, civil history, biography, and correspondence. Heraldry and genealogy are also found here.

A topic may fall into any of the three realms. Take, for instance, the Library of Congress. One could write about it scientifically; explain its present and future role in intelligence-gathering, estimate the date on which it will be filled from top to bottom, delineate its effect on the artistic life of America, describe the richer life of those who benefit from its program of talking books, and so on. One may say that these are not all scientific subjects. The assertion is uncontestable, and inappropriate. It is the mode of discussion that is scientific, not the subject. One could write about the Library of Congress historically: examine its past role in intelligence-gathering, investigate now long it took to build the Library of Congress Thomas Jefferson Building, list who helped in its construction, explain the source of the stone that makes up its walls, and so on. And, lastly, one could write about the Library artistically: devise a novel in which a descriptive cataloger spends his days in remembrance of things past and is subsequently fired; or pen a poem about the institution, which brings an artistic aspect.

DDC's Structure (the Schedules)

A basic premise of DDC is that it is arranged by discipline and not by subject. This frequently presents problems in classifying materials, but the Relative Index's job is to alleviate such difficulties.

The next basic premise is that of "tens." The Schedules are arranged in ten Classes, which are organized into ten Divisions, each of which is divided into ten Sections. The Schedules are found in Volumes 2 and 3 of *DDC* 22.

Each DDC notation is made up of three basic numbers that represent a particular place in the Schedules. The first digit indicates one of the ten classes. The second digit represents one of the ten divisions within the class. The third digit distinguishes one of the ten sections. Most notations require further refinement so a decimal is inserted following this three-part number to be followed by more digits representing a specific element of the topic.

DDC notation remains traditionally pure. That is, it consists only of the Arabic digits 0 through 9, plus the decimal point. The shortest possible number is three digits long, since lead zeros are written out in class 000, such as 006.

Number columns, Schedules, Index, and Table numbers are printed in groups of three, for example, 629.133 340 422 (Engineering of private airplanes), and –772 33 (Vanderburgh County, Indiana). The groupings merely facilitate reading. In common practice, the space is removed when writing the numbers as classifications. Brackets indicate recently or permanently vacated locations in the schedules.

Hierarchical Order

After the "slot-ification crisis" of Edition 16, the editorial policy has stressed disciplinary integrity, largely through the use of hierarchical subordination, or the logical progression from the general to the specific.

> The DDC is a hierarchical classification, which means that it develops progressively from the general to the specific in disciplinary and subject relationships. Even so, the overall arrangement is not necessarily theoretical or logical. The DDC is built on the premise that no one class can cover all aspects of a given subject. (Bloomberg and Weber 1976, 17)

This suggests that the hierarchical structure is not necessarily a linear one. The editors of *DDC* 20 claimed that any specific class has two or three sets of relationships: coordinate, subordinate, and sometimes superordinate (Dewey 1989, 1:xxviii–xxix). However, this is basically a hierarchical system that is more easily seen in the pure and applied sciences and is less evident in generalities, the humanities, or the social sciences.

This hierarchical or "tree" structure is echoed in the notation. Within this basic structure, the first level in the classification of an item is the first digit (Main Class); the second level of subdivision is the addition of the second digit (Division). The third level of subdivision is (Section) provided by the addition of the third digit added to the two previously selected digits.

3[00]	Social Sciences	(Main Class)
34[0]	Law	(Division)
342	Constitutional and Administrative Law	(Section)

At this point, Summary tables provide overviews of the hierarchies. Following is the Summary of Constitutional and Administrative Law.

342.001–.009	Standard subdivisions; laws, regulations, cases, procedures, courts
.02	Basic instruments of government
.03	Revision and amendment of basic instruments of government
.04	Structure, powers, functions of government
.05	Legislative branch of government
.06	Executive branch of government
.07	Election law
.08	Jurisdiction over persons
.09	Local government
.1	Socioeconomic regions
.2	Regional intergovernmental organizations
.3–9	Specific jurisdictions and areas

Centered Entries

Various subjects within the Schedules are encompassed in ranges of numbers. These entries are called *Centered Entries* because the range of numbers is centered on the page, with a ">" at the left margin.

> 342–349 Branches of law; laws, regulations, cases …

These Centered Entries are divided categories (*Facets*), which are further divided by various characteristics. Each Facet's specific notation is initiated by a digit, such as "0," which often precedes a Standard Subdivision. (Historical and Geographic Treatment is a Standard Subdivision.)

342.009	Historical, geographic, persons treatment
342.04 *	Structure, powers, functions of government
342.041 *	Powers and functions of government
342.0418 *	Police powers

The asterisk (*) beside a heading (topic) in the Schedules leads the user to a note at the bottom of the page.

* Add as instructed under 342–347

Discussions about notes found in the Schedules are found in Chapter 3.

Broad and Close Classification

One of the most notable features of DDC is its adaptability to libraries of every size. Smaller libraries may shorten their notations where they find it prudent by eliminating detailed subdivisions and retaining only main classes and subdivisions, which is referred to as broad classification. Larger libraries with more extensive collections generally use close classification, utilizing all of the detailed subdivisions that are applicable.

Libraries may use any method of shortening the notations, but the accepted one is that offered by the Library of Congress, which segments the numbers with marks indicating appropriate breaks for shortened notations.

Relative Index

Although both the Schedules and the Index of the classification system match linguistically with notational representations of the concepts, or the actual library materials being classified, they have reciprocal functions offering different insights. Schedules graph or delineate the structure, using notations to accent symmetries, analogies, and hierarchies. The Index offers random access through alphabetized primary and subordinated terms. Bloomberg and Weber, quoting the editors of DDC, offer the following evaluation:

> No other feature of the DDC is more basis than this: that it scatters subjects by discipline (DDC, Vol. 1, p. 18). The Editor's Introduction to the DDC further states that "the primary basis for DDC arrangement and development of subjects is by discipline . . . while subject, strictly speaking, is secondary" (DDC,

> Vol. 1, p. 17). One of the functions of classification is to bring together on the shelves materials on the same subject and on related subjects. It needs to be emphasized, however, that no classification accomplishes that function perfectly. It is important to remember that all material on a subject is seldom if ever classed together. . . . Thus, throughout the DDC various aspects of a topic or discipline may be placed in different numbers. . . . No attempt is made to place all aspects of a topic in one number in the schedule. . . . The device that brings together the various aspects and relationships of a topic is the Relative Index. . . . (1976, 20)

For example, some aspects of Agriculture are listed in the Relative Index as follow (Dewey 2003, 4:19):

Agriculture	630
applied science	630
economics	338.1
enterprises	338.763
law	344.095 7
public administration	354.5

Although all of the last four entries are related to Agriculture, they are actually in another class.

The backbone of the DDC Schedules are the disciplines, which are "organized fields of study or branches of knowledge" (Dewey 1996, 1:lix). These may be a main class of DDC such as Religion (200) or a division such as Psychology (150). As illustrated above, the various subjects, or topics, are found in the Schedules within the disciplines. The Relative Index is a guide to associate subjects or topics related to disciplines.

> The Relative Index brings together the various aspects and relations of a topic. It is an alphabetical listing of all the main headings in the DDC Schedules, showing also synonyms and, to a large degree, the relation of each subject to other subjects . . . Earlier it was pointed out that the DDC scatters aspects of subjects by discipline through the Schedules. The Relative Index brings together the various aspects of a topic. (Bloomberg and Weber 1976, 33)

In the Index, which is found in Volume 4 of *DDC* 22, subjects are listed in alphabetical order, with lists of disciplines under which the subjects are found. Many class numbers in the Index are not spelled out in the Schedules because they have been "synthesized," or built from Add Instructions, such as "Add to base number 339.48" (Dewey 2003, 2:520). Following is an example from the Relative Index (Dewey 2003, 4:454):

Law

arts	700.455 4
information systems	025.063 4
literature	808.803 554

Using the previous example, the notation for laws involving Information Systems is not found in the Schedules, but is built following instructions. The following example displays what is found under 025 in the Schedules (Dewey 2003, 2:54–55):

.06 Information storage and retrieval systems devoted to specific disciplines and subjects

Class here bibliographies of Web sites devoted to specific disciplines . . .

[.060 001–.060 009] Standard subdivisions

Do not use: class in 025.0401–025.0409

.060 01–.069 99 Specific disciplines and subjects

Add to base number 025.06 notation 001–999 . . .

There is no .063.4 specified, but it is included in .06001–.06999. Instructions indicate how to add numbers for the specific disciplines and subjects. In this case, 34 is added from the Schedules, indicating law (340).

The search for a class number begins with the Relative Index, which lists *subjects* in alphabetical order with disciplines identified underneath with their notations. Not all topics in the Schedules are in the Index, nor are all of the topics in the Index in the Schedules, but they are implied because the Schedules are not exhaustive. Some names from Table 2 are included, such as countries, states and provinces of many countries, U.S. counties, capitals and other important cities, and important geographic characteristics. Heads of State that are often used to denote historical periods are usually found in the Index.

Users are warned against assigning class numbers directly from the Index without examining their placement in the Schedules. For a satisfactory subject classification, it is necessary to verify the number within the context.

When Melvil Dewey produced the first edition of the DDC, he called the Index a "Subject Index," and that is exactly what it was. It was not an index of the terms found in the Schedules; it was a list of topics he thought to be important to the students and faculty of Amherst College.

A number on the same line as an Index term would naturally be thought to be for the *topic* given and thus for the *subject* being discussed in the work. This may or may not be true. The Relative Index is generally not a subject index in Melvil Dewey's sense of the phrase and it should not be confused with it.

The Manual

The Manual, like the Relative Index, assists classifiers in their search for proper notations. In *DDC* 21, the Manual shared the last volume with the Relative Index, but in *DDC* 22 it occupies the prominent status of page 1 of Volume 1. It is easily found among the introductory material and the Tables that follow it by grey "tab marks" on the edges of the pages. The Manual is arranged in the same order as the Schedules, although not all numbers are found there because its purpose is to provide further explanations about the proper use of numbers that may present problems. An example is (Dewey 2003, 1:62):

> **081–089**
>
> **General collections in specific languages and language families**
>
> Class collections originally written in one language or language family with that language or language family

In this example a paragraph of instructions describes where to class general collections of abstracts, addresses, lectures, essays, interviews, graffiti, and quotations. At 081–089 in the Schedules there is a note to "See Manual at 081–089." The following example demonstrates more complex instructions to analyze before assigning a notation (Dewey 2003, 1:121):

> **523 vs 559.9**
>
> **Earth sciences in extraterrestrial worlds**
>
> Use 523 for phenomena of celestial bodies when the celestial body has no distinct lithosphere. . . . Use 559.9 and notation 0999 from Table 1 in 551–553 for phenomena of celestial bodies that have distinct lithospheres.

In this example the user is guided in the decision of under which of the two subjects the work being classified fits. At 523 in the Schedules, there are instructions to "See Manual at 523 vs 559.9," however, at 559.9, the instructions read, "See Manual at 629.43, 629.45 vs 559.9, 919.904" (Dewey 2003, 2:971, 1075). The referenced numbers in the Manual have a heading "Space flight vs Earth science of, geography of, and travel in extraterrestrial worlds" and a paragraph of instructions about the use of the numbers (Dewey 2003, 1:142). Thus it is necessary to follow wherever any references or instructions may lead and analyze them in regards to the subject matter of the item being classified to arrive at the proper notation. Under 523 the discussion deals with only one aspect of Earth Sciences in extraterrestrial worlds, the existence of lithospheres. Under 559.9 the discussion broadens to include space flight, geography and travel in extraterrestrial worlds.

It is *always* important to refer to the Manual when encountering "See Manual" instructions. This is the only guarantee that the notation chosen will be the appropriate one.

Types of Changes Found in *DDC* 22

Controlled expansion, discontinuations, and relocations constitute the primary modes of changes found in Edition 22. These methods are combined in varying formats to make the system more responsive to contemporary needs or to implement the goal of subject integrity from a modern perspective. What seems to be a small readjustment may turn out to be nearly as far-reaching, or just as controversial, as a sudden large one. The recast Religion (200) Schedules appear to be the most revolutionary, but they differ only in degree, not in kind.

Tinkering with the Schedules is not the only way to modify a classification scheme. The semantic, and even the structural, peculiarities of the mediating language have their own laws and pose their own problems of change. In succeeding chapters, we examine adjustments made in *DDC* 22.

Expansions

Expansions introduce new numbers, or reintroduce numbers that have not been used recently. The first thought is that new notations reflect new concepts, and that the growth of knowledge, or growth of library materials on subjects, warrants the additions. An example is 006.8, a number that was not previously used, and is a new number for Virtual reality.

But there are other reasons for expansions of the Schedules. The further subdivision of a Class may be necessary. This occurs when the growth of knowledge, or the increase in materials written about a specific topic that was previously included under a broader subject, now warrants giving the subject a separate notation. An example is 005.722, which is a new number. This number represents Character sets, "including ASCII, Unicode." In *DDC* 21, ASCII was included under 005.72 and Unicode was not mentioned.

Sometimes deviations from Table 1 (Standard Subdivisions) indicate the need for new numbers. For example, Classification of Religious mythology is found in 201.4 under General classes of religions, a reused number, rather than at .012, which would be the usual number for the classification of a subject.

In some areas, the single zeros normally used for Standard Subdivisions are assigned to other subtopics or subdivisions, so additional zeros are added to form the Standard Subdivisions. An example is 324.243, which now is used for [Political] Parties of Germany. The notations with single zeros are used for specific political parties of Germany, or specific categories of parties such as Leftist and worker parties, which are found at 324.243 07. Notations for the Standard Subdivisions are 324.243 001–324.243 009 (Dewey 2003, 2:379, 381).

Discontinuations

A Discontinuation, formerly called a Reduction, may be the product of moving a topic to a number shorter than the notation previously used. The old number is no longer used and appears in the Schedules in brackets. An example is Socialization by father and mother [303.323 1–303.323 2], which was moved to 303.323, Socialization by family. A note at the old location in the Schedules reads, "Numbers discontinued; class in 303.323" (Dewey 2003, 2:319).

Discontinuations also have occurred when the content of a number becomes meaningless within the context of the *DDC* 22 Schedules. This discontinued number is enclosed in brackets. There are seventeen of these Discontinuations in this edition, contrasted with only three in Edition 21. An example is Mathematical systems [511.2], which displays the statement "Number discontinued because without meaning in context."

There are many "partial discontinuations" in this edition, in which only a part of a topic is moved to a smaller number. An example is found in general works on financial accounting, which have been moved from 657.48 to 657. The number 657.48 is retained in the Schedules for Inflation accounting, which was one of the topics included under that notation in Edition 21.

Relocations

A relocation occurs when a topic is shifted to a different number, not just a shorter one. The old number may be bracketed indicating that it is vacated and its use discontinued in this edition. These shifts may concern the users of the Schedules, and so are not done lightly. "Relocations . . . are made for various reasons in DDC, to keep pace with new knowledge or to rectify some of the structural irregularities which have developed in the system over the years" (Chan 1973, 38).

Figures indicating the number of relocations in previous editions range from 100 in Edition 2 to 1,098 in Edition 20. But there has been no consistent method of counting them because with systematic faceting the exact total of discontinued numbers and relocations cannot be precisely stated, and the total is often disputed by even such authorities as Benjamin A. Custer and John Philip Comaromi. In this work, no effort is made to develop a total number of relocations because the number is meaningless in relation to the effect on the various collections around the world. Some libraries, because of their focus, will experience little impact, but others may require the reclassing of vast sections of their holdings. In later chapters these relocations, as well as other alterations found in *DDC* 22, are discussed in detail to assist the users in reconciling their collections.

Some relocations are total, which is where the old number is no longer used. An example of this type of relocation is Judicial cooperation, letters rogatory [341.78], which is now found under 347.012. The old number is no longer being used for any meaning.

Another example is a split relocation in which only part of a meaning of a topic is shifted elsewhere, leaving the topic in its old location. An example is found in Anthropology and religion and ethnology and religion, which were moved from 215.7 to 218. The notation 215.7 is continued for Life sciences and religion.

A more radical relocation is where meanings or topics of a whole span of numbers are moved to another span. Obviously this radical change would not be done lightly, but it may be necessary to maintain the Schedules' currency. An example found in Edition 22 is the span 291 in which none of the numbers are used in *DDC* 22, but formerly was the number span for Comparative religion.

Another type of relocation is where topics with a single number or span of numbers are discontinued and their meanings distributed elsewhere. An example of this type of relocation is found at [305.906 949], which was the number used for Victims of war and crime. Victims of war are now located at 305.906 95, and Victims of crime are now found at 362.88. The old number is discontinued.

A partial relocation results when the original number retains some of its meaning, loosing only part of the meaning to a different class number. Instructions at the old location refer the user to the new number, which has a bracketed note beginning with *formerly*. An example of this relocation is found at 362.88, Victims of crimes. Prevention of violent crimes for individuals was moved to 613.66, which has the notation (*formerly* 362.88) (Dewey 2003, 3:42).

Scatter relocations are found where the meaning of a discontinued heading is dissipated so widely that full enumeration of its relocations would not be practical. In this edition, 544 (Qualitative analysis), 545 (Quantitative analysis), and 547.3 (Analytical organic chemistry) are scattered within 543, Analytical chemistry.

"Comprehensive works" are often shifted to a shorter number, or relocated completely to other hierarchies or other portions of their original hierarchy. An example is found under 617.05, "Surgery utilizing specific instruments and techniques or specific groups of instruments and techniques." Comprehensive works on geriatric surgery, pediatric surgery, military surgery, all utilizing specific instruments or techniques, are now found under this number. They have been moved from locations further down the 617 hierarchy (Dewey 2003, 3:133).

Overview of *DDC* 22 Revisions

As indicated in Chapter 1, Edition 22 continues an evolutionary path of gradual changes to keep pace with the rapid growth of knowledge as well as the shrinking of the world which results from the swift exchange of information now capable through technology and the easy movement of people. Significant changes were made in the following areas:

- Data processing and Computer science (004–006) has been updated to reflect the rapid changes in technology.
- The last planned changes have been made to Religion (200) to reduce the Christian bias.
- Medicine and Health (610) has been updated and expanded.
- Historical Periods have been updated in 930–990.
- American native peoples and languages have been expanded (Tables 5 and 6).
- Table 7 has been eliminated and replaced with notations from 08 in Table 1 and in other places in the Schedules.
- The Manual has been revised and condensed and reduced in size from 303 pages in Edition 21 to 181 pages in this edition.
- Table 2 (Geographic Areas, Historical Periods, Persons) has major changes that reflect the dynamics of today's world.
- Major revisions are found in Social Groups (305), Culture and Institutions (306), Law (341–344), Mathematics (510–519), Chemistry and Allied Sciences (540), and Earth Sciences (550).

Details about these and other changes are found in succeeding chapters.

Literature Cited

Bloomberg, Marty, and Hans Weber. 1976. *An Introduction to Classification and Number Building*. Littleton, CO: Libraries Unlimited.

Chan, Lois Mai. 1973. The Tenth Abridged DDC . . . and Children's Room/School Library Collections. *School Library Journal* 20 (1):38.

Dewey, Melvil. 1989. *Dewey Decimal Classification and Relative Index.* 20th ed. Albany, NY: Forest Press.

———. 1996. *Dewey Decimal Classification and Relative Index.* 21st ed. Albany, NY: Forest Press.

———. 2003. *Dewey Decimal Classification and Relative Index.* 22nd ed. Dublin, OH: OCLC Online Computer Library Center.

3

Principles of Number Building

Often, the subject of a work that is to be classed does not appear in either the Relative Index or the Schedules, thus it is often necessary to *build* the required number for the classification of the work. The process begins with the base number, which is then added to according to instructions that are found in the Schedules. "Adding" numbers come from the six Tables, Add Tables in the Schedules, and other parts of the Schedules. Table 1 (Standard Subdivision) notations can be added to any number in the Schedules unless there are specific directions not to use the Standard Subdivisions.

When more than one facet, or aspect, is needed to class a work, a series of added numbers may be required. These numbers are added in "citation order" taken from a whole sequence of hints in the Schedules on methodologies of choosing the order of "adds." Where there are no instructions for adding more than one aspect, Preference Order is used. This is the order indicated in Preference Notes or Instructions in the Schedules proper, auxiliary Tables, and in the Manual.

Principles of Book Classification

Classifying books has been defined "as the art of assigning books to their proper places in a system of classification in which the various subjects of human inquiry, or the descriptions of human life in its various aspects, are grouped according to their likeness or relation to one another" (Merrill 1939, 1). In practice, however, this is not an easy task. Catalogers use the following general principles when selecting a DDC number:

1. Class a book, or any other material, where it will be most useful to the patron. This can usually be accomplished by placing similar materials together. This may also be accomplished by the use of broad or close classification depending on library needs.

2. Class a book first by subject and second by form, except in the field of literature. For example, an encyclopedia of art will be classed in art and not with general encyclopedias. The subject, art, is more important than the form, an encyclopedia.

3. Class a work of literature first by its original language and second by its form. For example, a work on French poetry translated into English will be classed in the number for French poetry, not for English poetry, because the original language is French. After the original language of the work has been determined, it is then classed by form (drama, poetry, fiction, essays, speeches, and letters).

4. Class a book that covers two or three subjects under the *first* subject treated unless another subject receives more prominent attention. A book that treats first chemistry and then physics but that gives equal treatment to each is classed with the first subject treated, chemistry.

5. Class a book that covers more than three subjects in a general subject embracing all of the subjects. For example, a book treating mathematics, astronomy, physics, and chemistry will be classed with comprehensive works on science. A work treating arithmetic, algebra, trigonometry, and geometry is classed with comprehensive works on mathematics.

6. Class a book in the most specific number possible in the classification scheme. For example, a history of the American Civil War will be classed in a specific number for the Civil War and not in a more general number. A work on the banjo is classed in the specific number for the banjo and not in a general number for string instruments. Classifying a book in too general a number defeats the purpose of classification, because it places books on specific topics in meaningless order.

7. In general, class a book first by subject if there is a choice between subject and geographical location. For example, a book on German architecture is classed in the number for architecture, not in the number for Germany.

8. Class biographies, autobiographies, diaries, and reminiscences either together in a general biography number or with specific disciplines. For example, a biography of a lawyer is classed either in a general number covering biographies of people regardless of occupation or in a number in law used for biographies of lawyers, judges, etc.

9. Class a book according to the author's intent in writing it. For example, if an author produces a book of drawings of dogs the cataloger must examine the book to see if it is meant to emphasize the drawing of different breeds, or techniques of drawing dogs. Depending on the author's intent, the book could be classed in a number for dogs or a number for techniques of drawing. (Bloomberg and Weber 1976, 39–40)

The Theory of Number Building

The foundation of number building is the base number, which is a sequence of numbers that does not vary but remains the same, and digits from other parts of the schedule or from the Tables that can be added as instructed. For example, the base number for all languages is 4 and all numbers are added to base number 4. The base number for Tagalog language (Filipino) is 499.211. Instructions in the Schedules tell the classifier to "Add to 499 the numbers following –99 in notation 991–999 from Table 6 . . . then to the number for each language listed below add notation 01–8 from Table 4" (Dewey 2003, 2:936).

Thus, in any sequence the *base* number does not vary (e.g., Dictionary of Tagalog is 499.2113, or 499.211 + 3 for dictionaries). It is from the base numbers that the classifier builds more specific numbers for the materials being cataloged. Number building is the process of developing a number by the addition of numbers or segments of numbers from other parts of the schedule, from the Tables, or both.

Notes

A *scope note* usually appears after a major classification number, defining exactly what aspects of the subject are to be classed in the number. The following example is found under 361 Social problems and social welfare in general (Dewey 2003, 2:701).

361.1 Social problems

History, description, appraisal of areas and kinds of social breakdown, of problems endemic to human society.

The 361 section of the class Social sciences looks at only general aspects of social problems and social welfare. The scope note, "History, Description . . . " makes clear that the notation 361.1 is for works about aspects of social problems in general. Aspects about specific social problems, such as crime victims and environmental problems, are found in numbers 362 and 363.

Class here notes are intended for the same purpose: to specify what types of works should be classed in a particular number. The following example of a "class here note" is found under 333 Economics of land and energy (Dewey 2003, 2:474).

333.953 8 *Seaweeds

Class here algae, kelp

The "class here" note lists two well-known seaweeds that should be found under 333.9538 when economic aspects of their use is the subject of the work being classed.

The asterisk beside seaweeds refers to another type of note, an *add note*, found at the bottom of the page. "Add" notes give directions for building numbers for specialized subtopics.

* Add as instructed under 333.7–333.9.

This kind of reference is always found *within* the Schedules. Reviewing the Add Table before 333.7, there is more than a page of instructions as to use and what numbers can be added to further define Seaweeds and other types of natural resources found in 333.7, 333.8 or 333.9 and that are preceded by an asterisk (Dewey 2003, 2:460).

333.7–333.9 Natural resources and energy

Aspects other than ownership.

Class here raw materials.

Except for modifications shown under specific entries, add to each subdivision identified by * as follows:

01–09 Standard subdivisions

1 General topics

Class comprehensive works on specific topics in 333.71

[etc.]

"Class comprehensive works on specific topics in 333.71" is a *class elsewhere note*. This type of note will indicate that an aspect of the subject should not be classed in that particular number but "elsewhere."

Facets, or categories of a subject, are governed by notes in the Schedules to *Add to* or *Add from. Add to* notes replace the previously used "Divide likes," which refer to shifts in the Schedules. These notes usually refer the classifier to a part of the Schedules above the notation to which the "adding" is applied where instructions describe what should be added and under what conditions the adding should occur. An example found under 342 Constitutional and Administrative Law illustrates this process (Dewey 2003, 2:549).

342.04 * Structure, powers, functions of government

The asterisk (*) beside the topic in the Schedules leads the user to a note at the bottom of the page, " * Add as instructed under 342–347." In this particular part of the 300 class there are two Tables, one for 342–349 inclusive and another for 342–347 where two pages of detailed instructions guide the classifier in building numbers under these aspects of law (Dewey 2003, 2:546).

> **342–347 Branches of law**

Class here comprehensive works on specific subjects of law.

Except for modifications shown under specific entries, add to each subdivision identified by * as follows:

–01 Philosophy and theory

–02 Miscellany

–026 Laws, regulations, cases, procedure …

[etc.]

Using our example, a work on the regulation of the police powers of the government would be classed in 342.0418026. Looking in the schedules under 342.04, the classifier will find "Police Powers" at .0418 to which 026 is adding to indicate the regulations of the government's police powers.

Add from notes refer to adding numbers selected according to instructions from the six Tables found in Volume 1. These tables are discussed subsequently.

This discussion is an overview of the many kinds of notes found within the Schedules. *Always read and follow all notes* before using a DDC number. The notes are essential for number building and determining where to classify materials. Failure to read and carefully follow the notes in the DDC Schedules will result in incorrectly built numbers and incorrect classifications.

Tables

The six Tables in the full DDC are important devices used in number building. The Tables are a mnemonic (memory) feature in the DDC, which use the same combination of numbers to represent the same topic or have the same meaning throughout the Schedules. Thus, "05" represents "periodicals" wherever it is added to notations within the Schedules. This system provides a consistency of meaning in the various contexts or topics found in the DDC's approach to organizing knowledge. The numbers from the Tables are *never* used alone, but always in conjunction with numbers from the classification Schedules. A dash (–) proceeding the numbers emphasizes that they must be added to another number, but the dash is omitted when building notations.

Table 1 contains *Standard Subdivisions*, which are be added to any number in the Schedules unless instructions in the part of the Schedule used indicate otherwise. These subdivisions provide notations to identify works that may be in a historical or geographical approach, a philosophical or theoretical perspective, or a particular format or physical form. Examples of treatment by format or physical form are dictionaries, encyclopedias, and periodicals.

Table 2, Geographic Areas, Historical Periods, Persons, contains numbers that are used in combination with Standard Subdivision –09 from Table 1. The notations in this table, the largest one, allow a number to be expanded to indicate a geographical significance. Throughout the DDC Schedules there are instructions to add from Table 2 to build a more specific classification number. Where no specific instructions are given in the Schedules for adding the area notation, the Standard Subdivision –09 for Historical, Geographical, or Persons Treatment is added to the base number, and then the area notation added to –09.

Notation –1 in Table 2 is for places in general, oceans, and seas. The number –2 is used for biographical materials, and –3 represents the ancient world. Numbers –4 through –9 indicate first the continents and then are subdivided into countries. For example, the "4" in the notation for Greece (495) indicates Europe.

Table 3 contains notations that are used only with base numbers specified in 808–890, or where instructed in 700.4 (Special Topics in the Arts), 791.4 (Motion Pictures, Radio, Television under Public Performances). This Table consists of three Subtables whose notations are selected according to the type of literature being classified, the number of authors of the literature, themes or subject, and other facets or aspects of literature. Similar to the relationship between Tables 1 and 2, Table 3C is added to Table 3B according to the extensive instructions describing how to select the numbers.

Table 4 notations are used only where indicated with base numbers 420–490 (Languages). Add notes or and asterisk will indicate how the form divisions are applied.

Table 5, Ethnic and National Groups, contains numbers that are used as directed in the Schedules. These notations can be added to base numbers in the Schedules and to notations from other Tables. Adding from this is similar to adding geographical notations from Table 2 to Standard Subdivision –09 from Table 1. These numbers are generally added to –089 from Table 1, but can be added directly as instructed in the Schedules.

Table 6, Languages, is used as directed in the Schedules. These notations can be added to base numbers in the Schedules and to notations from other Tables. This Table is particularly important in the 400 and 800 classes. The mnemonic feature of the Schedules is evident in comparing Tables 2 and 6. For example, the designation for Spain in Table 2 is **6** under **4** (Europe), or **–46**. The number representing Spain in Table 6 is also **6**, Spanish language is **460**, and Spanish Literature is **860.**

Details about Tables 1 through 6 and examples of their use are found in Chapter 4.

Options

Recent emphasis on the international appeal of DDC, as well as increased sensitivities to various peoples, has expanded the number of options offered. They are often found in parenthesis at the beginning of a discipline. An example is found under 342 Constitutional and Administrative Law. Two separate options are available to the classifier, Options A and B. Using Option A, Instructions direct user to "class here comprehensive works on the law of preferred jurisdiction. . . ." Option B suggests that the classifier "class here comparative law and law without jurisdiction by adding to base number 342 . . . " (Dewey 2003, 2:548). These kinds of instructions may be complicated and are not for the faint of heart when classifying collections in this manner, but they do provide a flexibility that allows the Schedules to be applicable to all types of libraries.

Another type of Option is found under 420–490 Option B. "To give local emphasis and a shorter number to a specific language, place it first by use of a letter or other symbol, e.g., Arabic language 4A0" (Dewey 2003, 2:896). The first example gives options in placing materials within the Schedules. This example gives choice of actually modifying the notation to achieve local distinction.

Classifying and Building Numbers

Through these devices, classifications are possible for an infinite number of subjects. By using "Adds" and "Options," it is possible to make the notation as specific as practicable. However, many of the numbers will be too long for many small libraries. Libraries with smaller collections have a built-in option. Segmenting of DDC numbers is shown by spaces between digits in numbers; DDC numbers can be divided at these places without losing their meaning. Those that appear in one segment should generally be used without this reduction.

When classifying works, it is important to remember that it is necessary to use both the Schedules and the Relative Index. For example, when classifying works on survival skills, that subject will not be found anywhere in the Schedules. The Relative Index, however, directs the classifier to use 613.69, which lists only survival after accidents and disasters, and survival housekeeping in the Schedules. The successful classifier will use every part of *DDC* 22 to achieve the best notations for works in their libraries.

Literature Cited

Bloomberg, Marty, and Hans Weber. 1976. *An Introduction to Classification and Number Building in Dewey.* Littleton, CO: Libraries Unlimited.

Dewey, Melvil. 2003. *Dewey Decimal Classification and Relative Index.* 22nd ed. Dublin, OH: OCLC Online Computer Library Center.

Merrill, William Stetson. 1939. *Code for Classifiers: Principles Governing the Consistent Placing of Books in a System of Classification.* 2d ed. Chicago: American Library Association.

4

The Tables

The Tables were introduced in Edition 18, although a predecessor to Table 1 was found in the first edition. It was nicknamed "Form Divisions" despite the fact that several features were in no way expressive of physical format, but eventually the obvious misnomer was dropped. Other precursors of the modern Tables appeared and disappeared abruptly. Edition 2 (1885) included three new ones called "Geographic Divisions," which was little more than lists of topics that could be subdivided by region and utilized the history numbers in 930–999. The other two gave pattern lists of class numbers and subject divisions for the various languages identified in the 400 class. Edition 13 (1932) introduced a fifth, which subdivided literatures in the 800 class. All of these auxiliary aids lasted until Edition 15 dropped everything except a brief introduction to a method of subdividing "where consideration of the form or style in which the book is written, as well as the subject, is important" (Dewey 1951, 1:xiii).

Edition 16 restored the form divisions in a separate list similar to today's Table 1. The old "Geographic Table" appeared as a sequence of numbers "accompanied by instructions in the Schedules to 'divide like 930–999,' or 'like 940–999' " (Dewey 1958, 2:2421). Edition 17 renamed the "Form Divisions" and restructured the Geographic Table into an "Area Table" with all the characteristics of the present Table 2. Edition 18 reactivated the discontinued Tables 3, 4, and 6 for language and literature. It also added two more: Table 5 for racial, ethnic, and national groupings, and Table 7 for differentiating groups of persons.

Some writers urge that "the principle of separate Tables for certain subjects ought to be extended in future editions" (Croghan 1972, 120–21), much like the Add Tables found in many of the classes. This would mean Add Instructions for using notations from other parts of the Schedule and making almost no use of these Tables except for a rare reference to Table 2 for a location. DDC editors seem more concerned with refining and expanding the existing Tables. They are also aware that faceting inevitably tempts classifiers to use close classification to the limits of its practicability. Witness the excessively long DDC numbers often found in Library of Congress records. They may be justified for indexing uses for which the Universal Decimal Classification was designed.

One of the major changes found in *DDC* 22 is the deletion of a whole Table. Meanings previously added with notations from Table 7 Groups of Persons are now supplied by using numbers from Standard Subdivision –08 History and Description with Respect to Kinds of Persons, and in some areas, by adding other numbers from the Schedules.

Table 1. Standard Subdivisions

Table 1 notations are the most often used of the six Tables. From the first, Mr. Dewey applied a rudimentary pattern for "mode of treatment" subdivisions. Edition 2 gave it a fixed form, reflecting to some extent notable features built into the Schedule proper. The morphology of Table 1 has changed little over intervening years, although extensive expansions and several significant alterations took place.

Table 1 facets, or notations, can be attached to any notations from the Schedules, except where instructions direct otherwise. Some examples are:

155.2***01***	Theory of defense mechanisms
579.355***072***	Streptococcus research
614.432***05***	A serial publication on insects as disease carriers
297.***03***	An Islam concordance

The Standard Subdivisions are the only fully generalized faceting device offered in the DDC, the only Table by which Class numbers may be subdivided without specific instructions. However, frequently within the Schedules there are special instructions about the Table's application. For example, instructions in the Schedules under 297 (Islam, Babism, Bahai Faith) read (Dewey 2003, 2:289):

[06]	Organizations and management
	[Do not use; class in 297.6]

Sometimes part of the Table 1 meanings and notations are repeated in the Schedules under a particular class number. This practice may seem redundant, but closer examination shows that in every case certain Standard Subdivisions' meanings are expanded, negated, or superseded. The case of Standard Subdivision –04 (Special Topics) is unique because it is designed for local schedule manipulation. In Table 1 a note under the notation indicates that it is to be used only when indicated in the Schedules. Where the notation can and should be used, the

Special Topics related to the particular classification are listed. For example, under 613.7 (Physical Fitness), the Special Topics of the subject list physical fitness for the various ages and sexes.

Table 1 Summary and Applications

The following summary of the Standard Subdivisions found in Table 1 indicates the breadth of the facets that the Table provides and that these additions to a classification in the number building process can provide the most basic aspects of any topic (Dewey 2003, 1:186).

–01	Philosophy and theory
–02	Miscellany
–03	Dictionaries, encyclopedias, concordances
–04	Special topics
–05	Serial publications
–06	Organizations and management
–07	Education, research, related topics
–08	History and description with respect to kinds of persons
–09	Historical, geographic, persons treatment

The Standard Subdivisions provide possibilities for further division within each Subdivision. For example, Standard Subdivision –01 furnishes the following more specialized divisions (Dewey 2003, 1:186):

–01	Philosophy and theory
–011	Systems
–012	Classification
–014	Language and communication
–015	Scientific principles
–016	(Optional number for bibliographies)
–019	Psychological principles

Citation Order

Dewey interposed the "0" in front of his "form divisions" to prevent citation order problems and ensure their physical precedence over all other subdivisions of general Class numbers. By *DDC* 14 published in 1942, a variety of subdivision notations within the Schedules were needed to subdivide broad topics adequately. Variation in the number of intervening zeros was the solution to free single zero notations for Schedule use. Standard Subdivision notations, which are designed to be universally applicable, had to be adjusted to provide normal citation order. The double zero is the most common way to achieve this. More complicated situations require a third zero when the second one is, or may be, preempted for other use.

Thus, more than one "0" may be used for a Standard Subdivision, such as –03, –003, or –0003, with the number of " '0s" used in the Standard Subdivision varying to avoid conflict with other numbers within the Schedules. If more than one "0" is required, there will always be appropriate instructions provided. Even though the Standard Subdivisions generally can be used with any number in the Schedules, it is always necessary to check to see if there are special directions for their use in a particular classification number.

A good example of the increasing generality of content that multiple zeros reflect can be seen in the summary for the history of Central Europe, where the fewer the zeros the more particular the meaning of the number is. The most specific places have no zeros at all (Dewey 2003, 3:902).

943.000 1–.000 9	Standard subdivisions of central Europe
.001–.009	Standard subdivisions of Germany
.01–.08	Historical periods of Germany
.1	Northeastern Germany
.6	Austria and Liechtenstein
.7	Czech Republic and Slovakia
.8	Poland
.9	Hungary

There are also situations in which it seems that no zeros are used with a Standard Subdivision, such as under 200 (Religion), where the Standard Subdivisions are 200.1–.9. In reality, the zero is incorporated into the class number.

DDC prohibits adding one Standard Subdivision to another in the same classification number unless there are specific instructions to do so. When more than one applies to the same work, classifiers may find themselves in a quandary. There are instructions for such situations at the beginning of Table 1, a Table of Preference, which indicates the citation order for Table 1.

Special topics	–04
Persons	–092

Auxiliary techniques and procedures;
apparatus, equipment, materials (*except* –288) –028

Education, research, related topics –07

(*except* –074, –075)

Management –068

(Etc.)

DDC 22 Table 1 Revisions

Efforts to remove appearances of bias from Table entries are seen in –08 notations, such as "racial" being removed from –089, which now is Ethnic and National Groups, and –08905 through –0899 has become Specific Ethnic and National Groups. Also, the discontinuation of Table 7 has affected Table 1 in notations –088001 through –088999 where –001 through –999 replaces –09 through –99 from Table 7. Another effect of the removal of Table 7 on Standard Subdivisions involves notation –024, in which, like –088 notations, 001 through 999 and replaces –09 through –99 from Table 7.

Another change also under –08 is that dictionaries, encyclopedias, and concordances are added to –0801 through –0809, which makes a long list of eleven topics to which the notations apply.

Other revisions include Drafting at –0221 under Illustrations, Models, and Miniatures has been discontinued altogether because of the lack of any meaning within that context. And finally, reflecting the passage of time, a new notation, –90512, has been added for the years 2010 to 2019. Details of Table 1 changes follow (Table 4.1).

Table 4.1

Current Number	Current Topic	Old Topic/ Comment	Old Number
Add Table 1			
–01	Value		–013
–014	Etymology		–0142
–0221	[Drafting illustrations]	Discontinued	

Current Number	Current Topic	Old Topic/ Comment	Old Number
–024	Persons in specific occupations	001–999 and replaces –09 through –99 from Table 7	
–029	Trade catalogs and directories under commercial miscellany of Europe		–0294
–029	Buyers' guides and consumer reports under commercial miscellany of Africa		–0296
–029	Evaluation and purchasing manuals under commercial miscellany of North America		–0297
–029	Estimates of labor, time, materials under commercial miscellany of other parts		–0299
–07	Programmed texts		–077
–075	Organizing and preparing collections and exhibits and service to patrons		–0753 to –0755
–0863	Persons of medium cultural development		–08632
–086912	Immigrants	New number	
–086914	Displaced persons	New number	
–086918	Nomads	New number	
–088	Occupational and religious groups	Notations 001–009 replaces notations 09–99 from Table 7	–088001 to 088009

Table 2. Geographic Areas, Historical Periods, Persons

Table 2 notations are used in combination with Standard Subdivision –09 from Table 1 to denote geographic significance, historical periods, or biographical works. Geographic or political subdivisions were long dependent on the history divisions 930–990. Not only were subdivisions of 910 (Geography and Travel) drawn from that span but also regional divisions in any discipline were based on "Divide-like" instructions, which referred to those numbers for patterns. As time went on, two problems emerged. First, the WASP bias from which the DDC still struggles to extricate itself dominated the history schedule, stressing political units, especially in Europe and the United States, over physical and other regional areas. Second, the "Divide-like" instructions were hard to follow. *DDC* 17 initiated the now familiar Area Table, with a section for regions and places in general. Other parts of the table expanded jurisdictional sequences, especially those for Asia, Africa, and Oceania. Although it retained its Divide-likes to cite other additions from various parts of the Schedules, that edition referred to its auxiliary Tables by means of Add notes. Divide-likes gave way entirely in *DDC* 18 to instructions to "Add to" from within the Schedules, and "Add from" from the Tables.

Table 2 Summary and Applications

The summary of Table 2 gives the outline of notations used to signify locations on Earth, with extraterrestrial worlds occupying –9 along with Pacific Ocean islands, New Zealand, and Australia (Dewey 2003, 1:215–16).

–1	Areas, regions, places in general; oceans and seas
–2	Persons
–3	The ancient world
–4	Europe; Western Europe
–5	Asia; Orient; Far East
–6	Africa
–7	North America
–8	South America
–9	Other parts of the world; extraterrestrial worlds; Pacific Ocean Islands

The area notation –1 is used for areas not limited by continents, countries, or localities. Included are the treatment of a subject by region, areas, places, and groups in general. Also included here are such geographic features as frigid zones, land forms, oceans, and socioeconomic regions.

The demarcation between areas –3 and –4 to –9 is not always as clear as could be wished, especially in view of notes directing users to classify specific parts of the ancient world under –4 to –9. A British classifier offered some advice:

> Under –3 "The Ancient world" gathered those parts of the world which were more or less known *to* classical antiquity, and considered only during the period of "ancient history." The same areas in later times, as well as other areas such as America in both ancient and later times, are classed in –4 through –9. (Trotter 1980, 4)

Many class numbers can be geographically divided without specific instructions by going first to the Standard Subdivision –093 through –099 span, which is Treatment by specific continents, countries, localities, extraterrestrial worlds and is most frequently used. But twenty other Table 1 entries say to add notations from Table 2.

The discussion of Standard Subdivisions noted that two are not used in the same classification number except when so instructed. One of the most frequent exceptions is for catalogs of exhibits (with geographic facets) housed in museums (also characterized by geographic facets).

Persons, as individuals or as individual members of a class of people, have been indicated by means of either Table 1 or 2 for quite a while. Persons (–2) in Table 2 should not be confused with notation –8 (History and description with respect to kinds of persons) or –092 (Persons) in Table 1. The important word to note above is *kinds* of person and notations –081 to –089 distinguish persons by gender, age, social, occupational, or religious characteristics, or by ethnic group.

Table 1 notation –092 (Persons) is used for biography, autobiography, description and critical appraisal of a work, diaries, reminiscences, correspondence of persons regardless of place, *who are part of the subject or those that study the subject.*

The Table 2 persons notation is used for biographies, autobiographies, description and critical appraisal of a work, and so on of *persons associated with the subject*. Careful examination of the work being classified and the Schedules is necessary when determining which of the Tables is the correct one to use. For example, elementary school teachers is 372.92 not 372.092.

An example of using –09 from Table 1 and a geographic location from Table 2 is the classification for a work about hunting and fishing in Greece, 639.09495.

639	Hunting and fishing
.09	Standard subdivision (Table 1)
495	Greece (Table 2)

DDC 22 Table 2 Revisions

There have been numerous changes in Table 2 notations, many of which reflect massive political transformations, such as the breakup of the Soviet Union. England, Scotland, and Wales have been updated with many places shifted about under –411 through –414.

Throughout Table 2 specific names, such as a country name, have been added to more general designations. For example, –678 28 in Edition 21 was Western regions, but Western regions *of Tanzania* in Edition 22. These changes found throughout the Table help the classifier locate the correct notation.

As a result of the reduction in size of the Manual, more explanations are found under the various notations in Table 2. An example is found at –1648 (South Pacific Ocean), where Edition 21 referred the classifier to the Manual, but in Edition 22 there is no such instruction, but rather a paragraph indicating which bodies of water should be in this notation.

Place names have been updated to reflect changes occurring during recent years, such as –1717, formerly called Communist Bloc, now is Former Communist Bloc. Also, as in Table 1, the word "racial" has been removed from place names, such as –174, which now is Regions where Specific Ethnic and National Groups Predominate.

"Oceans and Seas" were added to the heading for –1 (Areas, Region, Places in General). Those bodies of waters had been buried in –162 through –169 but now are more evident from the new heading.

Place names that previously referred to Table 7 for adding numbers to the notation now indicate that notations 292–299 are to be used instead of 292–299 from Table 7. This results in new meanings for certain numbers, such as –1762 through –1769 (Other Religions).

Following is a detailed list of changes to Table 2.

Table 4.2

Current Number	Current Topic	Old Topic/Comment	Old Number
–1	Areas, regions, places in general; oceans and seas	Areas, regions, places in general	
–153	Grasslands planes	Plane regions	–145
–16338	French, Spanish, and Portuguese coastal waters to Strait of Gibraltar	French and Spanish coastal waters to Strait of Gibraltar	
–1717	Former communist bloc	Communist bloc	
–174	Regions where specific ethnic and national groups predominate	Regions where specific racial, ethnic, national groups predominate	
–1762 to 1769	Other religions	Notation 292–299 replaces notation 292–299 from Table 7	
–2	**Persons**		
–23	Collected persons treatment of members of specific ethnic and national groups (new number)	New Number	
–29	Persons treatment of nonhumans (new number)	New Number	
–411	**Scotland**		
–4113	Orkney and Shetland Islands	Orkney and Shetland Islands authorities	–4112

Current Number	Current Topic	Old Topic/Comment	Old Number
–4113	Orkney and Shetland Islands	Islands authorities	
–4118	[Western districts of Highland Region]	Discontinued	
–41152	Northern Highlands	Caithness District, Sutherland District, Kincardine and Wick	–4116
–41152	Northern Highlands	Ullapool	–41172
–41154	Skye and adjacent islands	Inner Hebrides	–4118
–41154	Skye and adjacent islands	Skye and Lochalsh District	–41182
–41154	Skye and adjacent islands	Canna, Eigg, Muck Rhum	–41185
–41156	Western Highlands	Inverness District, Ross and Cromarty District, Inverness, Great Glen, and Loch Ness	–4117
–41156	Western Highlands	Lochaber District and Fort William	–41185
–41158	Eastern Highlands	Badenoch and Strathspey District, Nairn District, and Spey River	–4119
–41158	Eastern Highlands	Grampian Mountains	–4121
–41158	Eastern Highlands	Western districts of the Highland Region discontinued (no meaning in this context)	–4118
–4122	Moray	Moray District	–41223
–4122	Moray	Northern districts of Grampian discontinued (without meaning in this context)	
–4123	Aberdeen City		–41235

Current Number	Current Topic	Old Topic/Comment	Old Number
–4123	Aberdeen City	Central districts of Grampian	
–4124	Aberdeenshire	Kincardine and Deeside District	
–4124	Aberdeenshire	Grampian Region, Cairngorm Mountains, and the Dee River	–4121
–4124	Aberdeenshire	Banff and Buchan District, Deveron River	–41225
–4124	Aberdeenshire	Gordon District and Don River	–41232
–4126	Angus	Angus District	
–4126	Angus	Strathmore	–4125
–4126	Angus	Monifieth	–4127
–4128	Perth and Kinross	Perth and Kinross District	
–4128	Perth and Kinross	Tayside Region	–4125
–4129	Fife	Fife Region	
–4129	Fife	Dunfermline, Kirkcaldy, and North East Fife Districts	–41292 and –41298
–4133	West Lothian	Western Lothian District	
–4133	West Lothian	Lothian Region	–4132
–4137	Scottish Borders	Borders Region	
–4137	Scottish Borders	Ettrick and Lauderdail District, and Tweeddale District	–4138
–4137	Scottish Borders	Berwickshire and Roxburgh Districts	–4139
–414	Southwestern Scotland	Strathclyde Region	–4141
–4142	Argyll and Bute		–41423

Current Number	Current Topic	Old Topic/Comment	Old Number
–4142	[Northwestern districts of Strathclyde]	Discontinued	
–4142	Argyll and Bute	Western part of Dumbarton District	–41425
–4143	[North central districts of Strathclyde]	Discontinued	
–41431	Inverclyde		–41428
–41432	West Dunbartonshire	Clydebank District	
–41432	West Dunbartonshire	Eastern part of the Dumbarton District, Alexandria, and Dumbarton	–41425
–41436	East Dunbartonshire	Strathkelvin District	
–41436	East Dunbartonshire	Bearsden and Milngavie District	–41434
–41437	Renfrewshire	Paisley, Renfrew, and the Renfrew District	–41441
–41439	East Renfrewshire	Barrhead	–41441
–41439	East Renfrewshire	Newton Mearns and the Eastwood District	–41451
–4144	Glasgow City		–41443
–4144	[Central districts of Strathclyde]	Discontinued	
–4145	[South central districts of Strathclyde]	Discontinued	
–41452	North Lanarkshire	Muirhead and Stepps	–41436
–41452	North Lanarkshire	Cumbernauld and Kilsyth District	–41438
–41452	North Lanarkshire	Monklands District, Airdrie, Coatbridge	–41446
–41452	North Lanarkshire	Motherwell District	–41449
–41457	South Lanarkshire	Hamilton District	

Current Number	Current Topic	Old Topic/Comment	Old Number
–41457	South Lanarkshire	Cambuslang and Rutherglen	–41443
–41457	South Lanarkshire	East Kilbride District	–41454
–41457	South Lanarkshire	Clydesdale District	–41469
–4146	[Southern districts of Strathclyde]	Discontinued	
–41467	South Ayrshire	Kilmarnock and Loudoun District	–41463
–4147	Dumfries and Galloway	Annandale, Eskdale District, Nithsdale District and the Nith River	–4148
–4147	Dumfries and Galloway	Stewartry and Wigtown Districts	–4149
–42	**England**		
–42232	Medway Borough	City of Rochester upon Medway	–422323
–42232	Medway Borough	Gillingham Borough	–422325
–42256	Brighton and Hove	Hove Borough	–42254
–4228	Isle of Wight	Medina Borough	–42282
–4228	Isle of Wight	South Wight Borough	–42285
–42391	South Gloucestershire	Northavon District	
–42391	South Gloucestershire	Kingswood Bourough	–42394
–42398	Bath and North East Somerset District	Wansdyke District	–42397
–4242	Herefordshire	The Leominister District	–42444
–4242	Herefordshire	South Herefordshire District and Ross-on-Wye	–42445
–4242	Herefordshire	Hereford City	–42446

Current Number	Current Topic	Old Topic/Comment	Old Number
–4242	Herefordshire	Western part of Malvern Hills District, Broomvard, and Ledbury	–42447
–42447	Malvern Hills District	Tenbury Wells	–42444
–42456	Telford and Wrekin	Wrekin District	
–42832	North Lincolnshire	Scunthorpe Borough	–42831
	North Lincolnshire	Southern part of Boothferry Borough, Crowle, and the Isle of Axholme	–42835
–42834	North East Lincolnshire	Cleethorpes Bourough	–42833
–42839	East Riding of Yorkshire	East Yorkshire Borough	
–42839	East Riding of Yorkshire	Boothferry Borough and Howden	–42835
–42839	East Riding of Yorkshire	Beverley Borough	–42836
–42839	East Riding of Yorkshire	Holderness Borough	–42838
–429	**Wales**		
–42925	Gwynedd	Arfon Borough.	
–42925	Gwynedd	Dwyer District	–42923
–42925	Gwynedd	Meirionnydd District	–42929
–42927	Conwy County Borough	Aberconwy Borough	
–42927	Conwy County Borough	Colwyn Borough, Abergele, and Colwyn Bay	–42931
–42933	Flintshire County	Alyn and the Deeside District	–42936
–42937	Denbighshire County	Glyndŵr District	

Current Number	Current Topic	Old Topic/Comment	Old Number
–42937	Denbighshire County	Rhuddlan Borough, Prestatyn and Rhyl	–42932
–42939	Wrexham County Borough	Parts of the Glyndŵr District	–42937
–42951	Northern Powys County	Montgomery District	
–42951	Northern Powys County	Parts of the Glyndŵr District	–42937
–42951	Northern Powys County	Radnor District and Llandrindod Wells	–42954
–42956	Southern Powys County	Brecknock Borough	
–4296	Southwestern Wales	Dyfed County	
–42962	Pembrokeshire County	Preseli District	
–42962	Pembrokeshire County	South Pembrokeshire District	–42963
–42965	Carmarthenshire County	Carmarthen District	
–42965	Carmarthenshire County	Llanelli Borough	–42967
–42965	Carmarthenshire County	Dinefwr Borough	–42968
–42976	Caerphilly County Borough	Rhymney Valley District	
–42976	Caerphilly County Borough	Islwyn Borough	–42993
–42978	Rhondda Cynon Taff County Borough	Rhondda Borough	–42972
–42978	Rhondda Cynon Taff County Burough	Cynon Valley Borough and Aberdare	–42973
–42982	City and County of Swansea	Lliw Valley Borough, Pontarddulais	–42983
–42982	City and County of Swansea	West Glamorgan	–42981
–42985	Neath PortTalbot County Borough	Afan Borough	

Current Number	Current Topic	Old Topic/Comment	Old Number
–42985	Neath PortTalbot County Borough	Eastern part of Lliw Valley Borough and Gwaun-cae-Gurwen	–42983
	Neath PortTalbot County Borough	Neath Borough	–429894
–42987	Cardiff County	South Glamorgan	–42986
–42987	Cardiff County	Creigiau and Pentyrch	–42978
–42989	St. Bride's Major		–42971
–42998	Monmouthshire	Monmouth District	
–42998	Monmouthshire	Clydach and Gilwern	–42995
–431 to 435	**Germany**		
–43154	Western Brandenburg	Potsdam District	–43157
–431552	Eastern Berlin	East Berlin	
–431554	Western Berlin	West Berlin	
–43172	Eastern Mecklenburg	Neubrandenburg District (Bezirk)	
–43174	Central Mecklenburg	Rostock District (Rostock Bezirk)	
–43176	Western Mecklenburg	Schwerin District (Bezirk)	
–43178	German Pomerania (Vorpommern)	Southern German Pomerania	–43172
–43178	German Pomerania (Vorpommern)	Northern German Pomerania	–43174
–43186	Dessau District (Dessau Reigierungsbezirk)	Northern Dessau District	–43182
–43186	Dessau District (Dessau Reigierungsbezirk)	Southern Dessau District	–43184
–43216	Chemnitz District	Karl-Marx-Stadt District	

Current Number	Current Topic	Old Topic/Comment	Old Number
–43222	Eastern Thuringia	Gera District	
–43224	Northern Thuringia	Erfurt District	
–43226	Southern Thuringia	Suhl District	
–4346	Baden-Wurttemberg	Swabia	–4337
–4346452	Mannheim		–434646
–43595	Hannover District	Hildesheim	–435958
–437	**Czech Republic and Slovakia**		
–43713	Jihočeský Region	New number	
–43714	Plzeňský Region	New number	
–43715	Karlovarský Region	New number	
–43716	Ústecký Region	New number	
–43717	Liberecký Region	New number	
–43718	Královéhradecký	New number	
–43719	Pardubičký Region	New number	
–43722	Vysočina Region	New number	
–43724	Jihomoravský Region	New number	
–43725	Zlínský Region	New number	
–43727	Olomoucký Region	New number	
–43728	Moravskoslezský Region	New number	
–43731	Bratislava Region	New number	
–43732	Trnavský Region	New number	
–43733	Nitrianský Region	New number	
–43734	Banskobystrický Region	New number	
–43735	Košický Region	New number	
–43736	Prešovský Region	New number	

Current Number	Current Topic	Old Topic/Comment	Old Number
–43737	Źilinsky Region	New number	
–43738	Trenčianský Region	New number	
–43812	Lubuskie Province	New number	
–43816	Zachodniopomorskie Province	New number	
–438	**Poland**		
–43822	Pomorskie Province	New number	
–43822	Pomorskie Province	Slupsk Province	–4381
–43826	Kujawsko-Pomorskie Province	New number	
–43832	Warminsko-Mazurskie Province	Elbląg Province	–4382
–43836	Podlaskie Province	New number	
–43841	Mazowieckie Province	New number	
–43845	Świętokrzyskie Province	New number	
–43847	Lódzkie Province	New number	
–43849	Wielkopolskie Province	New number	
–43852	Dolnóslaskie Province	New number	
–43855	Opolskie Province	New number	
–43858	Śląskie Province	New number	
–43858	Śląskie Province	Bielsko Province	–4386
–43862	Malopolskie Province	New number	
–43866	Podkarpackie Province	Tarnobrzeg Province	–4384
–441 to 448	France		

Current Number	Current Topic	Old Topic/Comment	Old Number
–44112	Brest	New number	
–44154	Rennes	New number	
–44162	Mayenne department	New number	
–44167	Loire-Atlantique department	New number	–4414
–44169	Vendée department	New number	–4461
–44184	Angers	New number	
–44212	Manche department	New number	
–44224	Caen	New number	
–44252	Rouen	New number	
–44262	Somme department	New number	
–442625	Amiens	New number	
–44264	Oise department	New number	–4435
–44266	Aisne	New number	–44345
–44312	Ardennes department	New number	
–44322	Reims	New number	
–4436	Ile-de-France	Paris metropolitan area	–4434
–443663	Versailles	New number	
–44385	Moselle department	New number	–443825
–443853	Metz	New number	
–44389	Vosges department	New number	–4439
–4439	Alsace	New number	–44383
–44393	Haut-Rhin department	New number	
–443933	Mulhouse	New number	
–44395	Bas-rhin department	New number	
–443954	Strasbourg	New number	
–44412	Yonne department	New number	
–44416	Nièvre department	New number	–4456

Current Number	Current Topic	Old Topic/Comment	Old Number
–44426	Dijon	New number	
–44466	Besançon	New number	
–44512	Eure-et-Loir department	New number	
–445124	Chartres	New number	
–44527	Orléans	New number	
–445525	Bourges	New number	
–445817	Saint-Etienne	New number	
–44583	Ain department	New number	–4444
–44584	Haute-Savoie department	New number	–4449
–44585	Savoie department	New number	–4448
–44586	Isère department	New number	–4499
–44586	Isère department	Dauphiné	–4496
–445865	Grenoble	New number	
–44587	Drôme department	New number	–4498
–44588	Valréas	New number	–4492
–44589	Ardèche department	New number	–4482
–445914	Clermont-Ferrand	New number	
–44595	Haute-Loire department	New number	–44813
–44597	Allier department	New number	–4457
–44634	Poitiers	New number	
–44642	La Rochelle	New number	
–44662	Haute-Vienne department	New number	
–446624	Limoges	New number	
–447144	Bordeaux	New number	
–44715	Landes department	New number	–44772
–44716	Pyrénées-Atlantiques department	New number	–4479
–44718	Lot-et-Garonne department	New number	–4476

Current Number	Current Topic	Old Topic/Comment	Old Number
–4473	Midi-Pyrénées	Lot department	–4486
–4473	Midi-Pyrénées	Gascony	–4477
–4473	Midi-Pyrénées	Pyrenees Mountains in France	–4489
–44733	Lot department	New number	
–44735	Ariège department	New number	–4488
–44736	Haute-Garonne department	New number	–4486
–447367	Toulouse	New number	
–44737	Tarn department	New number	–4485
–4477	Gers department		–44771
–4481	Lozère department	New number	–44815
–44837	Nîmes	New number	
–44842	Montpellier	New number	
–449	**Provence-Côte d'Azur, Monaco, Corsica**		
–44918	Arles	New number	
–4494	Alpres-Maritimes department and Monaco		–44941
–44941	Nice (city)		–449414
–4499	Corsica		–44945
–44992	Corse-de-Sud department	New number	
–44996	Haute-Corse department	New number	
–451 to 457	**Italy**		
–45165	Verbania	New number	

Current Number	Current Topic	Old Topic/Comment	Old Number
–45176	Biella province	New number	
–45219	Lodi province	New number	
–45237	Lecco province	New number	
–45519	Prato province	New number	
–45782	Vibo Valentia province	New number	–45781
–45787	Crotone province	New number	–45781
–481 to 484	**Norway**		
–483	Sørlandet		–4831
–484	Trøndelag and Nord-Norge	Trøndelag	–4841
–494	**Switzerland**		
–494524	Lausanne	New number	
–494572	Zurich	New number	
–497	**Serbia and Montenegro, Croatia, Slovenia, Bosnia and Hercegovina, Madedonia**	Yugoslavia, Croatia, Slovenia, Bosnia and Hercegovina, Macedonia	
–497	Serbia and Montenegro, Croatia, Slovenia, Bosnia and Hercegovina, Madedonia	Yugoslavia	–4971

Current Number	Current Topic	Old Topic/Comment	Old Number
–54	**India**		
–54123	Bihar	New number	
–54127	Jharkland	New number	
–54137	Chhattīsgarh	New number	–543
–5451	Uttaranchal	New number	–542
—5476	Dādra and Nagar Haveli	New number	—54796
–5477	Daman and Diu	Goa, Daman, and Diu	–54799
–5478	Goa	Goa, Daman, and Diu	–54799
–5479	Maharashtra		–54792
–54792	Bombay (Mumbai)		–547923
–54911	Federally Administered Tribal Areas	North-West Frontier	–54912
–549132	Northern Areas	New number	
–549138	Azad Kashmir	New number	
–549149	Islāmābād Capital Territory	New number	–549142
–54926	Barisāl Division	New number	
–54926	Barisāl Division	Khulna	–54925
–54927	Sylhet Division	New number	
–54927	Sylhet Division	Chittagong Division	–54923
–54929	Chittagong Hill Tracts Division	New number	
–54929	Chittagong Hill Tracts Division	Chittagong Division	–54923
–55	**Iran**		
–5512	Ardabīl province	New number	
–5512	Ardabīl province	East Azerbaijan province	–553

Current Number	Current Topic	Old Topic/Comment	Old Number
–5514	Gīlān province	New number	
–5516	Zanjān province	New number	
–5518	Qazvīn province	New number	
–5522	Golestān province	New number	–5523
–5524	Semnān province	New number	–5523
–5526	Qum province	New number	–5527
–5556	Kermānshāhān province	New number	–5552
–5558	Īlām province	New number	–5552
–5574	Būshehr province	New number	–5575
–5594	Yazd province	New number	–5595
–5597	Chahār Mahāll va Bakhtīarī province	New number	–5595
–561 to 566	**Turkey**		
–566 7	Southeast central Turkey	Northeastern Turkey	–5662
–5695	**Jordan and West Bank**		
–569542	Irbid Province	New number	
–569546	‘Ajlūn Province	New number	
–569548	Jarash Province	New number	
–569562	Ma’dabā Province	New number	
–569562	Ma’dabā Province	Amman Province	–56958
–569572	‘Aqabah Province	New number	

Current Number	Current Topic	Old Topic/Comment	Old Number
–569577	Ma'ān Province	New number	
–5987	**East Timor**	Lesser Sunda Islands	–5986
–621 to 623	**Egypt**		
–6215	Isthmus of Suez	Suez Canal	–16533
–624 to 629	**Sudan**		
–625	Northern states of Sudan	Eastern and Northern regions of Sudan	
–626	Khartoum state and east central states of Sudan	Khartoum province and Central region of Sudan	
–6262	Khartoum state	Khartoum province	
–6264	East central states of Sudan	Central region	
–627	Darfur region	Darfur region of Sudan	
–628	Kordofan region	Kordofan region of Sudan	
–629	Southern states of Sudan	Southern regions of Sudan	
–6293	Upper Nile states	Upper Nile region	
–6294	Southwestern states of Sudan	Bahr al Ghazal and Buhayrah regions	
–6295	Equatoria states	Equatoria region	

Current Number	Current Topic	Old Topic/Comment	Old Number
–632 to 634	**Ethiopia**		
–632	Central and eastern Ethiopia	Provinces east of Great Rift Valley	
–633	Western Ethiopia	Provinces west of Great Rift Valley	
–634	Northern Ethiopia	Northern provinces	
–641	**[Autonomous Communities of Spain]**		
–641	Ceuta and Melilla	New number	–642
–642 to 646	**Morocco**		
–642	Tangier-Tétouan region	Mediterranean region of Morocco	
–6432	Taza-Al Hoceïma-Taounate region	New number	–642
–6433	Nador province	New number	–642
–6434	Fès-Boulemane region	New number	
–6435	Gharb-Chrarda-Béni Hsen region	New number	
–6436	Rabat-Salé-Zemmour-Zaer region	New number	
–6438	Grand Casablanca region	New number	
–6439	Chaouia-Ouardigha region	New number	
–644	Tadla-Azilal region	Azilal and Beni Bellal provinces	
–645	Meknès-Tafilalt region	Rachidia province	

Current Number	Current Topic	Old Topic/Comment	Old Number
–645	Meknès-Tafilalt region	Ifrane, Khenifra, Meknes provinces	–643
–6462	Doukkala-Abda region	Jadida province	–643
–6464	Marrakech-Tensift-El Haouz region	New number	
–6466	Souss Massa-Draâ region	New number	
–6468	Guelmim-Es Semara region	New number	
–669	**Nigeria**		
–66927	Ekiti State	Nigeria	–66928
–66941	Bayelsa State	New number	–66942
–66947	Ebonyi State	New number	–66945
–66947	Northern part of Ebonyi	New number	–66949
–66953	Nassarawa State	New number	–66952
–66961	Zamfara State	New number	–66962
–66984	Gombe State	New number	–66982
–6751	Democratic Republic of the Congo	Zaïre	
–67511	Bas-Congo and Bandundu provinces and Kinshasa	Bas-Zaïre and Bandundu regions and Kinshasa	
–675114	Bas-Congo province	Bas-Zaïre region	
–67515	Orientale province	Haute-Zaïre region	
–67517	Maniema, Nord-Kivu, Sud-Kiva provinces	Kivu region	
–67518	Katanga province	Shaba region	

Current Number	Current Topic	Old Topic/Comment	Old Number
–678 2	**Mainland regions of Tanzania**	**Tanganyika**	
–67823	Dar es Salaam and Pwani regions	Coast and Dar es Salaam regions	
–682 to 687	**Republic of South Africa**		
–682	Gauteng, North-West, Limpopo, Mpumalanga, former homelands of Republic of South Africa	Transvaal	
–6822	Gauteng	Witwatersrand	
–68222	Krugersdorp, Oberholzer, Randfontein, Roodepoort, Westonaria districts	New number	
–68223	Heidelberg, Vaderbijl-park, Vereeniging districts	New number	
–68223	Heidelberg, Vaderbijl-park, Vereeniging districts	Vaal Triangle	–6821
–68224	Brakpan,Nigel, Springs districts	New number	
–68225	Alberton, Benoni, Boksburg, Germiston, Kempton Park districts	New number	
–68226	Ranburg district	New number	
–68227	Pretoria district	New number	
–68227	Pretoria district	Pretoria and Wonderboom	–68235
–68228	Soshanguve district	New number	
–68228	Soshanguve district	Central districts	–6823

Current Number	Current Topic	Old Topic/Comment	Old Number
–68228	Soshanguve district	Pretoria and Wonderbloom	–68235
–68229	Bronkhorstspruit and Cullinan districts	New number	
–68229	Bronkhorstspruit and Cullinan districts	Central districts	–6823
–6824	North-West	Western districts	
–6824	North-West	Bophuthatswana	–68294
–68241	Brits, Rustenburg, Moretele I and Odi districts	New number	
–68241	Brits and Rustenburg districts	Central districts	–6823
–68241	Moretele I and Odi districts	New number	–68294
–68242	Koster, Potchefstroom, Ventersdorp districts	New number	
–68243	Kerksdorp district	New number	
–68244	Ditsobotla district	New number	–68294
–68244	Coligny, Delareyville, Lichtenburg districts		
–68245	Bloemhof, Christiana, Schweizer-Reneke, Wolmaransstad districts	New number	
–68246	Ganyesa, Kudumane, Taung districts	New number	–68294
–68246	Vryburg district	Northern districts	–68711
–68247	Molopo district	New number	–68294
–68248	Northern districts of North-West	New number	
–68248	Northern districts of North-West	Central districts	–6823

Current Number	Current Topic	Old Topic/Comment	Old Number
–68248	Northern districts of North-West	Lehurutshe, Madikwe, and Mankwe districts, Pilanesberg National Park	–68294
–6825	Limpopo	Northern districts	
–68251	Warmbad and Thabazimbi districts	New number	
–68251	Warmbad and Thabazimbi districts	Central districts	–6823
–68253	Mokerong, Ellisras, Potgietersrus, Waterberg districts, Mogalakwena River	New number	
–68253	Mokerong, Ellisras, Potgietersrus, Waterberg districts, Mogalakwena River	Lebowa	–68293
–68255	Nebo, Sekhukhuneland, Thabamoopo districts, Sekhukhuneberg Range, Lebowa	New number	
–68255	Nebo, Sekhukhuneland, Thabamoopo districts, Sekhukhuneberg Range, Lebowa	Lebowa	–68293
–68256	Bochum, Seshego, Polokwane districts	New number	
–68256	Bochum, Seshego, Polokwane districts	Lebowa	–68293
–68257	Northeastern districts of Limpopo	New number	
–68257	Northeastern districts of Limpopo	Venda	–68291
–68257	Northeastern districts of Limpopo	Gazankulu	–68292
–68257	Northeastern districts of Limpopo	Lebowa	–68293

Current Number	Current Topic	Old Topic/Comment	Old Number
–68259	Southeastern districts of Limpopo	New number	
–68259	Southeastern districts of Limpopo	Eastern districts	–6826
–68259	Southeastern districts of Limpopo	Gazankulu	–68292
–68259	Southeastern districts of Limpopo	Lebowa	–68293
–6827	Mpumalanga	Southeastern districts	
–68271	Pelgrimsrus and Witrivier, Nsikazi districts, Kruger Natonal Park	New number	
–68271	Pelgrimsrus and Witrivier districts, Kruger Natonal Park	Eastern districts	–6826
–68271	Nsikazi district	KaNgwane	–68296
–68272	Barberton, Eerstehoek, and Nkomazi districts, Komati River, KaNgwane	New number	
–68272	Barberton district, Komati River	Eastern districts	–6826
–68272	Eerstehoek, Nkomazi districts KaNgwane	KaNgwane	–68296
–68273	Nelspruit district	New number	
–68273	Nelspruit district	Eastern districts	–6826
–68274	Lydenburg and Pelgrimsrus 2, Belfast and Waterval-Boven districts	New number	
–68274	Lydenburg and Pelgrimsrus 2, Belfast and Waterval-Boven districts	Eastern districts	–6826

Current Number	Current Topic	Old Topic/Comment	Old Number
–68275	Northwestern districts of Mpumalanga, Groblersdal district	New number	
–68275	Northwestern districts of Mpumalanga, Groblersdal district	Bophuthatswana–Central districts	–6823
–68275	Northwestern districts of Mpumalanga	Bophuthatswana	–68294
–68275	Northwestern districts of Mpumalanga	KwaNdebele	–68295
–68276	Middelburg and Witbank districts	New number	
–68277	Delmas district, Balfour, Hoëveldrif, Kriel districts	Witwatersrand	–6822
–68278	Bethal, Carolina Ermelo districts	New number	
–68279	Southern district of Mpumalanga	New number	
–6829	Former homelands (Former national states)	Homelands (National states) South Africa	
–684	KwaZulu-Natal	Natal	–6849
–684	KwaZulu-Natal	KwaZulu	–68491
–6842	North central districts of KwaZulu-Natal	Southeastern districts	–6827
–6842	North central districts of KwaZulu-Natal	KawZulu	–68491
–6843	Northeastern districts of KwaZulu-Natal	KawZulu	–68491
–6844	North Coast districts	KawZulu	–68491
–6845	Southern coastal districts of KwaZulu-Natal	KawZulu	–68491
–6846	Alfred and Mount Currie districts	Southern interior districts	
–6847	Natal Midlands districts	KawZulu	–68491

Current Number	Current Topic	Old Topic/Comment	Old Number
–685	Free State	Orange Free State	
–6851	Northern districts of Free State	Homelands (National states) South Africa	–6859
–6851	Northern districts of Free State	Northeastern districts	–68591
–6855	East central districts of Free State	Bophuthatswana	–68294
–687	Northern Cape, Western Cape, Eastern Cape	Cape of Good Hope	
–6871	Northern Cape	Interior and regions	
–68711	Northeastern district of Northern Cape	Northern districts	
–68719	Namaqualand district	New number	
–68719	Namaqualand district	Northwestern districts	–6872
–6873	Western Cape	Western and southwestern districts	–6872
–68731	Clanwilliam, Vanrhynsdorp, Vredendal districts	Western and southwestern districts	–6872
–68732	West central districts of western Cape	New number	
–68733	North central districts of Western Cape	New number	
–68734	Paarl, Somerset West, Stellenbosch, Strand, Wellington districts	New number	
–68736	South central districts of Western Cape	New number	
–68737	Southeastern districts of Western Cape	New number	
–68737	Southeastern districts of Western Cape	Southern districts	–6874
–68738	Little Karoo	New number	
–68738	Little Karoo	Southern districts	–6874

Current Number	Current Topic	Old Topic/Comment	Old Number
–68738	Little Karoo	Little Karoo districts	–68716
–68739	Great Karoo districts	New number	
–6875	Eastern Cape	Homeland (National states) South Africa	–6879
–68751	Southwestern districts of Eastern Cape	Cape Midlands districts	–68714
–68751	Southwestern districts of Eastern Cape	New number	
–68751	Southwestern districts of Eastern Cape	Great Karoo districts	–68715
–68751	Southwestern districts of Eastern Cape	Southern districts	–6874
–68752	Port Elizabeth and Uitenhage districts	Port Elizabeth	
–68753	Southeastern district of Eastern Cape	New number	
–68753	Southeastern district of Eastern Cape	Cape Midlands districts	–68714
–68754	Northwestern districts of Eastern Cape	New number	
–68754	Northwestern districts of Eastern Cape	Cape Midlands districts	–68714
–68754	Northwestern districts of Eastern Cape	Great Karoo districts	–68715
–68755	Central districts of Eastern Cape	Cape Midlands districts	–68714
–68755	Central districts of Eastern Cape	Northeastern districts	–6876
–68755	Central districts of Eastern Cape	Ciskei	–68792
–68756	North central districts of Eastern Cape	New number	
–68756	North central districts of Eastern Cape	Eastern Upper Karoo districts	–68713

Current Number	Current Topic	Old Topic/Comment	Old Number
–68756	North central districts of Eastern Cape	Cape Midlands districts	–68714
–68756	North central districts of Eastern Cape	Northeastern districts	–6876
–68756	North central districts of Eastern Cape	Transkei	–68791
–68757	Northeastern districts of Eastern Cape	Northeastern districts	–6876
–68758	Former Transket	New number	
–68758	Former Transket	Transkei	–68791
–68759	Eastern districts of Eastern Cape	New number	
–68759	Eastern districts of Eastern Cape	Transkei	–68791
–71	**Canada**		
–71133	Greater Vancouver Regional District	Lower Fraser Valley	–71137
–71336	Norfolk County	Regional Municipality of Haldimand-Norfolk	
–71337	Fraser Valley Regional District	Regional Municipality of Haldimand-Norfolk	–71336
–71352	City of Hamilton	Regional Municipality of Hamilton-Westworth	
–71384	City of Ottawa		–71383
–71411	Nord-du-Québec region	Mid-northern region	–714115
–714115	James Bay region	Mid-northern region	
–714117	Caniapiscau Regional County Municipality	Mid-northern region	–714115
–714132	Abitibi-Quest Regional County Municipality	New number	

Current Number	Current Topic	Old Topic/Comment	Old Number
–714134	Abitibi Regional County Municipality	New number	
–714135	City of Rouyn-Noranda	New number	
–714135	City of Rouyn-Noranda	Rouyn-Noranda Regional County Municipality	
–714137	Témiscaningue Regional County Municipality	New number	
–714139	Vallée-de-l'Or Regional County Municipality	New number	
–71414	Lac-Saint-Jean regional county municipalities	New number	
–714142	Le Domaine-du-Roy Regional County Municipality	New number	
–714145	Maria-Chapdelaine Regional County Municipality	New number	
–714148	Lac-Saint-Jean-Est Regional County Municipality	New number	
–714162	City of Saguenay	New number	
–714165	Le Fjord-du-Saguenay Regional County Municipality	New number	
–71417	Côte-Nord regional county municipalities	New number	
–71472	La Haute-Côte-Nord Regional County Municipality	New number	
–714174	Manicouagan Regional County Municipality	New number	
–714176	Sept-Rivières Regional County Municipality	New number	
–714178	Minganie Regional County Municipality	New number	

Current Number	Current Topic	Old Topic/Comment	Old Number
–7141782	Anticosti Island	New number	
–714221	City of Gatineau	Outaouais Regional Community	
–714223	Les Collines-de-l'Outaouais Regional Municipality	New number	
–714223	Les Collines-de-l'Outaouais Regional Municipality	New number	–714221
–714224	La Vallée-de-la-Gatineau Regional County Municipality	New number	
–714224	La Vallée-de-la-Gatineau Regional County Municipality	La Verendrye Wildlife Reserve	–71421
–714224	La Vallée-de-la-Gatineau Regional County Municipality	Gatineau River	–714221
–714241	Antoine-Labelle Regional County Municipality	New number	–714225
–714242	Les Laurentides Regional County Municipality	New number	
–714244	Les Pay-d'en-Haut Regional County Municipality	New number	
–714246	La Rivière-du-Nord Regional County Municipality	New number	
–714248	Thérèse-de-Blainville Regional County Municipality	New number	
–71425	Deux-Montagnes Regional County Municipality and City of Mirabel	Deus-Montagnes region	

Current Number	Current Topic	Old Topic/Comment	Old Number
–714252	Deux-Montagnes Regional County Municipality	New number	
–714254	City of Mirabel	New number	
–71431	Le Haut-Saint-Laurent Regional County Municipality	Huntingdon region	
–71432	Beauharnois-Salaberry Regional County Municipality	Beauharnois region	
–71434	Roussillon Regional County Municipality	Laprairie region	
–71434	Roussillon Regional County Municipality	Châteauguay County	–71433
–71435	Les Jardins-de-Napierville Regional County Municipality	Napierville Region	
–71436	Lajemmerais and La Vallée-du-Richelieu regional county municipalities	Vercheres region	
–714362	Lajemmerais Regional County Municipality	New number	
–714365	La Vallée-du-Richelieu Regional County Minicipality	New number	
–714365	La Vallée-du-Richelieu Regional County Minicipality	Chambly County	–71437
–71437	City of Longueuil	Champlain Regional County Municipality	
–71438	Le Haut-Richelieu Regional County Municipality	Saint-Jean region	
–71438	Le Haut-Richelieu Regional County Municipality	Iberville County	–71461

Current Number	Current Topic	Old Topic/Comment	Old Number
–71439	Le-Bas-Richelieu Regional County Municipality	New number	
–71439	Le-Bas-Richelieu Regional County Municipality		–71451
–714412	Les Moulins Regional County Municipality	New number	–71424
–714418	Matawinie Regional County Municipality	New number	
–71443	D'Autray Regional County Municipality	Berthier region	
–714451	City of Trois-Rivières	Saint-Maurice region	
–714451	City of Trois-Rivières	Cap-de-la-Madeleine	–714455
–714453	City of Shawinigan	New number	
–714453	City of Shawinigan	Le Centre-de-la-Mauricie Regional County	–714451
–714455	Les Chenaux Regional County Municipality	Champlain County	–714451
–714457	Mékinac Regional County Municipality	New number	
–714459	Le Haut-Saint-Maurice Regional County Municipality	New number	
–714471	City of Québec	Québec Urban Community	
–714474	La Jacques-Cartier Regional County Municipality	New number	
–714476	L'Île-d'Orléans Regional County Municipality	New number	–71448
–71448	La Côte-de-Beaupré Regional County Municipality	New number	

Current Number	Current Topic	Old Topic/Comment	Old Number
–714492	Charlevoix Regional County Municipality	New number	
–714494	Charlevoix-Est Regional County Municipality	New number	
–71452	Les Maskoutains and Acton regional county municipalities	Saint-Hyacinthe and Bagot regions	
–714523	Les Maskoutains Regional County Municipality	Saint-Hyacinthe region	
–714525	Acton Regional County Municipality	Bagot region	
–71453	Rouville Regional Coounty Municipality	Rouville Region	
–71454	Nicolet-Yamaska Regional County Municipality	Yamaska Region	
–71455	Bécancour Regional County Municipality		
–71456	Drummond and Arthbaska regional county municipalities	Drummond and Arthbaska regions	
–714563	Drummond Regional County Municipality	Drummond region	
–714565	Arthabaska Regional County Municipality	Arthabaska region	
–71457	Asbestos and L'Érable regional county municipalities	Wolfe and Megantic regions	
–714573	Asbestos Regional County Municipality	Wolfe region	
–714575	L'Érable Regional County Municipality	Megantic region	
–71458	Lotbinière Regional County Municipality	Lotbinière Region	
–71459	City of Lévis	Levis region	

Current Number	Current Topic	Old Topic/Comment	Old Number
–7146	Southern region of Quebec	Southern region	
–7146	Southern region of Quebec	Saint-François River	–7145
–71462	Brome-Missisquoi Regional County Municipality	Missisquoi region	
–71463	La Haute-Yamaska Regional County Municipality	Shefford region	
–71464	Memphrémagog Regional County Municipality	Brome region	
–71465	Le Val-Saint-François Regional County Municipality	Richmond region	
–71466	City of Sherbrooke	Sherbrooke region	
–71467	Coaticook Regional County Municipality	Stanstead region	
–71468	Le Haut-Saint-François Regional County Municipality	Compton region	
–71469	Le Granit Regional County Municipality	Frontenac region	
–7147	Eastern region of Quebec	Southeastern region	
–71471	L'Amiante, Beauce-Sartigan, Robert-Cliche, La Nouvelle-Beauce regional county municipalities	Beauce region	
–714712	L'Amiante Regional County Municipality	New number	–714573
–714714	Beauce-Sartigan Regional County Municipality	New number	

Current Number	Current Topic	Old Topic/Comment	Old Number
–714716	Robert-Cliché Regional County Municipality	New number	
–714718	La Nouvelle-Beauce Regional County Municipality	New number	
–71472	Les Etchemins Regional County Municipality	Dorchester region	
–71473	Bellechasse and Montmagny regional county municipalities	Bellechasse and Montmagny regions	
–714733	Bellechasse Regional County Municipality	Bellechasse region	
–714735	Montmagny Regional County Municipality	Montmagny region	
–71474	L'Islet Regional County Municipality	L'Islet region	
–71475	Kamouraska Regional County Municipality	Kamouraska region	
–71476	Témiscouata, Rivière-du-Loup, Les Basques regional county municipalities	Témiscouata and Rivière-du-Loup regions	
–714762	Témiscouata Regional County Municipality	New number	
–714764	Rivière-du-Loop Regional County Municipality	New number	
–714766	Les Basques Regional County Municipality	New number	
–71477	Gaspé Peninsula regional county municipalities	Gaspé Peninsula	
–714771	Rimouski-Neigette regional county municipalities	Rimouski region	
–714773	La Mitis Regional County Municipality	New number	–714771

Current Number	Current Topic	Old Topic/Comment	Old Number
–714775	Matane Regional County municipality	Matane and Matapédia regions	
–714778	La Matapédia Regional County Municipality	New number	–714775
–71478	Avignon and Bonaventure regional county municipalities	Bonaventure region	
–714783	Avignon Regional County Municipality	New number	
–714785	Bonaventure Regional County Municipality	New number	
–71479	Gaspé regional county municipalities and Municipality of Les Îles-de-la-Madeleine	Gaspé region	
–714791	La Haute-Gaspésie Regional County Municipality	New number	
–714793	La Côte-de-Gaspé Regional County Municipality	New number	
–714795	Le Rocher-Percé Regional County Municipality	New number	
–714797	Municipality of Les Îles-de-la Madeleine	Magdalen Islands	
–71695	Cape Breton Regional Municipality	Cape Breton County	
–7193	Northwest Territories	Fort Smith Region	
–7193	Northwest Territories	Thelon Game Sanctuary	–7194
–7193	Northwest Territories	Inuvik region	–7196
–7193	Northwest Territories	Holman	–7197
–7195	Nunavut	Northern territories	–7192
–71952	Baffin Region	New number	
–71955	Kitikmeot Region	New number	–7197

Current Number	Current Topic	Old Topic/Comment	Old Number
–71958	Keewatin Region	New number	–7194
–7285	**Nicaragua**		
–728532	Región Autónoma del Atlántico Sur	Zelaya department	
–728537	Región Autónoma del Atlántico Norte	New number	–728532
–7287	**Panama**		
–728717	Ngöbe Buglé comarca	New number	
–728717	Ngöbe Buglé comarca	Chiriquí province	–728711
–728717	Ngöbe Buglé comarca	Bocas del Toro province	–728712
–728717	Ngöbe Buglé comarca	Veraguas	–728722
–72877	Eastern Panama	New number	
–728772	Kuna Yala comarca	New number	
–728772	Kuna Yala comarca	Metropolitan provinces	–72873
–728773	Kuna de Madungandí comarca	New number	
–728773	Kuna de Madungandí comarca	Panama	–728731
–728774	Kuna de Wargandi comarca	New number	–72874
–728776	Emberá comarca	New number	–72874
–728778	Darién province	New number	–72874

Current Number	Current Topic	Old Topic/Comment	Old Number
–729 3	**Dominican Republic**		
–729343	Elisa Piña	La Estrelleta	
–747	**New York**		
–74727	Borough of the Bronx and Westchester County	Mainland east of Hudson River	
–755	**Virginia**		
–7551	Northampton and Accomack counties and Chesapeake Bay Region	Eastern Peninsula and Chesapeake Bay Region	
–7552	Potomac-Rappahannock region	Northern Neck	
–75541	Hampton and Newport News	Southern end of peninsula	
–755661	Halifax County	South Boston	–755662
–773	**Illinois**		
–7737	Southeastern and south central counties of Illinois	Southeastern counties	
–77379	South central counties of Illinois	Counties south of Decatur	
–788	**Colorado**		
–78864	Broomfield County, Colorado (Northwestern)	New number	

Current Number	Current Topic	Old Topic/Comment	Old Number
–78864	Broomfield County, Colorado (Northwestern)	Boulder County	–78863
–78864	Broomfield County, Colorado (Northeastern)	Weld County	–78872
–78864	Broomfield County, Colorado (Southeastern)	Adams County	–78881
–78864	Broomfield County, Colorado (Southwestern)	Jefferson County	–78884
–795	**Oregon**		
–7951	Western Oregon	New number	
–7955	Eastern Oregon	New number	
–797	**Washington**		
–7971	Eastern Washington	New number	
–7972	Northeastern counties of Washington	Northeastern counties	
–7976	Western Washington	New number	
–798	**Alaska**		
–7982	Panhandle region	Southeastern region (Panhandle)	
–85	**Peru**		
–8521	Ancash department	Ancash	
–8529	Ayacucho department	Ayacucho	–85292

Current Number	Current Topic	Old Topic/Comment	Old Number
–8538	Apurímac department	New number	–85294
–861	**Colombia**		
–86111	San Andrés y Providencia	New number	–8618
–86118	Cesar	New number	–86123
–8612	Northern departments of Andean Region	Northeastern region and Pacific Coast	
–8613	Southwestern departments of Andean Region	North central region	
–86139	Huila		–86154
–8614	Southeastern departments of Andean Region	Casanare, Cundinamarca, Bogota	
–86144	Boyacá		–86137
–86148	Capital District of Santa Fe de Bogotá	New number	
–8615	Pacific Coast Region	Northeastern region and Pacific Coast	–8612
–86151	Chocó	New number	–86127
–86158	Nariño	New number	–86162
–8616	Amazon Region	Southern region	
–8619	Orinoquia Region	New number	
–86192	Vichada	New number	–86139
–86194	Meta	New number	–86156
–86196	Casanare	New number	–86143
–86198	Arauca	New number	–86138

Current Number	Current Topic	Old Topic/Comment	Old Number
–866	**Ecuador**		
–8664	Oriente Region	Eastern region	
–881	**Guyana**		
–8811	Barima-Waini Region	North West district	
–8812	Pomeroon-Supenaam Region	Essequibo district	
–8813	Essequibo Islands-West Demerara Region	Essequibo Islands district	–8814
–8814	Upper Demerara-Berbice Region	East Berbice district	–8817
–8814	Upper Demerara-Berbice Region	Northeastern Rupununi district	–8818
–8814	Upper Demerara-Berbice Region	Mazaruni-Potaro district	–8819
–8815	Demerara-Mahaica Region	Northeastern West Demerara district	–8814
–8816	Mahaica-Berbice Region	Eastern East Demerara	–8815
–8817	East Berbice-Corentyne Region	Eastern Rupununi district	–8818
–8818	Upper Takutu-Upper Essequibo and Potaro-Siparuni regions	Rupununi	
–88184	Upper Takutu-Upper Essequibo Region	New number	
–88187	Potaro-Siparuni Region	Mazaruni-Potaro district	–8819
–8819	Cuyuni-Mazaruni Region		

Current Number	Current Topic	Old Topic/Comment	Old Number
–883	**Suriname**		
–8834	Para district	Suriname district	–8836
–8835	Paramaribo and Wanica districts	Paramaribo district	
–88352	Paramaribo district	New Number	
–88357	Wanica district	New number	
–8837	Commewijne district	Suriname district	–8836
–88392	Brokopondo district	New number	
–88395	Sipaliwini district	New number	–8831
–88395	Sipaliwini district	New number	–8833
–88395	Sipaliwini district	New number	–8838
–892	**Paraguay**		
–89212	Asunción Capital District and southern departments of Oriental region	South departments	
–892121	Asunción Capital District	Capital District	
–89224	Boquerón	Nueva Asuncion	–89225
–89227	Alto Paraguay	Chaco	–89226
–951 to 957	**New Guinea**		
–951	Papua	Irian Jaya	
–961 4	Samoa	Western Samoa	

Table 3. Subdivisions for the Arts, for Individual Literatures, for Specific Literary Forms

The notations in Table 3 are used only with base numbers specified in 808 to 890 (Literature of various languages and Rhetoric) and where instructed in 700.4 (Special Topics in the Arts) and 791.4 (Motion Pictures, Radio, Television). The Table consists of three subtables:

3A Subdivisions for works by or about individual authors

(Description, critical appraisal, biography, single or collected works of an individual author)

3B Subdivision for works by or about more than one author

(Description, critical appraisal, biography, collected works of two or more authors)

3C Notation to be added where instructed in Table 3B, 700.4, 791.4, 808–809

(Additional elements used in number building within Table 3B and as instructed)

Use of the Tables may be difficult for novices, so assistance is provided for 3A in four-step instructions, and 3B/3C have eight steps for application. In addition, flowcharts are available in the Manual to assist classifiers in using the Tables.

Table 3A

Table 3A contains the standard mnemonic notation for literary forms by a single author in specific languages. The following table lists Table 3A notations and examples of their use.

Table 4.3

Notation	Literary Form	Examples
–1	Poetry	821 (English poetry); 851 (Italian poetry)
–2	Drama	822 (English drama); 872 (Latin drama)
–3	Fiction	823 (English fiction); 863 (Spanish fiction)
–4	Essays	824 (English essays); 834 (German essays)
–5	Speeches	825 (English speeches); 814 (American speeches in English)
–6	Letters	826 (English letters); 846 French letters
–8	Miscellaneous writings	828 (English miscellaneous writings); 868 (Spanish miscellaneous writings)

Table 3B

Table 3B is used for works by or about more than one author in specific languages and includes the same literary forms as in Table 3A with the addition of –7 (Humor and satire). Table 3B is used in combination with Table 3C and is applied to works of more than one author in specific languages. The application of the Table is so complex that there are more than two pages of decision-making instructions in eight steps to ensure that the notations are applied properly in the number building process. Miscellaneous writings (–8) have an additional three and a half pages of instructions of how to apply notations, with extensive directions about notations for specific periods.

Table 3C

Table 3C is used according to instructions in 3B, and in 700.4 (Special Topics in the Arts), 791.4 (Motion Pictures, Radio, Television), and 808 (Rhetoric and Collections of Literary Texts from more than Two Literatures), and 809 (History, Description, Critical Appraisal of more than Two Literatures). When added, the numbers specify various aspects in the materials being classified. Following is the summary of Table 3C (Dewey 2003, 1:641).

–1 Arts and literature displaying specific qualities of style, mood, viewpoint

–2 Literature displaying specific elements

–3 Arts and literature dealing with specific themes and subjects

–4 Literature emphasizing subjects

–8 Literature for and by persons of ethnic and national groups

–9 Literature for and by other specific kinds of persons

Numbers developed using Table 3 notations can be phenomenally long. For example, 815.4083556 represents American speeches in the late nineteenth century dealing with social problems of the post–Civil War era.

81 American literature

5 Speeches

.4 Late 19th century

08 Specific subject

3556 Social problems

DDC 22 Table 3 Revisions

DDC 22 contains only nine changes in the three Table 3 subtables. Table 3B includes three changes, one of which is a new number, and Table 3C has six changes, one being a new number. Table 3A remains the same as in Edition 21.

In Table 3B, Specific periods of literary forms of Poetry (01), Drama (02), Fiction (03), Essays (04), Speeches (05), and Humor and Satire (07) have instructions that if there are "no applicable period" tables, no period notations are to be added (Dewey 2003, 1:629–36).

Table 4.4

New Number	New Topic	Old Topic/Comment	Old Number
Add Table 3B			
–1	Ephemeral and light verse		–108
–107	Light verse		–108
–30877	Picaresque fiction	New number	
–503	Debates	Debates and public discussions	
Add Table 3C			
–32	Travel (Places)	Places	–355
–3552	Sociology and anthropology	New number	
–3553	Economics	New number	
–3554	Law	New number	
–3556	Social problems and services	New number	
–3557	Education	New number	
–3559	Customs	New number	
–356	Technical themes	Scientific and technical themes	

New Number	New Topic	Old Topic/Comment	Old Number
–3561	Medicine, health, human body	New number	
–3561	Mental illness		–353
–3561	Physical disabilities		–355
–357	Artistic, recreational, literary themes	Artistic and literary themes	
–357	Dancing, sports		–355
–36	Agriculture, scientific themes, comprehensive works on scientific and technical themes.	Physical and natural phenomena	–356
–377	Magic and witchcraft	New number	
–8	Literature for and by persons of ethnic and national groups	Literature for and by persons of racial, ethnic and national groups	
–9205 to 9207	Persons by relationships, persons by miscellaneous social characteristics, persons with disabilities and illnesses, gifted persons	Persons of specific occupational and miscellaneous characteristics	–9204 to 9279
–921	Persons of specific occupational and religious groups	New number	
	Discontinued	[Persons occupied with geography, history, related disciplines]	[929]

Table 4. Subdivisions of Individual Languages and Language Families

As Table 3 is for application to Literatures, Table 4 is for use with Languages and Language families and is used only where indicated in 420–490.

Add Notes or an asterisk * will indicate how and when the form divisions are to be applied.

Table 4 Summary and Applications

Compared with Table 3, application of Table 4 notations is straightforward and easily mastered. For example, the notation for Modern Persian, or Farsi, dictionaries is 491.553.

491.55 Modern Persian (Farsi)

3 Dictionaries

Following is the summary of Table 4 notations (Dewey 2003, 1:651).

–1 Writing systems, phonology, phonetics of the standard form of the language

–2 Etymology of the standard form of the language

–3 Dictionaries of the standard form of the language

–5 Grammar of the standard form of the language; Syntax of the standard form of the language

–7 Historical and geographic variations, modern nongeographic variations

–8 Standard usage of the language (Prescriptive linguistics); Applied linguistics

DDC 22 Table 4 Revisions

Table 4 contains an unusual number of revisions compared with only one change in Table 4 in Edition 21. Except for a few rewordings of the headings, all changes are new numbers. Dictionaries (–3) has four new numbers, Grammar (–5) has fifteen, and Standard usage (–8) has nine new numbers.

Table 4.5

Current Number	Current Term	Old Term/Comment	Old Number
Add Table 4			
–019	Psychological principles	New number	
–312	Dictionaries of synonyms and antonyms	New number	
–313	Dictionaries of idioms	New number	
–315	Dictionaries of abbreviations and acronyms	New number	
–317	Picture dictionaries	New number	
–5	Grammar of the standard form of the language; Syntax of the standard form of the language	Grammar of the standard form of the language	
–501	Philosophy and theory	New number	
–5018	Schools and theories	New number	
–50182	Generative grammar	New number	
–50184	Dependency grammar	New number	
–55	Nouns, pronouns, adjectives, articles	New number	
–554	Nouns	New number	
–555	Pronouns	New number	
–56	Verbs	New number	
–562	Tense	New number	
–563	Aspect	New number	
–57	Miscellaneous word classes	New number	
–576	Adverbs	New number	

Current Number	Current Term	Old Term/Comment	Old Number
–59	Morphology	New number	
–592	Word formation	New number	
–595	Inflection	New number	
–813	Spelling (Orthography) and pronunciation	New number	
–864	Readers for persons whose native language is different from the language of the reader	Readers for persons whose native language is different	
–864024	Readers for persons in specific occupations	New number	
–8642 to 8649	Readers for specific native language speakers	New number	
–89	Use of a spoken language or a manually coded form of a spoken language for communication with and by deaf persons	New number	
–891	Manually coded language	New number	419
–8914 to 8919	Specific systems of manual coding	New number	
–895	Lipreading, cued speech, and oral interpretation (lipspeaking)	New number	
–8954	Lipreading	New number	
–8955	Cued speech	New number	

Table 5. Ethnic and National Groups

The notations from the fifth Table denote ethnic or national characteristics when added to the number representing a topic. They are applied following Standard Subdivision –089 from Table 1 or can be applied directly to topic notations where instructed. Adding from this Table is similar to adding geographic notation from Table 2 to Standard Subdivision –09.

To designate an ethnic or national group from areas other than those from which they originally came, such as Palestinian Arabs (9274) in the United States, 0 is added with notations from Table 2 (9274073).

Table 5 Summary and Applications

Applications of Table 5 notations can result in long classifications, but the process is not very complex. An example is a book on the survival skills of Cheyenne Indians (613.6908997353)

613.69 Survival skills

089 Standard Subdivision

97353 Cheyenne Indians

Following is the summary of Table 5 notations. Notice that the Table does not follow the mnemonic arrangement of Table 2, that is, North Americans are –1, not –7 (Dewey 2003, 1:661).

–05 Persons of mixed ancestry with ethnic origins from more than one continent

–09 Europeans and people of European descent

–1 North Americans

–2 British, English, Anglo-Saxons

–3 Germanic people

–4 Modern Latin people

–5 Italians, Romanians, related groups

–6 Spanish and Portuguese

–7 Other Italic people

–8 Greeks and related groups

–9 Other ethnic and national groups

DDC 22 Table 5 Revisions

The "Racial" aspect in the name of Table 5 as well as in the headings has been removed in Edition 22. Headings now concentrate on Ethnic and National Groups. Similarly, the use of –03 (Basic races) has been discontinued with the explanation, "without meaning in context" (Dewey 2003, 1: 661).

This edition of Dewey also includes eight new numbers to expand the details of national and ethnic groups.

Table 4.6

Current Number	Current Topic	Old Topic/Comment	Old Number
Add Table 5			
[–03]	Basic races	Discontinued (without meaning in context)	
–05	Persons of mixed ancestry with ethnic origins from more than one continent	Mixtures of basic races	–04
–09	Europeans and people of European descent	Caucasian race	–034
–396	Icelanders and Faeroese	West Scandinavians	
–687 to 688	Regional and national groups	National groups	
–9	Other ethnic and national groups	Other racial, ethnic and national groups	
–9275 to 9276	Regional and national groups of Arabs	National groups of Arabs	
–92761	Arabs of North Africa	New number	
–92761	Arabs of North Africa	North Africans	–93
–928	Persons who speak, or whose ancestors spoke, Ethiopian languages	Ethiopians and Eritreans	
–9289	Eritreans	New number	

Current Number	Current Topic	Old Topic/Comment	Old Number
–93	Non-Semitic Afro-Asiatic peoples	North Africans	
–9456	Mari, Chuvashes, Mordvin	Cheremis (Mari), Chuvashes, Mordvin	
–9594	Miao and Yao peoples	Miao (Hmong) and Yao peoples	
–96067	Africans of Central Africa and offshore islands	New number	
–966 to 968	Regional and national groups in Africa	National groups in Africa	
–969	Other regional and national groups of largely African descent	Other national groups of largely African descent	
–97078	Indians of Western United States	New number	
–9725	Apachean Indians	New number	
–974	Peoples who speak, or whose ancestors spoke, Penutian, Mayan, Mixe-Zoque, Uto-Aztecan, Kiowa-Tanoan languages	New number	
–98323	Quechuan (Keechauan) Indians	New number	
–99	Aeta, Andamanese, Semang; Papuans; Aboriginal people of Australia and Tasmania; Malayo-Polynesian and related peoples; miscellaneous peoples	Aeta, Andamanese, Semang; Papuans; Australian native peoples; Malayo-Polynesian and related peoples; miscellaneous peoples	
–991	Aeta, Andamanese, Semang	Aeta, Andamanese, Semang; Papuans; Australian native peoples	

Current Number	Current Topic	Old Topic/Comment	Old Number
–9915	Aboriginal people of Australia and Tasmania	Australian native peoples	
–99159	Aboriginal people of Tasmania	New number	
–992	Malayo-Polynesian and related peoples	People who speak, or ancestors spoke, Malayo-Polynesian languages	

Table 6. Languages

While most libraries using DDC seldom need to subdivide by language, it is a facet that should be recognized in any fully developed classification scheme. For instance, certain classic works are held in a variety of translations by special libraries, or in comprehensive collections. Table 6 stems from Class 400 (Language), although its notations do not necessarily correspond to the schedule spans 420 to 490 and 810 to 890.

Table 6 Summary and Applications

The following is the summary of Table 6, which shows how the arrangement of the languages reflects the basic structure of the 400 class.

Table 4.7

Table 6 Notation	Language	400 Class Notation	Language
–1	Indo-European languages		
–2	English and Old English (Anglo-Saxon)	420	English and Old English
–3	Germanic languages	430	Germanic languages; German
–4	Romance languages	440	Romance languages; French
–5	Italian, Sardinian, Dalmatian, Romanian, Rhaeto-Romanic	450	Italian, Romanian, and related languages

Table 6 Notation	Language	400 Class Notation	Language
–6	Spanish and Portuguese	460	Spanish and Portuguese languages
–7	Italic languages	470	Italic languages; Latin
–8	Hellenic languages	480	Hellenic languages; classical Greek
–9	Other languages	490	Other languages

Instructions indicate that classifiers should always select the notation for the source language for pidgin, creole, or dialects of the language. For example, French-based pidgins and creoles are to be indicated with –417 under the French language (–41). Directions also indicate the modern language number should be used unless there are specific provisions otherwise.

Uses of Table 6 are illustrated by the following examples:

897.557 Cherokee literature

897 Literatures of North America native languages

.557 Cherokee [from –975 in Table 6]

305.721052 English-speaking people of Japan

305 Social groups

.7 Language groups

2 England and Old English (Anglo-Saxon)

1 English

0 [geographic indicator]

5 Asia

2 Japan

DDC 22 Table 6 Revisions

Table 6 has been greatly expanded by the addition of 119 new numbers under Modern Indic, Afro-Asiatic, African, North American native, South American native, and Austronesian languages.

Table 4.8

Current Number	Current Topic	Old Topic/Comment	Old Number
Add Table 6			
–3	Germanic languages	Germanic (Teutonic) languages	
–395	North Germanic languages (Nordic languages)	West Scandinavian languages	–396
–395	North Germanic languages (Nordic languages)	Modern West Scandinavian languages	–3969
–396	Old Norse (Old Icelandic), Icelandic, Faeroese	West Scandinavian languages	
–3969	Icelandic and Faeroese	Modern West Scan-dinavian languages	
–397	Swedish	Revised	
–3982	Norwegian	New Norse, Landsmal	–3983
–49	Occitan, Catalan, Franco-Provençal	Provencal Franco-Provençal, Catalan	
–491	Occitan	Provençal	
–9146	Marathi and Konkani	Marathi	
–91461	Marathi	New number	
–91469	Konkani	New number	
–91497	Romani	Romany	

Current Number	Current Topic	Old Topic/Comment	Old Number
–92	Afro-Asiatic languages; Semitic languages	Afro-Asiatic (Hamito-Semitic) languages; Semitic languages	
–927	Arabic and Maltese	Arabic	
–963932	Mbundu group; Mbundu (Kimbundu)	Kimbundu (Mbundu) group; Kimbundu (Mbundu)	
–963976	Venda (Tshivenda)	New number	
–963989	Ndebele (South Africa)		–963977
–9725	Apachean languages	New number	
–97256	Mescalero-Chiricahua Apache	New number	
–9726	Navajo	New number	
–9727	Tlingit	New number	
–9728	Haida	New number	
–973	Algic and Muskogean languages	Macro-Algonkian languages	
–9731	Central Algonquian languages	New number	
–97312	Kickapoo	New number	
–97313	Menomini	New number	
–97314	Mesquakie	New number	
–973149	Sauk (Sac)	New number	
–97315	Miami	New number	
–97316	Potawatomi	New number	
–97317	Shawnee	New number	
–9732	Cree-Montagnais-Naska pi languages	New number	

Current Number	Current Topic	Old Topic/Comment	Old Number
–97323	Cree	New number	
–9733	Ojibwa languages	New number	
–97333	Ojibwa	New number	
–97336	Ottawa	New number	
–9734	Eastern Algonquian languages	New number	
–97343	Micmac	New number	
–97344	Mohegan-Montauk-Nar ragansett	New number	
–973449	Stockbridge	New number	
–97345	Unami and Munsee	New number	
–97347	Powhatan	New number	
–97348	Wampanoag	New number	
in0–9735	Plains Algonquian languages	New number	
–97352	Blackfoot	New number	
–97353	Cheyenne	New number	
–97354	Arapaho languages	New number	
–9738	Moskogean languages	New number	
–97385	Muskogee (Creek) and Seminole	New number	
–973859	Seminole	New number	
–97386	Chickasaw	New number	
–97387	Choctaw	New number	
–9741	Penutian languages	Penutian, Mixe-Zoquean, Mayan languages	

Current Number	Current Topic	Old Topic/Comment	Old Number
–97412	Plateau Penutian languages, Tsimshian languages	New number	
–974122	Klamath-Modoc	New number	
–974124	Nez Percé	New number	
–974127	Yakama	New number	
–974128	Tsimshian	New number	
–97413	Yok-Utian languages	New number	
–974133	Miwok	New number	
–9742	Mayan languages		–97415
–97422	Cakchikel	New number	
–97423	Ouiché	New number	
–97427	Yucatecan languages	New number	
–97428	Cholan-Tzeltalan languages	New number	
–974287	Tzotzil	New number	
–9743	Mixe-Zoque languages	North American native languages	–9741
–97454	Sonoran languages	New number	
–974542	Yaqui	New number	
–974544	Huichol	New number	
–974546	Tarahumaran languages	New number	
–97455	Tepiman languages	New number	
–974552	Tohono O'Odham and Akimel O'Odham	New number	
–974552 9	Akimel O'Odham (Pima)	New number	
–97457	Numic languages	New number	

Current Number	Current Topic	Old Topic/Comment	Old Number
–974572	Comanche	New number	
–974574	Shoshoni	New number	
–974576	Ute and Southern Paiute	New number	
–974576 9	Southern Paiute	New number	
–974577	Northern Paiute	New number	
–97458	Hopi	New number	
–97492	Kiowa	New number	
–97494	Tewa	New number	
–97496	Northern Tiwa	New number	
–97497	Southern Tiwa	New number	
–975	Siouan, Iroquian, Hokan, Chumash, Yuki languages	Siouan, Iroquian, Hokan, Yukian languages	
–97522	Mandan	New number	
–97524	Dakota languages	New number	
–975243	Dakota	New number	
–975244	Lakota	New number	
–97525	Dhegiha languages	New number	
–975253	Omaha and Ponca	New number	
–9752539	Ponca	New number	
–975254	Osage	New number	
–97526	Winnebago	New number	
–97527	Missouri Valley Siouan languages	New number	
–975272	Crow	New number	
–975274	Hidatsa	New number	

Current Number	Current Topic	Old Topic/Comment	Old Number
–97554	Five Nations languages	New number	
–975542	Mohawk	New number	
–975543	Oneida	New number	
–975546	Seneca	New number	
–97555	Wyandot	New number	
–97557	Cherokee	New number	
–97572	Yuman languages	New number	
–975722	Mohave	New number	
–975724	Havasupai-Walapai-Yavapai	New number	
–97574	Pomo languages	New number	
–97576	Washo	New number	
–9758	Chumash languages	New number	
–976	Oto-Manguean languages	Otomanguean languages	
–9763	Mixtecan languages	New number	
–9783	San Blas Kuna	New number	
–9788	Misumalpan languages	New number	
–97882	Mískito	New number	
–9792	Arawakan languages of Central America and West Indies	New number	
–97922	Taino	New number	
–9793	Chaddoan languages	New number	
–97932	Arikara	New number	
–97933	Pawnee	New number	
–9794	Salishan languages	New number	

–97943	Interior Salish languages	New number	
–979435	Kalispel-Pend d'Oreille (Salish)	New number	
–9795	Wakashan languages	New number	
–97953	Kwakiutl	New number	
–97954	Makah	New number	
–97955	Nootka	New number	
–9796	Tarascan languages	New number	
–9799	Kutenai and Zuni	New number	
–97992	Kutenai	New number	
–97994	Zuni	New number	
–982	Chibchan, Barbacoan, Paezan languages	Chibchan Paezan languages	
–98372	Shuar	Jivaro proper; Shuar	
–98382	Narrow Tupí group	Narrow Tupí group; Guarani	
–9842	Carib languages	New number	
–98422	Carib (Galibi)	New number	
–987	Araucanian, Alacalufan, Chon, Lule-Vilela, Mataco-Guaicuru languages	New number	
–9872	Araucanian languages	New number	
–989	Other South American languages	New number	
–9892	Yanomam languages	New number	
–99159	Tasmanian languages	New number	
–992	Austronesian languages	Austronesian languages; Malayo-Polynesian languages	

Literature Cited

Croghan, Antony. 1972. The Dewey Decimal Classification and its eighteenth edition. *Library Association Record* 74 (7):120–21.

Dewey, Melvil. 1951. *Decimal Classification.* 15th ed. Lake Placid Club, NY: Forest Press.

——— 1958. *Dewey Decimal Classification and Relative Index.* 16th ed. Lake Placid, NY: Forest Press.

——— 2003. *Dewey Decimal Classification and Relative Index.* 22nd ed. Dublin, Ohio: OCLC Online Computer Library Center.

Trotter, Ross. 1980. Dewey 19—a subjective assessment. *Catalogue & Index* 59:4.

5

Class 000: Generalities

This class bore no name in Dewey's first edition (1876), but it has long been called the "General works" or "Generalia" class. As indicated by its name, it is a mixture of related and only vaguely related subjects, the least of which is Library and Information Science (020). It contains also news media, journalism, and publishing at 070, and within Generalities (000–009) there is Knowledge (001), The Book (002), and Systems in 003. "Systems" in this context does not refer to computer systems, but is a mixture of subjects, such as forecasting; forecasts and stochastic systems and their relation to each other is rather uncertain. Some have doubts about this mixture, such as Bloomberg and Weber, who remarked that news media and journalism might better be located with the disciplinary material in sections for specific kinds of communication, such as postal and telecommunications (383–384) (Bloomberg and Weber 1976, 43).

Computer-oriented subjects are found in 004 (data processing), 005 (computer programming and computer programs), and 006 (special computer applications, such as artificial intelligence). Computers and related topics found their home at last in the Generalities Class with Edition 20. Data Processing and Computer Science have wandered throughout the Schedules, appearing in 001.64 as late as Edition 19 and in various places in 600 in Edition 14. Computation Instruments and Machines were found at 510.78 in Edition 15, while other aspects remained in 651.26 and 621.34. Edition 16 split the topics among 510.78, 681.14, and 651.2. Edition 17 found the machines and their use scattered around the 600 Class of Technology, while 510.78 was retained for Mathematics and Comprehensive Works. Edition 18 moved Data Processing (its general parts) to 001.6, while Office Applications remained at 651.8. These various aspects remained separated in Edition 19 with few changes.

By 1983, the editor pointed out the difficulties in this situation to the Editorial Policy Committee, which quickly decided that it had to take action to put this problem in order. By 1985, the publication of *004–006 Data Processing and Computer Science and Changes in Related Disciplines*, produced primarily by assistant editor Julianne Beall, was released with an enthusiastic response from users. However, even with this improvement 651.8 continued to be used for office functions, and word processing was found in 652.5.

The following examples from the Relative Index indicate how computer topics are distributed among the various classes.

Computer architecture	004.22
engineering	621.392
Computer communications	004.6
communications services	384.3
engineering	621.398 1
programming	005.711
programs	005.713
public administration	354.75
sociology	302.231
Computer control	629.89
Computer engineering	621.39
Computer games	794.8
Computer graphics	006.6
engineering	621.399 6
instructional use	371.334 66
statistical presentation	001.422 602 856 6
Computer graphics programs	006.68
Computer hardware	004
engineering	621.39
Computer-human interaction	004.019
engineering	621.398 4
Computer input devices	004.76
engineering	621.398 6
Computer input-output devices	004.75
engineering	621.398 5
Computer interfacing	004.6
programming	005.711
programs	005.713
software	005.71

Computer interfacing equipment	004.64
engineering	621.398 1
Computer languages	005.13
microprogramming	005.18
Computer literacy	004
Computer mathematics	004.015 1
Computer modeling	003.3
instructional use	371.397
Computer mice	004.76
Computer music	786.76
Computer network resources	025.04
Computer network security	005.8
Computer networks	004.6
communications services	384.3
processing modes	004.3
security measures	005.8
Computer output devices	004.77
engineering	621.398 7
Computer peripherals	004.7
engineering	621.398 4
Computer printers	004.77
engineering	621.398 7
Computer programming	005.1
Computer programs	005.3
Computer science	004
Computer software	005.3
Computer systems	004
engineering	621.39
networks	
processing modes	004.3
Computer terminals	004.75
engineering	621.398 5
Computer viruses	005.84
Computers	004
access control	005.8
management	658.478
engineering	621.39

The topics are comfortably situated in 004–006 for software or users' aspect, and 621.39 for engineering and manufacturing. Applications, such as computer network resources (025.04) and computer art (776) are classed in the discipline of the application.

Within the Generalities Class, Data Processing and Computer Science (004) includes hardware (except for repair, which is in 621.39) and programs and data, which relate directly to the hardware, such as interfacing and communications. The 005 section includes programming, programs, and data, while special computer applications, such as artificial intelligence and computer graphics, are located in 006.

Recognizing the complexity of the subject, the comps provided extensive direction in the application of the Schedules, devoting nearly thirteen pages of the Manual to guidelines and examples. A series of inquiries provide pathways to the appropriate places in the schedules. Sample titles, their class numbers, and the reasoning behind the class assignments should answer any final questions about how to class a computer science title.

Summary and Details of Class 000

000	Computer Science, Information, General Works
010	Bibliography
020	Library and Information Sciences
030	General Encyclopedic Works
040	[Unused]
050	General Serial Publications
060	General Organizations and Museology
070	Documentary Media, Educational Media, News Media; Journalism; Publishing
080	General Collections
090	Manuscripts, Rare Books, Other Rare Printed Materials

Division 000: In the first Subdivision of the Schedules the true generalities of the class reside, including broad, fundamental concepts of learning, culture, and research as well as disputable or questionable information such as UFOs (001). The second Section contains general concepts and interdisciplinary pieces about monographs (002), followed by general concepts of prediction, computerized representations, intercourse and information, and theories of making decisions (003). Needing a good home, the topics of data processing and computer science found this a welcoming

place in 004–006 with plenty of room to grow and one that eliminates the need to decide the argument of whether computers should be considered more science (500) than technology (600). The engineering aspects of computers are found in 621.3 under Applied physics (Technology).

Division 010: The next Division is reserved for bibliographies or lists of titles that may appear in any format or a particular format, or from a particular place (010–016). Also found here are such lists as specific collections, or catalogs (017–019).

Division 020: The third Division in the Schedules contains all information involving libraries and related disciplines (020–027) and one Section on the use of informational materials and reading as an activity (028).

Division 030: Encyclopedias that include information on broadly diverse topics are found in the fourth Division. The first Section is for books of general facts, such as almanacs, the Standard Subdivisions of the Division (030), followed by encyclopedias by language (031–039).

Division 040: Unused in this edition.

Division 050: All publications that are periodical issues are found in this Division and are arranged like 030 with general publications and Standard Subdivisions first (050), followed by works organized by language (051–059).

Division 060: Organizations that are not related to specific fields or disciplines are located in this Division with an arrangement similar to 030 and 050 with general organizations and Standard Subdivisions of the Division first (060), then works arranged by country (061–068). Museums, because they are considered general organizations or perhaps because there was no other logical place to put them, conclude the Division (069).

Division 070: Journalism in all forms, including newspapers, periodicals, motion pictures, and broadcast media, is in this Division. It is organized like the previous three Divisions with general aspects (070.1–.4) and Standard Subdivisions (070.01–.09) for the Division first then the remaining Sections are arranged by place (071–079). Historical and persons treatment of journalism and newspapers are found separate from this geographic treatment at 070.9. All aspects of publishing, including book publishing, are also included in the first section (070.5).

Division 080: As in the preceding Divisions, collections of addresses, lectures, essays, interviews, graffiti, and quotations in general and the Standard Subdivisions for the Division are first (080) and such collections grouped by language follow (080–089). Works that emphasize the literary form and quality of these formats are not included in this Division but are placed with the literature of the language used.

Division 090: This Division is used for rare materials or works that are unusual for some reason, such as through their ownership or origin, and titles that are forgeries or hoaxes are in the concluding Sections of the first Class of the Schedules. Manuscripts are found in 091, Block books in 092, Incunabula in 093, and Printed books 094. Books notable for particular characteristics are found in 095, 096, 097, and 099. Finally, Prohibited works, forgeries, and hoaxes are found in 098.

The Number Building Process

Examining the procedures for building a number for a work about activity or media programs in elementary school libraries in the United States will demonstrate how the schedules are used in the classification process. The library and information sciences are found in the 020 division with their relational aspects in 021; administration, management, and operations in 022 to 025; libraries with collections in a particular subject in 026; and libraries with general collections in 027. Reading and the use of other information media found at 028 may be a possibility since this book is about media in school libraries. However, when examined the section concerns the users' end of the topic, their interests and use of mostly printed materials.

Even though the particular topics are activities and media programs, the work is actually concerned with the library itself. School libraries have multidiscipline collections, so 027 appears to be an appropriate beginning for the classification number. School libraries are found at 027.8, with the elementary level found at **027.8222.**

Because this book discusses school libraries in the United States, the Standard Subdivision for the treatment by specific continents, countries, and localities, or **09,** should be added followed by the notation for the United States, **073.**

LC Classification: **027.82220973**

Primary sources in the library: a collaboration guide for library media specialists, by Mary J. Johnson.

DDC 22 Class 000 Revisions

Revisions in Edition 22 for Class 000 are more widely distributed than in the last division, where almost all changes were within the computer sciences notations. This edition includes changes in each of the subtopics, although some are just changes in one topic heading. Finally, there are a total of twenty-two new numbers within the 000 Class.

004–006 Computers Revisions

It is not surprising that Data Processing and Computer Science (004–006) continues to be revised and expanded, but at a much slower rate than Edition 21 in which there were seventy-three changes compared with thirty-four in this edition. A small heading change has been made in topics in which "digital" has been removed from terms involving computers, such as Digital Supercomputers now being called Supercomputers, and Digital Microcomputers are now Microcomputers.

Table 5.1

Current Number	Current Topic	Old Topic/Comment	Old Number
	Data Processing/ Computer Science		
004.33	Systems analysis and design, computer architecture, performance evaluation of real-time computers	Real-time processing	004.338
004.35	Systems analysis and design, computer architecture, performance evaluation of multiprocessor computers		004.358
004.357	Systems analysis and design, computer architecture, performance evaluation of specific multi-Processor computers	Specific multiprocessor computers	004.3585

Current Number	Current Topic	Old Topic/Comment	Old Number
004.36	Systems analysis and design, computer architecture, performance evaluation of distributed computer systems	Distributed processing	004.368
004.678	Internet (World Wide Web)	Internet	
004.682	Intranets	New number	
004.693	Discussion groups	Electronic bulletin boards	
004.7	Peripherals for digital computers		004.71
	Computer Programming, Programs, Data		
005.116	Constraint programming	New number	
005.18	Microprogramming and microprograms		005.6
005.29	Programming for hybrid and analog computers	Programming for hybrid computers	
005.3	(Programs) Special tropics		005.304
005.36	Specific programs (for microcomputers)		005.369
005.434	Process management programming		005.424
005.435	Memory management programming		005.425
005.436	File system management programming		005.426
005.5	General purpose application programs		005.3

Current Number	Current Topic	Old Topic/Comment	Old Number
005.5	Specific programs with interdisciplinary applications		005.304 2
005.52	Word processing		652.5
005.54	Electronic spreadsheets	New number	
005.55	Statistical programs	New number	
005.57	Personal information management programs	New number	
005.58	Presentation software	New number	
005.722	Character sets	New number	
005.75	Flat-file databases		005.752
005.759	Full-text database management systems	Hypertext databases	005.759 2
005.759	Full-text database management systems	Specific full-text database management systems	005.759 8
	Special Computer Methods		
006.3	Comprehensive works on artificial intelligence and cognitive science		153
006.312	Data mining	New number	
006.5	Digital audio	Computer sound synthesis	
ctlpar006 .696	Digital video	Computer animation	
006.74	Markup languages	New number	
006.8	Virtual reality	New number	

010 Bibliographies Revisions

There are nine changes in Bibliographies, with five being new numbers. Three topics have new numbers assigned.

Table 5.2

Current Number	Current Topic	Old Topic/Comment	Old Number
	Bibliographies and Catalogs		
011.372	Motion pictures	New number	
011.373	Video recordings	New number	
011.376	Pictures and related illustrations	New number	
011.384	Audio or talking books	New number	
011.39	Electronic resources	New number	
011.56	Underground publications (Clandestine publications)	Publications of underground presses	
011.8	General bibliographies of works by specific kinds of authors		013
015	Bibliographies and catalogs of works of authors resident in specific regions, continents, countries, and localities		013.9
016.0053	Bibliographies of computer programs and software		011.77

020 Library Sciences Revisions

There have also been eighteen changes in the numbers relating to Libraries and Information Sciences, including three new numbers and five added notations resulting from the removal of Table 7.

Table 5.3

Current Number	Current Topic	Old Topic/Comment	Old Number
	Libraries and Library Science		
020.62	Permanent organizations	Permanent non-government organizations	
020.621	International organizations	International non-government organizations	
020.622	National organizations	National non-government organizations	
020.623	Regional, state, provincial organizations	Regional, state, provincial non-government organizations	
020.7155	Comprehensive works on in-service training		023.8
021.65	Networks	Networks, systems, consortia	
022	Plant management	Administration of the physical plant	020.682
023	Personnel management (Human management)	Personnel administration	
025.02	Technical services	Technical processes	
025.344	Electronic resources	Machine-readable materials	
027.42	Library outreach programs	New number	
027.652	Legislative reference bureaus	New number	
028.108	Reviews with respect to kinds of persons	New number	

Current Number	Current Topic	Old Topic/Comment	Old Number
028.5	(Use of books and other information media as sources of recreation and self-development) Young people	Reading and use of other information media by young people	028.8083
028.532	(Reading and use of other information media by young people) By infants		028.5342
028.533	(Reading and use of other information media by young people) By children 3 to 5		028.5343
028.534	(Reading and use of other information media by young people) By children 6 to 11		028.5344
028.55	(Reading interests and habits) Young people		028.9083

030–060 Serials and Museums Revisions

General Serial Publications and Encyclopedic Works each have the same change in the topic heading. Museology's only changes are three new numbers.

Table 5.4

Current Number	Current Topic	Old Topic/Comment	Old Number
	General Encyclopedic Works		
034	General encyclopedic works in French, Occitan, and Catalan	General encyclopedic works in French, Provençal, and Catalan	

Current Number	Current Topic	Old Topic/Comment	Old Number
	General Serial Publications		
054	General serial publications in French, Occitan, and Catalan	General serial publications in French, Provençal, and Catalan	
	General Organizations and Museology		
069.07	Education, research, and related topics	New number	
069.074	Museums, collections, and exhibits	New number	
069.075	Museum activities and services; Collecting	New number	

070–080 Journalism and General Collections Revisions

Journalism has fifteen changes, eight of which are changes in names of topics and only one new number. General Collections has one topic heading change

Table 5.5

Current Number	Current Topic	Old Topic/Comment	Old Number
	Journalism		
070.43	Newsreels		070.18
070.43	Radio news programs		070.194
070.43	Television news programs		070.195
070.435	News agencies	Wire services	

Current Number	Current Topic	Old Topic/Comment	Old Number
070.483 2	(Journalism directed to special groups) Children 0 to 11	(Journalism directed to special groups) Children	
070.483 3	(Journalism directed to special groups) Young people 12 to 20	(Journalism directed to special groups) Young adults	
070.483 36	(Journalism directed to special groups) Males 12 to 20	(Journalism directed to special groups) Young men	
070.483 37	(Journalism directed to special groups) Females 12 to 20	(Journalism directed to special groups) Young women	
070.483 4	(Journalism directed to special groups) Adults		070.483 3
070.484	Foreign-language and nondominant ethnic and national groups	Foreign-language and nondominant racial, ethnic and national groups	
070.579 7	Electronic publications (Digital publications)	Machine-readable publications	
070.579 73	Web publications	New number	
071 to 079	(Historical and persons treatment of journalism and newspapers) Treatment by specific continents, countries, localities		070.93 to .99
075	(Historical and persons treatment of journalism and newspapers) Journalism and newspapers in Italy and adjacent islands in Italy	Journalism and newspapers in Italy and adjacent territories	
079.1	(Historical and persons treatment of journalism and newspapers) Treatment by areas, regions, places in general		070.91

Current Number	Current Topic	Old Topic/Comment	Old Number
	General Collections		
084	General collections in French, Occitan, Catalan	General collections in French, Provençal, Catalan	

Exercises in the Use of Class 000

The following exercises are given for practice in interpreting and assigning DDC numbers. They have been selected from Library of Congress cataloging to demonstrate the nature and relative quantity of its DDC classification. The class numbers are assigned by the LC, as are all examples in this work, and is not the author's responsibility. Utilizing all Schedules, Tables, and methodologies discussed in previous chapters, assign class numbers then check them with those assigned by the Library of Congress, which are found in "Answers to the Exercises" in the Appendix.

1. A work on interactive multimedia.
2. A work on operating systems for IBM computers.
3. A work on assigning Dewey classification numbers.
4. A work on archives in the U.S. Virgin Islands.
5. A bibliography on young adult literature.
6. A work on computer programs for Web servers.
7. A work on parallel processing and supercomputers.
8. A work on Microsoft Windows.
9. A work on parallel computers.

Literature Cited

Bloomberg, Marty, and Hans Weber. 1976. *An Introduction to Classification and Number Building in Dewey.* Edited by John Phillip Immroth. Littleton, CO: Libraries Unlimited.

6

Class 100: Philosophy, Parapsychology and Occultism, Psychology

The traditional branches of philosophy are scattered throughpout the Divisions of the 100 Class rather than found cohesively adjoining each other.

Metaphysics	110	The study of the source and substance of reality
Aesthetics	111.85	The study of beauty
Epistemology	120	The study of what one can know about reality
Logic	160	The study of valid inference
Ethics 1	70	The study of proper conduct

The Specific Philosophical Schools (140) are separated from the other elements of philosophy on one side by Paranormal Phenomena (130) and the other by Psychology (150). Paranormal Phenomena began in the first edition as Anthropology then changed to Mind and Body in the second edition. Classed here were the manifestations of the physical world on the mind, including the brain.

Psychology (150) was originally known as Mental Faculties, which were completely separate from physical considerations. These included what the mind did, such as think and feel, so it appears to be situated in the proper place, amid other subjects that deal with the mind.

Summary and Details of Class 100

100	Philosophy, Parapsychology and Occultism, Psychology
110	Metaphysics
120	Epistemology, Causation, Humankind
130	Parapsychology and Occultism
140	Specific Philosophical Schools and Viewpoints
150	Psychology
160	Logic
170	Ethics (Moral Philosophy)
180	Ancient, Medieval, Eastern Philosophy
190	Modern Western and other Non-Eastern Philosophy

Only the Standard Subdivisions for philosophy in general are found in the first Division, 101–109.

Division 110: Metaphysics, or the study of that outside of the physical world, is found in the first of the branches of philosophy in the Schedules, and includes Ontology (111); the character of the universe including the origin and nature of life, or Cosmology (113); and physical concepts of the universe such as correlation of space and matter (114); eternity, the relationship between time and motion (115); evolution, motion, and process (116); matter, form, order, and chaos (117); power and force (118); and concepts of quantity (119). Section 112 is unused in this edition.

Division 120: This Division also contains philosophical works. These include philosophical aspects of knowledge, faith, and values, or Epistemology (theory of knowledge) (121); chance, cause, purpose, and freedom of will (122–124). Also found in this Division are features of the human race such as aspects of perception (126–127); and works on attributes of human life including emotions and human souls (128–129). Section 125 is unused in this edition.

Division 130: The fourth Division moves away from the discipline of philosophy and contains works on the supernatural and topics that are outside scientifically known phenomena. Themes found here include ways to achieve a successful life that are outside of natural law or are in the realm of the supernatural (131). However, these would be "secular phenomena" as opposed to that involved in a religious experience, which is found in 200. Next come ghosts and haunted places (133.1); various methods of fortune-telling (133.3); devil worship, witchcraft, and magic (133.4); astrology (133.5); palmistry (133.6); psychic phenomena (133.8); and spiritualism (133.9). Other such phenomena are nonpsychological aspects of dreams (135), and unusual methods of ascertaining character and mental abilities such as handwriting (137); analysis of physical features (138); and the skull (139). Sections 132, 134, and 136 are unused in this edition.

Division 140: This Division returns to the discipline of philosophy and contains specific schools and viewpoints. These include idealism and related topics (141); critical philosophy (142); Bergsonism and intuitionism (143); humanism and related topics (144); sensationalism (145); natural philosophies (146); pantheism, monism, dualism, and pluralism (147); dogmatism, eclecticism, liberalism, syncretism, and traditionalism (148). Other philosophical schools, such as realism and mysticism conclude the Division (149).

Division 150: The Schedules leave philosophy once more in this Division, which is used for the discipline of psychology. The first Section contains only the Standard Subdivisions of psychology (150.1–9). Aspects of psychology follow, such as sensation, movement, emotions, and drives (152); intellectual processes (153); and aspects of the subconscious mind (154). Applications of psychology conclude the Division. These are the study of growth and individualization (155); the psychological comparison of humans and other living organisms (156); and the application of psychology to effect individual improvement (158). Sections 151, 157, and 159 are not used in this edition.

Division 160: This Division, which contains logic, is short as pages go but is filled with ideas and theories. The important principles of induction (161) and deduction (162) lead off, followed by errors and fictions (165); syllogism (166); hypotheses (167); controversy, debate, and influencing by reason (168). The Division ends with analogy (169). Sections 163 and 164 are unused in this edition.

Division 170: This Division, used for ethics, returns to philosophy because ethics is the same as moral philosophy. The first Section is used for Standard Subdivisions of ethics (170.1–.9), with the Specific topics of metaethics and normative ethics (170.4). Various systems of ethics are next (171), with the remaining Section numbers used for the various categories of ethics. These are ethics involving the political state (172) followed by ethics within the family (173); ethics of work or professions (174); social activities, amusement, and entertainment (175); ethics involving procreation and other sexual activities (176); ethics involved in social relationships (177); the ethics of gluttony, greed, and the use of addictive substances (178); and the treatment and respect for other life, foul speech, vices, and virtues (179) conclude the Division.

Division 180: This Division is used for ancient, medieval, and Eastern philosophy. The first Section contains the Standard Subdivisions for the Division (180.01–.09) and for ancient philosophy (180.1–.9). Eastern philosophy follows (181) with the Standard subdivisions of Eastern philosophy (181.001–.009) and philosophies based on specific religions (181.04–.09), followed by the philosophies of various geographic areas (181.1–.9). The ancient philosophies are next, including pre-Socratic (182), Sophistic, and Socratic philosophies (183), Platonic (184), Aristotelian (185), Skeptic and Neoplatonic (186), Epicurean (187), and Stoic (188). Medieval Western philosophies conclude the Division (189).

Division 190: The last Division of the Class is for post-Medieval Western and all other philosophies, including Christian philosophy. The arrangement is by geographic location, with the United States and Canada in 191, Europe and Russia in 192–197, and 198 for Scandinavia and Finland. Philosophies of all other geographic areas are found in 199.

The Number Building Process

A work on demoniac possession in sixteenth-century England is a good example of number building in Class 100. According to the Relative Index, demoniac possession as part of the occult is found at 133.426 and under religion the number is 204.2. Looking under the number for religion we find "Religious experience, including conversion, enlightenment" (Dewey 2003, 2:166). That does not seem to fit the subject matter of this book, but demoniac possession is found under the number for occultism thus the notation should begin **133.426.**

Because the locality is specified, it is expected that Standard Subdivisions should be employed, but it is first necessary to review the Schedules to be sure that there is not a note indicating a change in the usual practice. There is no such indication under 133.426, which indicates demoniac possession. Thus the next part of the notation will be **09** for the geographic division and **42** for England from Table 2 Geographic areas with the notation now **133.4260942.**

The next thing to consider is that this is a work about sixteenth-century England. In Table 1 Standard Subdivisions, we find the number **09031** represents the sixteenth century, so that number is added to the notation.

LC Classification: 133.426094209031

Demonic possession and exorcism in early modern England: contemporary texts and their cultural contexts, compiled by Philip C. Almond.

DDC 22 Class 100 Revisions

There are only twenty changes in the 100 Class, and most are not significant. There are only four new numbers, all under psychology. As in other classes and some of the Tables, the word "racial" has been removed from topic names, usually leaving "ethnic" and "national" to cover those aspects of differentiation.

130–150 Parapsychology and Psychology Revisions

Parapsychology has a change in one heading. Psychology has four new numbers and eleven other changes, most of which were changes in the topic names. Three notations have been enlarged with one digit added to the number.

Table 6.1

Current Number	Current Topic	Old Topic/Comment	Old Number
	Parapsychology and Occultism		
130	Comprehensive works		133
	Psychology		
150.1986	Humanistic psychology	New number	
150.1987	Transpersonal psychology	New number	
152.188	Proprioceptive and visceral perceptions	Proprioceptive perceptions	

Current Number	Current Topic	Old Topic/Comment	Old Number
152.1882	Proprioceptive perception	Kinesthetic and vestibular perceptions	
152.4	Emotions	Emotions and feelings	
152.44	Guilt and shame	New number	
152.8	Threshold, discrimination, reaction-time studies	Quantitative threshold, discrimination, reaction-time studies	
153.758	Face perception	New number	
153.93	Individual and group intelligence tests	Individual intelligence tests	153.932–.933
154.2	Id, ego, superego; activities	The subconscious	154.22–.24
0155.45	Exceptional children; children distinguished by social and economic levels, by level of cultural development, and by ethnic and national origins	Exceptional children; children distinguished by social and economic levels, by level of cultural development, by racial, ethnic, and national origins	
155.457	Children distinguished by ethnic and national origins	Children distinguished by racial, ethnic, and national origins	
155.45705 to .4579	Specific ethnic and national groups	Specific racial, ethnic, and national groups	
155.8	Ethnopsychology of nonliterate peoples		155.81

170–190 Ethics and Philosophy Revisions

There are five changes dealing with medical ethics, four of which involve moving the topics within the section. Modern Western Philosophy has one minor heading change.

Table 6.2

Current Number	Current Topic	Old Topic/Comment	Old Number
	Ethics		
174.2	Medical professional ethics	Medical professions	
174.29	Innovative procedures of medical professionals		174.25
174.297 954	Organ transplants		174.25
174.295 895	Gene therapy		174.25
179.7	Questions of life and death of medical ethics		174.24
	Modern Western Philosophy		
198	Scandinavia and Finland	Scandinavia	

Exercises in the Use of Class 100

Utilizing the following brief summaries, test your skills at number building then compare your classification with LC's found in the section "Answers to the Exercises" in the Appendix.

1. A work on American naturalist philosophy.
2. A work on the parapsychologist/occultist Edgar Cayce.
3. A work on counseling techniques and procedures.
4. A work on ancient Mesopotamian cosmology.
5. A work on Aristotelian ontology.

6. A work on the ancient Greeks' philosophy of nature.
7. A work on the psychology of African Americans.
8. A work on imagination in the Middle Ages.
9. A work on sixteenth-century philosophy of individualism.
10. A work on intelligence tests of American minorities.

Literature Cited

Dewey, Melvil. 2003. *Dewey Decimal Classification and Relative Index.* 22nd ed. Dublin, OH: OCLC Online Computer Library Center.

7

Class 200: Religion

Criticisms of Dewey's personal religious biases and of the shortcomings of class 200 are not wanting. They arose early on, from most types of libraries and most faiths. Doctrinal, textual, philosophic, psychological, and social aspects were interminably shuffled and rebalanced in successive DDC editions. According to one voice of reason:

> There surely have been inadequacies and religious biases in Dewey's Decimal Classification. Some of these faults are attributable to the personal peculiarities of Dewey himself; some to the kinds of libraries for which early editions of the system were designed; and some to the later editors of the scheme. Most of these biases are forgivable because they were inevitable—or at least human.
>
> Probably any general library classification is more likely to be—or seem—biased in religion than in any other discipline. Several factors account for this distortion: the large number of materials to be classified; the parochial and controversial vein of many books in the field; the fact that, traditionally, people are likely to be narrow-minded in religion—not considering beliefs other than their own to be particularly important. Any hierarchical classification is, as we have been reminded so often, always unsatisfactory to most users, but its faults are likely to be magnified when it is examined by religionists. (Broadus 1970, 574–78)

There is no point to ponder belief. A battery of techniques was supplied in *DDC* 18 to allow preferred treatment, with shorter numbers, for any belief. The options are summarized in Bloomberg and Weber (1976, 59). They include two permanently unassigned numbers for local use: 289.2 and 298. Terminology changes show up regularly throughout the class, sometimes signifying conceptual shifts, but at other times merely conforming to modern usage.

The 200 class should be labeled Theology, or the study of a god or gods, as Dewey did in the first edition. Religion is the worship of a god or gods, and there are many things other than gods that are worshipped.

Summary and Details of Class 200

200	Religion
210	Philosophy and Theory of Religion
220	Bible
230	Christianity; Christian Theology
240	Christian Moral and Devotional Theology
250	Local Christian Church and Christian Religious Orders
260	Christian Social and Ecclesiastical Theology
270	Historical, Geographic, Persons Treatment of Christianity; Church History
280	Denominations and Sects of Christian Church
290	Other Religions

Division 200: This Division is used for the Standard Subdivisions of religion in general (200.1–.9). Standard Subdivisions of Christianity have been moved from this Division into 230, 260, or 270 in the continuing effort to remove the Christian bias in the Schedules.

Division 210: This Division is used for the theories of religion and contains those works in which religious convictions or viewpoints are achieved through "reason, observation of nature, and speculation instead of revelation" (Bloomberg and Weber 1976, 69). A further analysis of the breadth of the Division shows that it includes the concepts of natural and philosophical theology. The Standard Subdivision, Philosophy and Theory of Religion, is found in Sections 210 to 219 and is concerned with concepts and characteristics of God, including such disparate "isms" as polytheism, monotheism, humanism, and skepticism in addition to creation, science, and religion, theodicy, and humankind.

Division 220: The Bible, the Holy Scriptures used by Judaism and Christianity, is found in this Division. Standard Subdivisions (220.1–.09), and generalities, such as sources and verification (220.1), are found in this very crowded Section, followed by versions and translations (220.4–.5); introductions to the Scriptures, literary and historical criticism (220.6); commentaries (220.7); nonreligious subjects in the Scriptures (220.8); and ending the Section with the geographic and historic treatments, chronology, and persons of biblical lands and time (220.9). The Old Testament, or Tanakh, is covered next with general works (221) followed by the historical book (222), poetic books and wisdom literature (223), and prophetic books (224). The Manual suggests an optional arrangement for the Tanakh, of Jewish scriptures, which includes the Torah (222), Nevi'im (223), and Ketuvim (224). Christianity's New Testament is next with general aspects first (225), Revelation (228), and concluding the Division with Apocryphal or noncanonical works (229).

Division 230: General aspects of Christianity and Christian theology are found in this Division. Standard Subdivisions of Christianity are first (230.002–.007), followed by Standard Subdivisions of Christian Theology (230.01–.09), and Doctrines of Specific Denominations and Sects (230.1–.9). Aspects of Christian theology include God (231), Jesus Christ, and his family (232). In addition, this Divisions covers human beings and their place in Christianity, including the creation, original sin, good and evil (233); salvation and grace (234); saints, angels, and devils (235); humankind's purpose and destiny (236); creeds (238); and ends logically with arguments in defense of precepts of Christianity and attacks upon its detractors (239).

Division 240: Christian moral (241) and devotional theology are found in this Division. Included are meditations and prayers for devotional use (242); evangelical works (243); art in Christianity (246); church furnishing (247); and spiritual worship and Christian life and practices (248–249).

Division 250: This Division is for the local Christian church and the religious orders. As usual, Standard Subdivisions are first (250.1–.9), then followed by all aspects of the local church including preaching and sermons (251–252); pastoral life, duties, and administration (253–254, 259). Religious orders (255) conclude the Division.

Division 260: Aspects of Christianity are in the next Division. These are Christian social and political roles (261); church organization and government (262); religious observances and worship (263–265); missions (266); organizations that are part of Christianity but are not necessarily Christian organizations (267).

The Division ends with religious education (268) and Evangelism and Pentecostalism (269).

Division 270: This Division is used for the history of the Church (271–273). The geographic treatment of Christianity (274 to 279) is found in the last six Sections of the 270 Division, using Table 2 notations.

Division 280: Denominations and sects of the Christian Church are in the next to last Division. The Standard Subdivisions (280.01–.09) and branches (280.2–.4) are in the first Section and are followed logically by early and Eastern churches (281). The Roman Catholic Church (282); Anglican churches (283); and Protestant denominations and other sects (284–289), which are the most recent, conclude the Division.

Division 290: This last Division in the class contains comparative religion (291) and all non-Christian religious faiths. Classical religions come first (292), naturally followed by Germanic religions (293). Religions of Eastern original (Buddhism, Jainism, Hinduism, and Sikhism) are in 294, with Zoroastrianism (295) next. The other two great religions that, besides Christianity, recognize the Old Testament's Abraham are Judaism (296) and Islam. Islam shares the 297 Section with Babism and Baha'i Faith. All other religions are crowded into 299, arranged by ethnic orientation (299).

The Number Building Process

An excellent example of number building in the 200 Religion class is a work on missions and missionaries in Medieval Europe during the period 400 to 1050. The Relative Index helps guide us to our beginning point with the number **266** for Christian missions.

With a specific area emphasized, the next step is to add the Standard Subdivision for the geographic treatment of the subject. Checking the schedules, we find that Standard Subdivisions for Christian missions are found in .001 to .009, thus the next number added is **009.** The number to indicate Europe, or **4,** is added resulting in the notation **266.0094.**

The final step is to add the notation for the time period. Under Table 1 Standard Subdivisions we find that the number **09021** represents the sixth to the twelth centuries, or 500 to 1199, which is about where the period of this work falls.

LC Classification: 266.009409021

The missionary life: saints and the evangelisation of Europe, 400–1050, by Ian Wood.

DDC 22 Class 200 Revisions

At the time that the Dewey classification was being developed, the thought of it being used outside of the American continent did not exist. Its use and structure was based on the knowledge and culture of late-nineteenth-century United States, which was that of the WASP, or white Anglo-Saxon Protestant. Since then the culture of this country has broadened to include almost all ethnic groups and races found in the world, as well as their religions. Also, libraries around the world have used the Dewey classification as a tool in organizing their collections. The changes have necessitated major revisions in the classification, which enable it to fit more readily into other cultures.

The major efforts in this direction in the last decade have been in the area of religion, moving topics about in an effort to reduce the bias toward Christianity found in the schedules. The result shows marked improvement; however, with Christianity still occupying divisions 220 through 280 and all other religion stuffed into the last division of 290, it is still not perfectly balanced.

This edition contains the last planned major changes in this area, most of which involve moving topics in comparative religion from 291 to 200. However, there are twenty-four new numbers, most of which are in the section for the Baha'i Faith. Also, there were many changes in the notations for aspects of the religions originating among Africans and North and South American native religions, all of which are found in the 299 Section.

Table 7.1

Current Number	Current Topic	Old Topic/Comment	Old Number
200	**Religion**		
200	Comparative religion		291
200.1	Value		200.13
200.8	History and description with respect to kinds of persons	Relations of the sexes, social classes, language, ethnic, age groups	291.17834
200.8	History and description with respect to kinds of persons		306.608
200.9034	Religions of 19th- and 20th-century origin		291.046

Current Number	Current Topic	Old Topic/Comment	Old Number
201	Religious mythology, general classes of religion, interreligious relations and attitudes, and social theology		291.1
201.3	Mythology and mythological foundations		291.13
201.4	General classes of religion		291.14
201.42	Prehistoric religions and religions of nonliterate peoples		291.042
201.43	Goddess religions		291.14
201.44	Shamanism		291.144
201.5	Interreligious relations		291.172
201.6	Religions and secular disciplines		291.175
201.6001 to .6199	Computer science, information, philosophy, parapsychology and occultism, and psychology	New number	
201.64 to .69	Language, natural sciences, mathematics, technology, arts, literature, rhetoric, geography, and history	New number	
201.7	Attitudes of religions toward social issues	Social theologies and interreligious relations and attitudes	291.17
201.7	Role of organized religions in society		291.171
201.7	Communications media		291.175

Current Number	Current Topic	Old Topic/Comment	Old Number
201.7	Sexual relations, marriage, divorce, and family		291.17835
201.7	Population		291.178366
201.72	Political affairs	Religions and political affairs	291.177
201.721	Theocracy		291.1773
201.723	Civil rights		291.177
201.727	International affairs		291.1787
201.7273	War and peace		291.17873
201.7275	Nuclear weapons and nuclear war		291.178732
201.73	Economics	The economic order	291.1785
201.76	Social problems and services	Religions and socioeconomic problems	291.178
201.76	Socioeconomic problems	Social problems	291.1783
201.7625	Poor people		291.178325
201.76276	Child abuse and neglect		291.1783271
201.76276	Sexual abuse		291.1783272
201.762764	Adults who were victims of abuse as children		291.1783273
201.7628292	Abuse within the family		291.178327
201.76287	Refugees and victims of political oppression		291.178328
201.7638	Hunger		291.178326
201.764	Crime and punishment		291.17833
201.77	Environment	New number	

Current Number	Current Topic	Old Topic/Comment	Old Number
201.77	Ecology	Attitude of religions toward ecology	291.178362
202	Doctrines		291.2
202.1	Objects of worship and veneration		291.21
202.11	God, gods, goddesses, divinities, and deities		291.211
202.112	Attributes of God, of the gods		291.2112
202.113	Male gods		291.2113
202.114	Female goddesses		291.2114
202.117	Relation to the world		291.2117
202.118	Theodicy		291.2118
202.12	Nature		291.212
202.13	Persons		291.213
202.14	Personified abstractions		291.214
202.15	Good spirits		291.215
202.16	Evil spirits		291.216
202.18	Images		291.218
202.2	Humankind		291.22
202.3	Eschatology		291.23
202.37	Reincarnation		291.237
202.4	Creation and cosmology		291.24
203	Public worship and other practices		291.3
203.1	Religious healing		291.31
203.2	Divination		291.32
203.3	Witchcraft		291.33
203.4	Offerings, sacrifices, penances		291.34

Current Number	Current Topic	Old Topic/Comment	Old Number
203.42	Human sacrifice	New number	
203.5	Sacred places and Pilgrimages		291.35
203.5093 to .5099	Treatment by specific continents, countries, localities		291.35093 to .35099
203.51	Pilgrimages		291.351
203.6	Sacred times		291.36
203.7	Symbolism, symbolic objects, sounds		291.37
203.8	Rites and ceremonies		291.38
203.81	Birth rites	New number	
203.82	Initiation rites	New number	
203.85	Marriage rites	New number	
203.88	Funeral and mourning rites	New number	
204	Religious experience, life, and practice		291.4
204.2	Religious experience		291.44
204.22	Mysticism		291.447
204.3	Worship, mediation, and yoga		291.43
204.32	Devotional literature		291.432
204.33	Prayer books		291.433
204.35	Meditation		291.435
204.36	Yoga		291.436
204.4	Religious life and practice		291.44
204.4086	Persons by miscellaneous social characteristics		291.44086
204.4087	Gifted persons	New number	
204.41	Marriage and family life		291.441

Current Number	Current Topic	Old Topic/Comment	Old Number
204.42	Persons experiencing illness, trouble, addiction, and bereavement		291.442
204.46	Individual observances		291.446
204.47	Asceticism		291.447
205	Religious ethics	Moral theology	291.5
205.6	Specific moral issues, sins, vices, and virtues		291.56
206	Leaders and organization		291.6
206.1	Leaders and their work		291.61
206.3	Founders of religions		291.63
206.5	Organizations and organization		291.65
206.57	Monasticism and monasteries		291.657
207		Missions and religious education	291.7
207.2	Missions		291.72
207.5	Religious education		291.75
208	Sources		291.8
208.2	Sacred books and scriptures		291.82
208.3	Oral traditions		291.83
208.4	Laws and decisions		291.84
208.5	Sources of sects and reform movements		291.85
209	Sects and reform movements		291.9
218	Humankind	Life sciences	215.7

Current Number	Current Topic	Old Topic/Comment	Old Number
220.52083	Living Bible and New Living Translation	Living Bible	
248.83	Young people		248.8083
248.84	Persons in specific stages of adulthood		248.8084
248.842	Men		248.8081
248.843	Women		248.8082
248.844	Married persons		248.808655
248.845	Relatives		248.8085
248.846	Separated and divorced persons		248.808653
248.88	Occupational groups	Occupational classes	
248.89	Clergy or persons in religious orders	Religious groups	
261.513	Parapsychology and occultism	Paranormal, occult phenomena and arts	
261.83	Social problems and services	Social problems	
261.836	Population	Ecology and population	
261.85	Economics	The economic order	
261.88	[Christianity and the] Environment	Ecology and population	261.836
261.88	Ecology	New number	261.836
262.98	Branches and other denominations and sects	New number	
270.08	Christian attitudes toward social groups	Relations of age groups, the sexes, social classes, and language groups	261.834
284.0943	Evangelische Kirche in Deutschland		284.143
287.536	Methodist Church of Great Britain	New number	

Current Number	Current Topic	Old Topic/Comment	Old Number
290	Other religions	Comparative religion and religions other than Christianity	
294.54	[Hinduism] Religious experience, life, practice, and religious ethics	Religious experience, life, practice, and moral theology	
294.548	[Hinduism]Religious ethics	Moral theology	
297.45	Sufi ethics	Sufi moral theology	
297.931 to .937	[Baha'i Faith] Specific aspects	New number	
297.938	[Baha'i Faith] Sources	New number	
297.9382	[Baha'i Faith] Sacred books	New number	
297.93822	[Baha'i Faith] Works by Bahá'u'lláh	New number	
297.93824	[Baha'i Faith] Works by 'Abdu'l-Bahá	New number	
297.9386	[Baha'i Faith] Authoritative interpretation	New number	
297.9387	[Baha'i Faith] Elucidation and legislation	New number	
299.1	Religions of Indo-European origin	New number	
299.16	Celtic religions	New number	
299.161	Specific aspects of Celtic religions	New number	
299.3	Religions of Non-Semitic Afro-Asiatic origin	New number	
299.31	Ancient Egyptian religion	New number	

Current Number	Current Topic	Old Topic/Comment	Old Number
299.511	Specific aspects of Chinese religions	New number	
299.61	[Religions originating among Black Africans . . .] Specific aspects	New number	
299.6113	[Religions originating among Black Africans . . .] Mythology and mythological foundations		299.62
299.612	[Religions originating among Black Africans . . .] Doctrines		299.63
299.613	[Religions originating among Black Africans . . .] Practices		299.64
299.6138	[Religions originating among Black Africans . . .] Rites and ceremonies		299.64
299.67	[Religions originating among Black Africans . . .] Mythology and mythological foundations		299.62
299.67	[Religions originating among Black Africans . . .] Doctrines		299.63
299.67	[Religions originating among Black Africans . . .] Practices, rites, ceremonies		299.64

Current Number	Current Topic	Old Topic/Comment	Old Number
299.675	[Religions originating among Black Africans . . .] Zombiism		299.64
299.68	[Religions originating among Black Africans . . .] Mythology and mythological foundations of religions of specific groups and peoples		299.62
299.68	[Religions originating among Black Africans . . .] Mythology and mythological foundations		299.62
299.68	[Religions originating among Black Africans . . .] Doctrines		299.63
299.68	[Religions originating among Black Africans . . .] Practices, rites, ceremonies		299.64
299.683001 to .685008	[Religions of peoples who speak, or whose ancestors spoke, Niger-Congo, Nilo-Saharan languages] Standard subdivisions		299.68301 to .68308
299.683009 to .685009	[Religions of peoples who speak, or whose ancestors spoke, Niger-Congo, Nilo-Saharan languages] Historical, geographic, persons, treatment		299.68309 to .68509

Current Number	Current Topic	Old Topic/Comment	Old Number
299.7	[Religions of North American native origin] Specific cults		299.77
299.7113	[Religions of North American native origin] Mythology and mythological foundations		299.72
299.712	[Religions of North American native origin] Doctrines		299.73
299.713	[Religions of North American native origin] Practices		299.74
299.7138	[Religions of North American native origin] Rites and ceremonies		299.74
299.78	[Religions of North American native origin] Religions of specific groups and peoples		299.72
299.78013	[Religions of North American native origin] Mythology and mythological foundations		299.72
299.7802	[Religions of North American native origin] Doctrines		299.73
299.7803	[Religions of North American native origin] Practices		299.74
299.78038	[Religions of North American native origin] Rites and ceremonies		299.74
299.8	Religions of South American native origin	Specific cults	299.87

Current Number	Current Topic	Old Topic/Comment	Old Number
299.8113	[Religions of South American native origin] Mythology and mythological foundations		299.82
299.812	[Religions of South American native origin] Doctrines		299.83
299.813	[Religions of South American native origin] Practices		299.84
299.8138	[Religions of South American native origin] Rites and ceremonies		299.84
299.88013	[Religions of South American native origin] Mythology and mythological foundations		299.82
299.8802	[Religions of South American native origin] Doctrines		299.83
299.8803	[Religions of South American native origin] Practices		299.84
299.88038	[Religions of South American native origin] Rites and ceremonies		299.84
299.94	Religions based on modern revivals of witchcraft	New number	

Exercises in the Use of Class 200

Test your skills by assigning classifications to the follow works, being careful to use all of the applicable number building tools that have been discussed in this manual. Check your results against the classifications assigned by the Library of Congress found in "Answers to the Exercises" in the Appendix.

1. A work on the equality and sex roles of women in the Baha'i Faith.
2. A work on the theological view of revelation of a reformed Jew.
3. A work on readings and interpretations of Genesis.
4. A work on the ordination of women in the Catholic Church.
5. A work on Puritans in England.
6. A work on sex in the Bible.
7. A work on revivals and evangelicalism in New Zealand.
8. A work on Taoism and Taoist ethics.

Literature Cited

Broadus, Robert N. 1970. Dewey and Religion. *Library Resources & Technical Services* 14 (4):574–78.

Bloomberg, Marty, and Hans Weber. 1976. *An Introduction to Classification and Number Building*. Littleton, CO: Libraries Unlimited.

8

Class 300: Social Sciences

Social Sciences is a wide-ranging Class that includes such diverse subjects as general statistics, law, military science, and etiquette. One may say that it is a catch-all for categories not covered by the other nine Classes. It ranks second in size to Technology (Applied Sciences), but in complexity it ranks first.

Placing Economics (330) between Political Science (320) and Law (340), and distant from Commerce, Communications, Transportation (380) is regrettable, but it would not serve a useful purpose to revamp the Divisions (and put the users in a tizzy) to rectify the predicament. However, it is certain that those working in the Pentagon would question whether the military is a social science. Situating Public Administration and Military Science (350) in the same Division is puzzling and almost amusing. Is it a comment on our civilization that implies that if the government does not function properly, then military will step in and assume the authority, as well as the reverse, where military juntas are overthrown and constitutional governments instated? A parallel paradox is figuring out whether social problems and services are the same as associations (360). What relationship is there between penal institutions and insurance, or social problems and clubs?

Customs, Etiquette, Folklore (390) is the oddest of the DDC Divisions. Customs are a part of culture and consequently belong in 306, Culture and Institutions. Costume and Personal Appearance (391) both belong in the 640s, Home Economics and Family Living. Folklore is also culture, but Folk Literature belongs in Literature, not the Social Sciences Class, for it is a compendium of literary works of the imagination. Etiquette (little ethics) belongs with "big ethics," 170, and the customs of war and diplomacy are with other customs in 390 rather than with war in 355 and diplomacy in 327.

All and all, it is a strange and badly conceived Class. Probably only DDC classifiers could see motion pictures as communication rather than purely an art. Valiant efforts have been made to fix the problems, but these have always failed, perhaps because of the impact on the users. Even when the redoubtable Benjamin

A. Custer tried to remove Folk Literature to the 800s, he was unable to win the battle. The only explanation for these paradoxes is that this is the resting ground for the misfits that do not belong in other classes and have some sort of relationship to society, thus creating this strange mélange of topics that are merged together like adopted children in a comfortable home of disparate members.

Summary and Details of Class 300

300 Social Sciences

310 Collections of General Statistics

320 Political Science (Politics and Government)

330 Economics

340 Law

350 Public Administration and Military Science

360 Social Problems and Services; Associations

370 Education

380 Commerce, Communications, Transportation

390 Customs, Etiquette, Folklore

Division 300: As usual, the Standard Subdivisions of Social Sciences are found in the first Division (300.1–.9) followed by books in sociology and anthropology that are general in nature (301). More specific topics come next, such as interpersonal and social relationships and nontechnical concepts of communication (302). Socialization, social change, and natural and demographic factors affecting society are in 303 and 304. Specific groups that make up societies and their beliefs, values, mores, and institutions are in 305 and 306. The study of communities (307) concludes the Division, 308 and 309 not being used in this edition.

Anthropology is in its pre–Edition 20 state with general aspects (or comprehensive works) in 301 with Sociology, and specific topics being mixed and blended throughout 302–307.

Division 310: This Division is used for works on the various statistics of societies, such as censuses. The arrangement mirrors Table 2, with Europe in 31***4***, Asia in 31***5***, Africa 31***6***, North America 31***7***, South America 31***8***, and all other places in 31***9***. Statistics of specific subjects are found with the subject plus the notation from Table 1 for statistics (–021).

Division 320: The third Division is used for political science, or the study of politics and government. The first Section contains Standard Subdivisions (320.01–.09), and general aspects of the discipline, such as the structure and functions of government, and political conditions (320.1–.9). The various types of government (i.e., Democratic or authoritarian) are found in the next Section (321) followed by relationship of the government to its peoples (322) and their rights (323). Works on political parties and elections are next (324) followed by the international movement of peoples, including colonization (325). It is strange to think of slavery in the twenty-first century, but it does exist and books on the subject are found in 326. Relationships between countries and topics of laws, lawmaking, and the governmental bodies that are responsible for them (328) conclude the Division. Section 329 is not used in this edition.

Division 330: This Division is used for economics, the first Section being reserved for Standard Subdivisions (330.01–.09). The "systems" part of the first Standard Subdivision (–011) is in a separate Section (330.1) as are the geographic and historic treatments of economic conditions (330.9). The next Section is reserved for topics concerning the work force (331), followed by books on banking and money (332). The next Section is used for the economic aspects of natural resources, including land and forms of energy (333), then various types of economic cooperation in banking, housing, and other forms (334). All types of socialism are found in 335. Finance of governments is in the next section (336), followed by international economic cooperation by governments (337). The Division ends with all types of economic production in 338, and economics on a more universal scale, such as the distribution of wealth and aspects of the national product, as well as macroeconomics in 339.

Division 340: The next Division is used for law or jurisprudence, and like the previous Divisions, the Standard Subdivisions (340.02–.09) are in the first Section. However, the philosophy and theory of law is separate (340.1) and found with the general aspects of law (340.2–.9). The next Section is reserved for international law (341) and the remaining Sections encompass specific kinds of law. Laws that are constitutionally based and those dealing with government duties and responsibilities are in 342. Military law, public property, tax law, and the law of commerce (343); law concerning the workforce, education, and other social and cultural activities (344) end the various types of civil law. All aspects of criminal law are in 345. Noncriminal law involving persons, civil trials and procedures, statutes, and regulations are in 346 through 348. The Division ends with laws and regulations of specific localities (349), which utilize Table 2 notations to distinguish the locations.

Division 350: This Division holds such unlikely companions as the executive branch of government, civil service, and military and naval sciences. Standard Subdivisions of public administration are found in 351 (351.01–.09), followed by administration of areas in general (351.1) and by specific places (351.3–.9). Finances, personnel, and other aspects of public administration are in the next Section (352), followed by administration of specific services or functions (353) and of the economy and environment (354).

The military sciences begins in the next Section, and because of limited number ranges in the Class, seems fragmented. General aspects are first in 355, followed by land-based services and warfare including the infantry (356.1). Cavalries and mounted forces are found in 357, missile, artillery, and armored forces in 358.1. Engineering services are under 358.2. The rest of 358 includes unconventional warfare, such as chemical, biological, and radiological (358.3), followed by air and space warfare and forces (358.4 and 358.8). The last Section is used for seaborne forces and warfare (359), including marine forces (359.96).

Division 360: This Division is reserved for societies' problems and the services that are available to help alleviate them (361–365) and associations (366–369). In the first Section, Standard Subdivisions for social problems and social welfare (361.001–.008) are followed by free and fee-based services, then material and guidance assistance (361.02–.06). General aspects of these services, such as social, private, governmental, and community actions follow (361.1–.8), with the historical, geographic and persons treatment concluding the Section.

Illnesses, disabilities, the poor, the aged, and other groups are in the next Section (362), followed by public safety, housing, environmental, and population problems (363). The problems involving crime, its prevention, and the treatment of criminals are in the next two Sections (364–365).

Supposing that there was no better Class in which to place them then to follow economics, public administration, military sciences, and associations conclude the 360 Division. Philanthropic and social organizations (366–367). Insurance considered as a type of mutual help association rather than a financial institution (368). The Division ends with miscellaneous types of associations, such as patriotic, military, racial, ethnic, and clubs for youths (369).

Division 370: Education is found in the next Division, with Standard Subdivisions, as usual, being in the first Section (370.1–.9). Schools are found in 371, including teachers, students, the physical plant, and special education. Four out of the next five sections contain works about the levels of education, beginning with elemental education (372), then secondary education (373), and adult education (374), and higher education (378). General aspects of curricula (375), is shoved in between adult and higher education. The Division concludes with financial and policy issues of education (379).

Division 380: The next to last Division is used for trade, communications, and transportation. The first Section is reserved for Standard Subdivisions (380.01–.09). Works on trade in general, including domestic trade (381), and trade between countries (382) conclude that subject.

The next Section begins communication with intercourse by mail (383), then telecommunication by telegraph (384.1), by computer (384.3), wireless methods, including radio and television (384.5); by telephone (384.6), and motion pictures (384.8).

Railroads (385) begin transportation, followed by inland water transportation (386), and water (387.1–.5), air (387.7), and space transportation (387.8). Ground transportation of all types concludes works on transportation beginning with roads (388.1), vehicular (388.3), and urban transportation (388.4). Pipelines considered as a transit system end the ground transportation sections (388.5)

The division ends with another of those strangely placed topics, Metrology (389.1) and Standardization (389.6), which one may conclude should be better placed in 530.81 with measurement.

Division 390: The final Division is reserved for practices, manners, and conventions that are common to societies, in addition to tradition, lore, and folktales that are common to a culture. The first Section contains the Standard Subdivisions for the Division (390.01–.09), followed by practices and conventions of social classes and those of occupations (390.1–.4). Works that are concerned with people's clothing and other ways that they adorn themselves are in the second Section (391), followed by practices and conventions concerning the stages of life from birth to marriage and the home (392), and to death (393). Conventions involving such diverse activities as consumption of food, drink, and drugs; holidays and other special days; recreation; suicide; and cannibalism are all in the next section (394). Etiquette and manners come next (395), followed by folk literature, riddles, proverbs, and rhyming games (398). Customs of war and diplomacy conclude the Class.

The Number Building Process

The demonstration of number building in the 300 Class is a work on America's espionage through aerial reconnaissance during the Eisenhower administration. According to the Relative Index, espionage is found at **327.12,** under International Relations. Since this book deals with espionage by the United States, the next part of the notation should involve a geographic subdivision. Looking further under 327.12 to be sure that there are no special instructions or changes for the geographic subdivisions, notes are found instructing the classifier: "Do not use for espionage and subversion by specific nations, class in 327.123–327.129," and "Add to base number 327.12 notation 3–9 from Table 2" (Dewey 2003, 2:392). Thus the geographic notation is added directly to the base number without the Table 1 notation –09. The notation for the United States is –73, which now brings the classification number to **327.1273.**

The next aspect to add to the number is the date, which is during the Eisenhower presidency, or the 1950s. Table 1 indicates that the number for that time period is –09045. Returning once more to the Schedules to see if there are instructions that may effect the adding of this notation, an instruction indicates "for espionage and subversion by that country in another area add 0*," then checking the bottom of the page for the asterisk "*Add 00 for Standard Subdivisions." Thus an additional zero must be added to distinguish Standard Subdivisions from these geographic notations; in this case the notation is **–009045.**

LC Classification: 327.1273009045

Secret empire: Eisenhower, the CIA, and the hidden story of America's space espionage, by Philip Taubman.

DDC 22 Class 300 Revisions

The March 1976 Decimal Classification Editorial Policy Committee reviewed a survey report pinpointing eleven areas that were in need of extensive revisions, more than half of which were in Class 300 (Comaromi 1977, 94). Edition 20 began this mission with vast changes, but many were left for succeeding editions. Significant efforts were made in Edition 21 to completely revise Public Administration, 350–354, and Education, 370. Insurance (368) also contained notable modifications, and there was much shifting around in 324, The Political Process.

Division 310, Collections of General Statistics, has no modifications in Edition 22. The big change here took place in Edition 20 when the heading became General Statistics, such as censuses, which clearly indicates the scope as it now exists. Statistics of populations, or demography, is now found scattered with the subjects, with addition of 021. Demography in general is found in 304.6.

300 Social Sciences Revisions

As in other Classes, the word "race" has been removed from all topic names leaving "ethnic" and "national" as the characteristics. Social Sciences (300) has seen similar changes appear in Editions 19 and 20, focusing in the 305–306 area, which continues to present difficulties to DDC users. In Edition 22 there are seventy-eight changes including twenty-three new numbers in social groups (305) and seventy-six changes in Culture and Institutions (306) with twenty new numbers. The movement of topics between the two sections continues in Edition 22 with thirty-eight topics moved from 305 to 306. A detailed list of changes follows.

Table 8.1

Current Number	Current Topic	Old Topic/ Comment	Old Number
	Social Sciences		
302.2	Failures and disruptions of communication		302.25
302.23	Electronic media		302.234
302.231	Digital media	New number	
302.234	Motion pictures, radio, television		306.485
302.5	Relation through reference groups		302.52
303.32	Socialization	Socialization other than by peer group	303.327

Current Number	Current Topic	Old Topic/ Comment	Old Number
303.323	Socialization by father and mother		303.3231 to .3232
303.327	Socialization by peer group	Socialization by instrumentalities	
303.37	Social norms	Normative methods	
303.386	Opinions held by miscellaneous groups	New number	303.388
303.388	Opinions held by occupational groups	Opinion held by occupational and miscellaneous groups	
303.388	Opinions held by occupational groups	Notation 001–999 replaces 09–99 from Table 7	
303.66	War and peace	War	
304.237	Time factors	New number	
304.63	Family size		304.634
305	**Social Groups**		
305	History and description with respect to kinds of persons		306.08
305.2	Age groups		305.80083 to .80084, 305.90083 to .90084
305.2 to .9	History and description with respect to kinds of persons		305.08, 305.308
305.23 to .26	Men, women, age groups		305.2081 to .2084
305.23081	Boys	New number	
305.23082	Girls	New number	

Current Number	Current Topic	Old Topic/ Comment	Old Number
305.23086	Children by miscellaneous social characteristics	New number	
305.2308692	Predelinquent and runaway children	New number	305.906923
305.23086945	Abandoned children, abused children, orphans		305.906945
305.235	Age groups		305.235083 to .235084
305.235087	Persons with disabilities and illnesses, gifted persons		305.235087
305.2351	Men	New number	305.235081
305.2352	Women	New number	305.235082
305.242	Young adults		305.242083 to .242084
305.2421	Men	New number	305.242081
305.2422	Women	New number	305.242082
305.244	Age groups		305.244083 to .244084
305.2441	Men	New number	305.244081
305.2442	Women	New number	305.244082
305.26	Age groups		305.26083 to .26084
305.261	Men	New number	305.26081
305.262	Women	New number	305.26082
305.33	[History and description with respect to kinds of people] Men		305.90081
305.388	[Ethnic and national groups] Men		305.80081

Current Number	Current Topic	Old Topic/ Comment	Old Number
305.43	Women's occupations	Notation 001–999 replaces 09–99 from Table 7	
305.43	[History and description with respect to kinds of people]Women		305.90082
305.488	[Ethnic and national groups] Women		305.80082
305.4896	Women by social, economic, cultural level; special social status	New number	
305.5	Social classes	Persons by level of cultural development	305.9063
305.522	Upper class by birth	Royalty	305.5222
305.522	Upper class by birth	Nobility	305.5223
305.55	Middle class (Bourgeoisie)	Persons of medium cultural development	305.90632
305.552	Intelligentsia	Persons of high cultural development	305.90631
305.56	Lower, alienated, excluded classes		305.90694
305.562	Working class	Laboring class (Proletariat)	
305.565	Culturally disadvantaged persons	New number	305.90633
305.5688	Dalits	New number	
305.5692	Homeless people	New number	
305.6	Religious groups	Notation 230–299 replaces notation 2 from Table 7	305.80088, 305.90088
305.696	Jews as a religious group	New number	
305.8	Ethnic and national groups	Indigenous ethic and national groups	306.089

Current Number	Current Topic	Old Topic/ Comment	Old Number
305.8	Ethnic and national groups		305.80089, 305.90089
305.8	Ethnic and national groups	Indigenous ethic and national groups	306.08
305.805 to .89	Specific ethnic and national groups	Ethnic and national groups	306.089
305.9	Occupational groups		305.80088, 305.90088
305.906	Persons with social status	Persons by cultural level, marital status, sexual orientations, special social status	
305.9069	Persons with status defined by changes in residence; antisocial, asocial, unemployed persons; victims of war; veterans	New number	
305.90691	Persons with status defined by changes in residence	New number	
305.906912	Immigrants	New number	
305.906914	Displaced persons	New number	325.21
305.906918	Nomads	New number	
305.90692	Antisocial and asocial persons	New number	
305.90694	Unemployed persons		305.906941
305.90695	Victims of war	New number	305.906949
305.90697	Veterans of military service	New number	
305.908	Persons with disabilities and illnesses, gifted persons	Persons by physical and mental characteristics	305.2087 305.242087, 305.244087, 305.26087, 305.80087, 305.90087

Current Number	Current Topic	Old Topic/ Comment	Old Number
305.908	Persons with disabilities and illnesses, gifted persons	The numbers following –087 in notation –0871 to –0879 from Table 1 replace the numbers following –08 in notation –081 to –082 from Table 7	
305.909	Generalists	The numbers following 0 in 001 to 099 replace the numbers following –09 in notation –0901 to –097 from Table 7	
305.91 to .99		Notations 100 to 999 replaces notation –1 to –9 from Table 7	
305.963	Farmers		305.555
305.963	Farmers	Agricultural workers	305.563
305.963	Farmers	Agricultural occupations	306.364
306	**Culture and Institutions**		
306.34	Systems of production and exchange	Cooperation	306.344
306.34	Systems of production and exchange	Syndicalism	306.347
306.36	Free labor systems		306.366
306.362	Slaves		305.567
306.365	Serfs, sharecroppers		305.563
306.38	Retired persons		305.90696
306.44	Language	Ethnolinquistics	306.44089
306.461	Medicine and health	Medicine	

Current Number	Current Topic	Old Topic/ Comment	Old Number
306.4613	Personal health	New number	
306.47	Arts and crafts		306.489
306.48	Recreation and performing arts	Recreation	
306.48125	Vacations (Holidays)	New number	
306.4819	Travel and tourism	New number	
306.4842	Music	New number	
306.48422 to .48429	Traditions of music	New number	
306.4846	Dance	New number	
306.4848	Theater	New number	
306.63 to .69	Institutions of specific religions	New number	
306.7	Sexual relations	Institutions pertaining to relations of the sexes	
306.73	Free love		306.735
306.733	Premarital sexual relations	New number	
306.734	Courtship and engagement		305.906523
306.734	Engaged persons		305.906523
306.734081	Engaged men	New number	305.3896523
306.734082	Engaged women	New number	305.4896523
306.76	Persons by sexual orientation	Men by sexual orientation	305.38966
306.76	Persons by sexual orientation	Women by sexual orientation	305.48966
306.76	Persons by sexual orientation		305.9066
306.76	Men by sexual orientation		305.38966
306.762	Asexuality	Neutral sexual orientation	

Current Number	Current Topic	Old Topic/ Comment	Old Number
306.7662	Gay men		305.389664
306.7663	Lesbianism		305.489664
306.768	Transsexuality	New number	
306.77	Sexual and related practices	Sexual practices	
306.77	Sodomy		306.773
306.778	Transvestism	New number	
306.81	Marriage and marital status	Marriage	
306.81	Marriage and marital status	Marriage status	305.9065
306.815	Single marital status	New number	
306.815	Single persons		305.90652
306.8152	Single men	New number	305.389652, 306.815081
306.8153	Single women	New number	305.489652, 306.815082
306.84	Types of marriage and relationships	Types of marriage	
306.841	Cohabitation		306.735
306.8423	Ménage à trios		306.735
306.8423	Polygamy	Polygamy and polyandry	
306.8423	Polygamy	Polygamous persons	305.90659
306.848	Same-sex marriage	Gay marriage	
306.85	Suburban family		306.853
306.87	Intrafamily relationships	Relatives; Parents	305.085
306.87	Intrafamily relationships	Relatives; Parents	305.3085
306.87	Intrafamily relationships	Men by kinship characteristics	305.3894
306.87	Intrafamily relationships	Women by kinship charactistics	305.4894

Current Number	Current Topic	Old Topic/ Comment	Old Number
306.87	Intrafamily relationships	Relatives; Parents	305.80085
306.87	Intrafamily relationships	Youngest child	306.874
306.87	Intrafamily relationships	Relatives; Parents	305.90085
306.87	Intrafamily relationships	Persons by kinship characteristics	305.904
306.872	Husband-wife relationship	Married people	305.90655
306.8722	Husbands	Married men	305.389655
306.8723	Wives	New number	305.489655
306.874	Parent-child relationship	Children of unmarried parents	305.906945
306.87422	Single fatherhood	New number	
306.87432	Single motherhood	Unmarried mothers	305.4896947
306.8747	Stepparent-stepchild relationship	New number	
306.88	Alteration of family arrangements	Widowed persons	305.90654
306.88081	Men	New number	
306.88082	Women	New number	
306.882	Widowers		305.389654
306.883	Widows		305.489654
306.89	Separation and divorce	Separated and divorced persons	305.90653
306.892	Separated and divorced men		305.389653, 306.89081
306.893	Separated and divorced women		305.489653

Current Number	Current Topic	Old Topic/ Comment	Old Number
307	**Communities**		
307.77	Self-contained communities	Voluntary socialist and anarchist communities	335.9
307.776	Kibbutzim and moshavim	Kibbutzim	

320 Political Science Revisions

Political Science (320) was a Division cited as being in need of revision in the 1974 survey of the DDC in the United States and Canada. The political process or decisions regarding who is to wield power underwent a complete revision for Edition 19, additional changes in Edition 20, and rather substantial changes in Edition 21. Edition 22 continues with improvements with the majority of changes being new numbers, twenty-three of which are found under the [political] Parties of Germany (324.243)

Table 8.2

Current Number	Current Topic	Old Topic/Comment	Old Number
320	**Political Science**		
320.546	Black nationalism	New number	
320.557	Islamic fundamentalism	New number	
320.58	Environmentalist political ideologies	New number	
320.588	Black Muslim movement	New number	
320.6	Policy making	Decision making	320.019
323.042	Citizen participation	Participation of citizens in governmental processes	

Current Number	Current Topic	Old Topic/ Comment	Old Number
323.448 3	Freedom from misuse of information in databases and government records	Freedom from misuse of information in databases	
323.62	Acquisition of citizenship	Citizenship by marriage	323.636
323.62	Acquisition of citizenship	Citizenship by birth	323.622
323.62	Acquisition of citizenship	Other ways of acquiring citizenship	323.629
323.63	Relation of the state to aliens and persons with citizenship problems	Stateless persons, persons with dual nationality	323.632 to .634
323.63	Relation of the state to aliens and persons with citizenship problems	Married people of differing nationality	323.636
324.22	Politics as a profession, occupation, hobby		324.023
324.243	Parties of Germany	New number	
324.243001 to .243009	[Parties of Germany] Standard subdivisions	New number	
324.24301	[Parties of Germany] General topics	New number	
324.24302	[Parties of Germany] Historical parties	New number	
324.243023	[Parties of Germany] Rightist parties	New number	
324.2430238	[Parties of Germany] National Socialist German Labor Party (Nazi Party)	New number	
324.243024	[Parties of Germany] Conservative parties	New number	

Current Number	Current Topic	Old Topic/Comment	Old Number
324.243025	[Parties of Germany] Centrist parties	New number	
324.243026	[Parties of Germany] Liberal parties	New number	
324.243027	[Parties of Germany] Leftist and worker parties	New number	
324.24303	[Parties of Germany] Rightist parties	New number	
324.24303	[Parties of Germany] Rightist parties	National Democratic Party of Germany	324.243083
324.243038	[Parties of Germany] Neofascist and neo-Nazi parties	New number	
324.24304	[Parties of Germany] Conservative parties	New number	
0324.24304	[Parties of Germany] Conservative parties	Conservative religious parties; Christian Democratic Union of Germany; Christian Social Union (CSU)	324.243082
324.24305	[Parties of Germany] Centrist parties	New number	
324.24306	[Parties of Germany] Liberal parties	New number	
324.24307	[Parties of Germany] Leftist and worker parties	New number	
324.243072	[Parties of Germany] Social democratic parties	New number	
324.243074	[Parties of Germany] Socialist parties	New number	
324.243075	[Parties of Germany] Communist parties	New number	
324.24308	[Parties of Germany] Other recent parties	New number	

Current Number	Current Topic	Old Topic/Comment	Old Number
324.243082	[Parties of Germany] Religious parties	New number	
324.243083	[Parties of Germany] Nationalist parties	New number	
324.243084	[Parties of Germany] Regionalist and separatist parties	New number	
324.243087	[Parties of Germany] Environmentalist (Green parties)	New number	
324.2737	[Parties of United States] Leftist and labor-oriented parties	Leftist and worker parties	
324.274703	[Parties in New York] Nationalist parties of the right		324.2747093
324.274707	Leftist and worker parties		324.2747097
324.274708	Other recent parties	New number	324.274709
324.274708		Conservative Party	324.274703
324.274708		Liberal Party	324.274707
324.29404	National Party of Australia	Country party	
324.623	Women's suffrage		324.62082
324.7	Conduct of election campaigns	Public relations for conduct of political election campaigns	659.293247
324.73	Use and effect of media	Advertising for political election campaigns	659.1932473
327.3–.9	Foreign relations of specific continents and localities	Foreign relations of specific nations	327.093 to .099, 327.1093 to .1099
328.4–.9	Legislative process in specific continents and localities in modern world		328.094 to .099

330 Economics Revisions

John Phillip Comaromi listed Economics (330) as needing revisions second only to sections 301–307. Many changes, some sweeping in scope, were made in both Editions 20 and 21, especially section 333, which was changed from Land Economics to Economics of Land and Energy; and 333.95 Biological Resources, which was revised and expanded. Changes in Edition 22 are quite extensive, with more than 160 changes including expansions resulting in fifty-six new numbers, most of which are found under Labor Economics (331).

Table 8.3

Current Number	Current Topic	Old Topic/Comment	Old Number
330	**Economics**		
330.092	Persons treatment		330.90092
330.15	Schools of economic thought	Historical and mathematical schools	330.154
330.15	Schools of economic thought	Ethical, romantic, social justice schools	330.155
330.1552	Institutional economics	New number	
330.1553	Chicago school of economics (Monetarism)	New number	
330.1554	Supply-side economics	New number	
330.9	Comprehensive works on geographic treatment		330.9009
331.11	Nongovernmental, nonagricultural occupations		331.119042
331.1142	[Labor force] Qualifications	Qualifications by level of experience	331.11424
331.114224	Skilled workers	New number	
331.114233	High school graduates	New number	

Current Number	Current Topic	Old Topic/Comment	Old Number
331.114235	College graduates	New number	
331.12	Nongovernmental, nonagricultural occupations		331.129042
331.120424	Full employment policies	New number	
331.1261	Labor turnover in industries and occupations other than extractive, manufacturing, construction	New number	
331.12610001 to .12610009	[Labor turnover] Standard subdivisions	New number	
331.1261001 to .1261999	Subdivisions for turnover in industries and occupations other than extractive, manufacturing, construction	New number	
0331.1262 to .1269	Labor turnover in extractive, manufacturing, construction occupations	New number	
331.137	Unemployment	Labor surpluses	331.136
331.137	Unemployment	Distribution and incidence of unemployment	331.1374
331.21647	Profit sharing	New number	
331.21649	Employee stock ownership plans	New number	
331.236	Guaranteed annual wage	New number	
331.2524	Pension funds	New number	
331.2552	Unemployment compensation	New number	

Current Number	Current Topic	Old Topic/Comment	Old Number
331.2554	Health services	New number	
331.256	Work environment	New number	
331.2567	Home labor	New number	
331.2568	Telecommuting	New number	
331.257	Hours	[Alternative work schedules] Comprehensive works on workdays and workweek	331.2572
331.257	Hours	[Compressed workweek] Comprehensive works on workweek	331.25722
331.25724	Flexible hours	New number	
331.25725	Shift work	New number	
331.25727	Part-time work	New number	
331.257277	Job sharing	New number	
331.25729	Temporary employment	New number	
331.28132833	Compensation of legislators		328.333
331.318	Children through age 13 by industry and occupation		331.38
331.34	Persons aged 21 through 35		331.348
331.3981 to .3982	Specific aspects on employment of older workers	New number	
331.71	Professional occupations		331.712
331.761658	Managerial occupations		331.714

Current Number	Current Topic	Old Topic/Comment	Old Number
331.79	General occupation groups and government occupations	Specific groups of occupations	
331.88	Labor unions (Trade unions)	Special topics	331.8804
331.88	Blue collar unions		331.88042
331.8836	White collar unions		331.88041
331.8892	Open and closed shop	Right to work	331.898
331.8896	Other union security issues	Control of hiring, layoffs, apprenticeships	331.8894
331.8896	Other union security issues	Preferential hiring, sole bargaining rights	331.8892
331.891	Contracts and related topics	Procedures	
331.8912	Organizing and contract negotiation	Negotiation during life of contract	331.8915
331.892	Strikes	Strike votes	331.8921
331.892	Strikes	Authorized, unauthorized, sympathetic strikes	331.8922 to .8924
331.892	Strikes	Protest stoppages, sit-down strikes	331.8926
331.898	Strike requirements		331.8982
332.024	Personal finance	Management of household finance	640.42
332.024	Personal finance	Other personal financial problems	332.02402
332.0240081 to .0240088	Miscellaneous specific kinds of persons		332.02404 to .0249
332.0240089	Ethnic and national groups		332.02403

Current Number	Current Topic	Old Topic/Comment	Old Number
332.02401081 to .02401088	Miscellaneous specific kinds of persons		332.02404 to .0249
332.024014	Retirement planning	New number	
332.0240145	Retirement investment plans	New number	332.6042
332.024016	Estate planning	New number	
332.02402081 to .02402088	Miscellaneous specific kinds of persons		332.02404 to .0249
332.0240081 to .0240088	Personal finance with respect to miscellaneous specific kinds of persons		332.02404 to .0249
332.0240089	Personal finance with respect to ethnic and national groups		332.02403
332.02401081 to .02401088	Increasing income, net worth, financial security with respect to miscellaneous specific kinds of persons		332.02404 to .0249
332.02402081 to .02402088	Personal debt management with respect to miscellaneous specific kinds of persons		332.02404 to .0249
332.0415	Comprehensive works on external sources of capital		332.04154
332.0424	Capital movements	New number	
332.06	Organizations	Organizations and management	
332.113	Relation to commercial banks	Relation to private banks	

Current Number	Current Topic	Old Topic/Comment	Old Number
332.123	Private banks	Incorporated banks	
332.153094	[International banks] Europe; Western Europe	New number	
332.153097	North America	New number	
332.16	Banks with multiple outlets	Multiple banking	
332.17522	Checking accounts	New number	
332.404	Decimalization of currency		332.4048
332.4142	Devaluation	New number	
332.42	Monetary standards		332.4204
332.42	Monetary standards	Symmetallic and composite commodity standards, fiat money	332.424 to .427
332.45	Foreign exchange with a paper standard		332.454
332.4562	Floating exchange rates (Fluctuating exchange rates)	Determination by supply and demand	
332.4564	Fixed and flexible exchange rates	Determination by government regulation of exchange rates	
332.5	Barter, commercial paper, social credit money	Other mediums of exchange	
332.54	Barter	New number	
332.6	Investment	Comprehensive works on forms of investment	332.63
332.6	Investment	Investment by specific private investors in general or by individual investors	332.67153

Current Number	Current Topic	Old Topic/Comment	Old Number
332.6	Investment	Comprehensive works on domestic investment	332.672
332.6	Investment	Domestic investment by private investors in general, by individual investors	332.67253
332.601 to .609	[specific forms of investment] Standard subdivision		332.6301 to .630 9
332.601 to .609	[Investment in specific industries] Standard subdivision		332.67201 to .67209
332.60422	Tax shelters	New number	
332.632	Securities, real estate, commodities	Corporate securities	332.632044
332.6322	Common stock		332.63223
332.632283	[stock] Options	New number	
332.6452	Futures	New number	
332.64524	Hedging	New number	
332.6453	Options	New number	
332.6457	Derivatives	New number	
332.67	Investments in specific industries, in specific kinds of enterprise, by specific kinds of investors; international investment; investment guides		332.671
332.672	Investment in specific industries, in specific kinds of enterprises, by specific kinds of investors	Domestic investment	

Current Number	Current Topic	Old Topic/Comment	Old Number
332.6722	Investment in specific industries and kinds of enterprises		332.6712
332.67222	Small business	New number	
332.6725	Investment by specific kinds of investors		332.6715
332.67253	Investment by institutional investors	Domestic investment in specific kinds of institutions other than person funds	332.67254
332.672532	Insurance companies	New number	
332.67254	Investment by pension funds	Domestic investment by specific kinds of institutions	
332.673	International investment	International investment by private investors in general	332.67314
332.6731	International investment by specific kinds of investors	International investment by individual investors	332.67314
332.67322	Incentives and obstacles in country of investment	Incentives and obstacles in specific continents and region of investment	332.6732093 to .6732099
332.67324	Incentives and obstacles in country of investor	Incentives and obstacles in specific continent and region of investor	332.6732093 to .6732099
332.678	Investment guides	Guides to domestic investment in general	332.672
332.678	Investment guides	Guides to investment by private investors in general by individual investors	332.67253
332.75	Insolvency and credit restrictions	Credit restrictions and collapse	

Current Number	Current Topic	Old Topic/Comment	Old Number
332.8	Interest		332.82
333.7	Land, recreational and wilderness areas, energy	Natural resources and energy	
333.74	Grasslands	Pasture (Grazing) lands	
333.7511	Reserves	New number	
333.7512	Requirements	New number	
333.7513	Consumption (Utilization)	New number	
333.7515	Development	New number	
333.79137	Abuse and wastage	New number	
333.91	Water and lands adjoining bodies of water	Comprehensive works on bodies of water	333.916
333.91001 to .91009	[Bodies of water] Standard subdivisions		333.91101 to .91109, 333.91601 to .91609
333.91411	Reserves	Energy-producing potential of water	
333.91415	Requirements	Development and generation of energy	
333.917	Lands adjoining bodies of water	Shorelands and related areas	
333.9523	[Biological resources] Nonnative species	New number	
333.9533	[Plants and microorganisms] Nonnative and native plants	Native plants	
333.95411	Reserves	New number	
333.95415	Development	New number	
333.9543	[Animals] Nonnative animals	New number	

Current Number	Current Topic	Old Topic/Comment	Old Number
334.682 to .688	Producer's cooperatives extractive, manufacturing, construction industries		334.6813801 to .681382
335.40904	[Marxian systems] 20th century, 1900–1999	New number	
335.409041	[Marxian systems] 1917–1919	New number	
335.42	Marxian systems, 1848–1917	Early period	
335.42	[Marxian systems] 19th century, 1800–1899		335.409034
336.12	Commercial revenues from public lands	Revenue from rent	336.11
336.16	Administrative revenues	Revenue from franchises	336.11
336.2424	Capital gains	Income from property transfers	
336.243	Corporate income taxes	Comprehensive works on profits taxes	336.2432
336.2432	Profits taxes	Excess and undistributed profits taxes	
336.31	Government securities	Short-term securities	336.32
336.4 to .9	[Public finance] Treatment by specific continents, countries, localities in modern world		336.094 to .099
338.09	[Production] Historical, geographic, persons treatment		338.009

Current Number	Current Topic	Old Topic/Comment	Old Number
338.17498	Forest products	New number	
338.4	Secondary industries and services	Comprehensive works on products	338.47
338.69	Worker control of industry	New number	
338.749	Government corporations	New number	
338.888 to .889	Geographic treatment		338.88109, 338.88309, 338.88409
338.889	Multinational business enterprises by location of owners	Foreign-owned enterprises by owner	
339.23	Input-output analysis (Interindustry analysis)	Input-output accounts (Interindustry accounts)	
339.33 to .39	Product and income accounts of specific continents	Treatment by specific continents, countries, localities	339.3093 to .3099, 339.31093 to .31099, 339.32093 to .32009
339.42	Cost of living	Purchasing power	339.41
339.46	Poverty	Economic causes and effects of poverty	
339.49	Conservation of economic resources	Conservation of national resources	
339.5	Macroeconomic policy	Incomes policy (wage-price policy)	331.21

340 Law Revisions

There have long been questions about the structure of Law (340), and indecision has wreaked havoc on the Dewey Division.

> When work on the 340s began, it was thought that there were three ways to arrange the materials in it. Using traditional Dewey practice, jurisdiction could be attached to type of law by means of –09. Thus, 345.0973 would be

> used for a work on criminal law in the United States. A second method was to add jurisdiction directly to 34, thus gathering law books together first by jurisdiction and the by type of law, as law is generally studied (i.e., 347.305 would be the number of criminal law in the United States). A third way was to add jurisdiction directly to type of law (i.e., 345.73 for the same subject as above). This would be followed by standard subdivisions or the special subdivisions peculiar to that type of law. Of the three ways, the third was the second choice of librarians in the United States, who preferred arrangement by the –09 method, and of librarians in Great Britain and elsewhere outside the United States, who preferred arrangement by jurisdiction first. British law librarians in particular called for a citation order that reflected the way law was actually studied—first by jurisdiction, then by type of law. The opinion of American law librarians—who usually do not use the DDC—and of American librarians of general collections—in which law is of secondary importance—weighed equally, however, in the scales of judgment. Hoping to alienate no one, the Decimal Classification Division opted for everyone's second choice, namely, number three. The editors reasoned that in this way no one would be offended by having someone else's first choice allowed. It appears, however, that two second choices do not make a first, for many British librarians have called for reversal on the decision in favor of the second method. The Americans have said little on the matter. (Comaromi 1976, 594)

The British eventually broke with the Dewey-preferred practice; they chose the option of putting jurisdiction before type of law. Edition 20, under Comaromi's guidance, put in place the Division policy of assigning in the classification legal materials, both the British first choice (which the British National Bibliography uses) and the American second choice. The American first choice was never honored.

Edition 22 continues with extensive changes, almost 170 changes, with thirty-seven new numbers. Most of the changes occur in 343 and 344 involving civil law, but the major changes involve relocating whole ranges of numbers formerly under 341 to other parts of the law schedule. An example is under Human rights (341.48) where aspects of the subject are now found under 342 and 343.

There have also been changes in terminology, including international law which is now called Law of nations, "associations and organizations" in topics is now just "organizations, " and "treaties and cases" is now "treaties, codes, cases."

Finally, Regional Intergovernmental Organizations is a new topic found in each Section at .2. A detailed list of changes follows.

Table 8.4

Current Number	Current Topic	Old Topic/Comment	Old Number
340	**Law**		
340.5	Jewish law		340.58
341.2325	[United Nations] Economic and Social council	New number	
341.4	Jurisdiction over physical space; Human rights	Jurisdiction and jurisdictional relations of states	
341.4	Jurisdiction over physical space; Human rights	Conservation and development of extraterritorial natural resources	341.762
341.455	Seabed (Ocean bottom)		341.7621
341.48	Human rights		341.481
341.4801 to .4809	[Rights of specific social groups] Standard subdivisions		341.48501 to .48509
341.483	Specific human rights	New number	
341.4832 to .4838	[Specific human rights] Standard subdivisions	New number	
341.485	Rights of specific social groups	New number	
341.485	Rights of specific social groups	History and description with respect of kinds of persons	341.4808
341.4852 to .4858	[Rights of specific social groups] Subdivisions	New number	
341.67	Humanitarian law	Individuals	
341.68	Law of nations and civil war	International law and civil war	

Current Number	Current Topic	Old Topic/Comment	Old Number
342–347 + 0261	Treaties		341.2 to .7 + 026
342–347 + 02632	Individual and collected laws; codes		341.2 to .7 + 0267
342–347 + 0264	Cases		341.2 to .7 + 0264
342–347 + 0601	International organizations	New number	
342.041 2	Conduct of relations with foreign governments	Military assistance and missions	341.728
342.08	Jurisdiction over persons		341.48
342.082	Entrance to and exit from national domain	Immigration, passports, visas	341.4842
342.083	Citizenship and nationality		341.482
342.083	Citizenship and nationality	Status of aliens	341.484
342.083	Citizenship and nationality	Jurisdiction over stateless persons and refugees	341.486
342.083	Citizenship and nationality	Right of asylum	341.488
342.0877	[Jurisdiction over] Age groups	New number	
342.08772	Young people	New number	
342.08774	Persons in late adulthood	New number	
342.2	Regional intergovernmental organizations	New number	
343.01	Military and defense law		341.72
343.01	Military and defense law	Comprehensive works on military services	343.013

Current Number	Current Topic	Old Topic/Comment	Old Number
343.013	Military life, customs, resources	Military services	
343.0153	Organization		343.013
343.0155	Training		343.013
343.0157	Military installations and bases		341.725
343.0252	Nationalization of alien property		341.4846
343.03	International financial law		341.751
343.032	Monetary law		341.7514
343.0321 to .0326	Specific aspects of monetary law	New number	
343.0325	Foreign exchange		341.75145
343.0326	Monetary policy		341.75145
343.034	Budgeting and expenditure	International financial law	341.751
343.0526	Income taxes by incidence	Double taxation	341.4844
343.053	Death and gift taxes	Inheritance taxes	343.0532
343.056	Customs taxes (Tariff)		341.7543
343.056	Customs taxes (Tariff)	Custom taxes (Tariff) on specific commodities	341.7547
343.07	Regulation of economic activity	International economic law	341.75
343.07	Regulation of economic activity	International economic organizations	341.7506
343.072	Unfair practices	Monopoly	341.753
343.0723	Restraint of trade		341.753
343.074	Economic assistance		341.759
343.075	Production controls	Standardization	341.754
343.076	Agricultural industries	Agricultural assistance	341.7592

Current Number	Current Topic	Old Topic/Comment	Old Number
343.07692	Products of fishing		341.7622
343.076928	Products of whaling		341.7622
343.076929	Products of sealing		341.7622
343.07694	Products of fishery of invertebrates		341.7622
343.07891	Regulation of tourist industry		341.754
343.08	Regulation of commerce (Trade)	Commodity exchanges	341.75244
343.08	Regulation of commerce (Trade)	Internal commerce (Domestic trade)	343.088
343.081	Retail and wholesale trade, interstate commerce	New number	
343.0811	Retail trade	New number	343.0887
343.0812	Wholesale trade	New number	343.0888
343.0815	Interstate commerce	New number	343.088
343.0851 to .0855	Subdivisions for specific commodities	Domestic trade of specific commodities	343.0881 to .0885
343.087	International commerce (Foreign trade)		341.754
343.0871 to .0875	International commerce in specific commodities		341.7547
343.0925	Nuclear energy		341.755
343.093	Transportation		341.756
343.093	Transportation	Comprehensive works on ground transportation	343.094
343.0932	Freight services		341.756
343.0932	Freight services	Transportation of specific goods	341.7569
343.0933	Passenger services		341.756

Current Number	Current Topic	Old Topic/Comment	Old Number
343.0939	Pipeline transportation	New number	
343.09395	Oil (Petroleum)	New number	
343.09396	Natural gas	New number	
343.09397	Coal	New number	
343.094	Road transportation		341.7568
343.094	Road transportation	Highway transportation	341.7568
343.095	Railroad transportation		341.7565
343.096	Water transportation		341.7566
343.0962	Ocean transportation		341.75662
343.097	Air transportation		341.7567
343.0976	Air navigation and traffic control		341.75676
343.0979	Space transportation		341.75679
343.0982	Vehicular traffic	Street traffic	
343.099	Communications		341.757
343.0992	Postal services		341.7573
343.0994	Telecommunication		341.7577
343.0994	Telecommunication	Telegraph	343.09942
343.09943	Telephone		341.7577
343.09944	Computer communications		341.7577
343.09945	Radio		341.7577
343.09946	Television		341.7577
343.2	Regional intergovernmental organizations	New number	
343.2407		Economic law of European Union	341.750614
344.01	Labor		341.763
344.01	Labor	Social law	341.76

Current Number	Current Topic	Old Topic/Comment	Old Number
344.03	Social service		341.766
344.0327	Problems of and service to young people		
344.0327	Problems of and service to young people	UNICEF	341.76
344.04	Miscellaneous social problems and services	Comprehensive works on Public health	341.765
344.046	Environmental protection		341.762
344.04632	Pollution		341.7623
344.046336	Acid rain		341.7623
344.04634	Pollution of specific environments		341.7625
344.046342	Air pollution		341.76252
344.046343	Water pollution		341.76253
344.047	Safety		341.765
344.0534	Disasters		341.766
344.0535	Civil defense		341.72
344.07	Education	Education, schools, students	341.767
344.08	Educational and cultural exchanges		341.7673
344.09	Culture and religion		341.767
344.09	Culture and religion	Information exchange	341.7672
344.094	Historic preservation	Archaeology	341.7677
344.095	Science and technology		341.7675
344.0952	Astronomy and space research	New number	
344.0953	Physics and applied physics	New number	

Current Number	Current Topic	Old Topic/Comment	Old Number
344.0954	Chemistry and chemical technology	New number	
344.0955	Geology	New number	
344.0955	Geology	Weather control	341.762
344.0957	Agriculture and biology	New number	343.076
344.097	Arts		341.7677
344.2	Regional intergovernmental organizations	New number	
345	International criminal law		341.77
345.01	Criminal courts	Criminal jurisdiction	341.488
345.02	Crimes (Offenses)	Terrorism	341.773
345.0235	International offenses		341.77
345.0251	Genocide		341.778
345.02552	Hijacking		341.772
345.0264	Piracy		341.772
345.0277	Drug traffic		341.775
345.052	Criminal investigation and law enforcement	Extradition	341.488
345.052	Criminal investigation and law enforcement	Interpol	341.77
345.052	Criminal investigation and law enforcement	Judicial assistance	341.78
345.2	Regional intergovernmental organizations	New number	
346.01662	Prenuptial contracts (Antenuptial contracts)	New number	
346.01663	Support	New number	
346.01664	Marital property	New number	
346.01664	Marital property	Community and separate property	346.042

Current Number	Current Topic	Old Topic/Comment	Old Number
346.0168	Same-sex marriage	New number	
346.0171	Unborn children	New number	
346.040 8691	Property of persons with status defined by changes in residence	Alien property	341.484
346.044	Government control and regulation of real property	Conservation of natural resources	341.762
346.046	Protection of specific resources		341.7625
346.04679	Control of power and power resources		341.755
346.046956	Conservation of fisheries		341.7622
346.047	Personal property		341.48
346.048	Intangible property		341.758
346.06	Organizations (Associations)	General considerations of organizations	346.062
346.065	Business enterprises and combinations		341.753
346.065	Business enterprises and combinations	Combinations	341.753
346.0662	Organization	Investment banking	341.7526
346.07	Commercial law	Commercial contracts and conduct of business	341.753
346.073	Loan		341.75115
346.082	Banks		341.7511
346.08215	International banks		341.75115
346.0822	Specialized banking institutions		341.7512
346.0823	Credit and loan institutions		341.7513
346.092	Investment		341.752

Current Number	Current Topic	Old Topic/Comment	Old Number
346.0922	Specific types of investments	Securities	341.75232
346.0926	Marketing agents and arrangements	Securities brokers	341.7522
346.0926	Marketing agents and arrangements	Exchange of securities, stock exchanges	341.75242
346.2	Regional intergovernmental organizations	New number	
347.012	General considerations of courts	Judicial cooperation, letters rogatory	341.78
347.2	Regional intergovernmental organizations	New number	
348.00601	International organizations	New number	
348.0201 to .0208	[Laws and regulations] Standard subdivisions		348.001 to .008
348.022	Laws arranged in chronological order	Statutes	
348.02501 to .02508	[Regulations] Standard subdivisions		348.001 to .008
348.2	Regional intergovernmental organizations	New number	
349.2	Law of regional intergovernmental organizations	New number	

350 Public Administration and Military Science Revisions

Unlike Edition 21, there have been few changes in the 350 Division. There were no changes in military science and just three under the topic of Public Administration.

Table 8.5

Current Number	Current Topic	Old Topic	Old Number
350 to 354	**Public Administration**		
352.23	Comprehensive works on heads of state		321
352.266		Management	338.749 068
352.4	Financial administration and budgets	Management of public finance	336.0068

360 Social Problems, Services, and Associations Revisions

The 360 Division was pinpointed by a Comaromi survey as fourth among the 300 class needing revisions. The word "associations" in the caption is often puzzling to users. However, when one joins a group that has a purpose of some sort, one has *associated* himself with it. The association is volitional, which is why such groups do not fall in 301–307 but still does not explain why the topic is here.

All twelve of the thirteen changes in Edition 22 are within the 362 and 363 sections, which are concerned with specific social problems and services. Half of those changes are new numbers. The last change moves Bank Deposit Insurance out of Economics (332) to Insurance at 368.

Table 8.6

Current Number	Current Topic	Old Topic/Comment	Old Number
360	**Social Problems and Services**		
361.4	Group work	Self-help groups	374.22
362.104 2584	Health maintenance organizations	New number	
362.16	Extended medical care facilities	Institutions providing complete medical care	362.61

Current Number	Current Topic	Old Topic/Comment	Old Number
362.61	Residential care	Comprehensive works on life care communities and rest homes	362.16
362.88	Victims of crimes		305.906949
363.22	Personnel	[Police services] Personnel management	363.206 83
363.34926	Disasters caused by ice storms	New number	
363.73849	Specific types of toxic chemicals	New number	
363.738492	Lead	New number	
363.738494	Asbestos	New number	
363.738498	Pesticides	New number	
368.854	Bank deposit insurance	Government guarantee of deposits	332.1

370 Education Revisions

The structure of the 370s is so poor that a complete recasting of the Division was done early in the development of Edition 20 but was shelved for a variety of reasons, then resurrected in Edition 21. Some changes are continued into this edition, including nine new numbers. Conscious mental process and intelligence was expanded with four new numbers further describing aspects of educational psychology.

380 Commerce, Communications, Transportation Revisions

Unlike the 21st edition, this edition has quite a few changes in the 380 Division, with the majority found in commerce and trade (381). All of these changes but one were moving aspects of the topic from within the 380 division to a newly ordered structure for commerce. In this shuffling, four new numbers were also added.

Table 8.7

Current Number	Current Topic	Old Topic/Comment	Old Number
370	**Education**		
370.15	Educational psychology	Subconscious processes, Comprehensive works on behavior	370.153
370.152	Conscious mental process and intelligence	Cognition	
370.1528	Behavior modification	New number	370.153
370.1529	Intelligence	New number	
370.1532	Personality	New number	
370.1534	Emotions	New number	
370.155	Perception, movement, psychological drives	Psychomotor and sensory processes in learning	
371.26013	Validity and reliability of test	Value	
371.895	School assemblies	New Number	
371.91246	Instructions in lipreading		371.9127
371.926	Students with moderate mental disabilities	Slow learners	
371.928	Students with sever mental disabilities	Students with mental retardation	
371.94	Students with emotional disturbances	Hyperactive students	371.93
372	**Elementary Education**		
372.37	Personal health and safety	Health (Hygiene)	

Current Number	Current Topic	Old Topic/ Comment	Old Number
372.373	Nutrition and food	New Number	
372.373	Nutrition and food	Cooking	372.82
372.378	Substance abuse	New Number	
373	**Secondary Education**		
373.238	Upper level	Comprehensive works on sixth-form colleges	378.1543
378	**Higher Education**		
378.1213	Academic freedom	New number	
378.1214	Tenure	New number	

The remaining changes were one each under international commerce, communications and telecommunications, and inland waterways and ferry transportation.

Table 8.8

Current Number	Current Topic	Old Topic/ Comment	Old Number
381	**Commerce (Trade)**	Internal commerce (Domestic trade)	380.1
381.1	Marketing channels	Retail trade	
381.101 to .105	Standard subdivisions		381.1401 to .1405
381.106	Organizations and management		381.1406
381.107 to .109	Standard subdivisions		381.1407 to .1409
381.11	Shopping centers	New number	
381.142	Teleshopping	Mail-order, telephone-order, television selling organizations	

Current Number	Current Topic	Old Topic/Comment	Old Number
381.149	Discount stores	Supermarkets not predominantly food stores	381.456413
381.149	Convenience stores	Supermarkets	381.148
381.15	Outlet stores	Discount outlet stores	381.149
381.177	Online auctions	New number	
381.186	Street fairs	New number	
381.347	Better business bureaus	New number	
381.41	Products of agriculture		380.141
381.42	Products of mineral industries		380.142
381.43	Products of other extractive industries		380.143
381.431	Products of culture of invertebrates and cold-blooded vertebrates		380.1431
381.432 to .439	Products of fishing, whaling, hunting, trapping		380.1432 to .1439
381.44	Slave trade	Human beings (Slave trade)	380.144
381.45	Products of secondary industries and services		380.145
381.456413	Food trade	Food retailing in supermarkets	381.148
381.456413 0068	Management	Management of food retailing in supermarkets	658.878

Current Number	Current Topic	Old Topic/Comment	Old Number
382	**International Commerce (Foreign Trade)**		
382.78	Tariff exemptions (Duty-free importation)	Specific kinds of exemptions	382.782-.788
384	**Communications; Telecommunications**		
384.35	Videotex	Broadcast and interact videotext	384.352-.354
386	**Inland Waterway and Ferry Transportation**		
386.82 to .86	Physiographic location, facilities, activities, services, free ports	New number	

390 Customs, Etiquette, Folklore Revisions

The majority of the changes in the 390 Division were found under dwelling places where a second zero was added in the subdivisions. There were also added zeros in the Standard Subdivisions under 390. Customs of people by occupation (390.4) was affected by the elimination of Table 7, where notations 001 to 999 replace Table 7 notations –09 to –99. Finally, four new numbers were added under general customs.

Table 8.9

Current Number	Current Topic	Old Topic/ Comments	Old Number
390	**Customs, Etiquette, Folklore**		
390.01 to .07	Standard subdivisions		390.001 to .007
390.08	History and description of customs, etiquette, folklore with respect to kinds of persons together		390.008
390.09	Historical, geographic, persons treatment of customs, etiquette, folklore together		390.009
390.4	Customs of people by occupation	Notation 001–999 replaces notation -09 to –99 from Table 7	
392	**Customs of Life Cycle and Domestic Life**		
392.3601	[Dwelling places] Philosophy and theory		392.36001
392.3602	[Dwelling places] Miscellany		392.36002
392.3603	[Dwelling places] Dictionaries, encyclopedias, concordances		392.36003
392.3605 to .3607	[Dwelling places] Standard subdivisions		392.36005 to .36007
392.3608	Dwelling places with respect to kinds of persons		392.36008

Current Number	Current Topic	Old Topic/Comments	Old Number
392.360862	[Dwelling places] Persons by social level	[Dwelling places] Persons by economic levels	392.3601
392.360862	[Dwelling places] Persons by social level	[Dwelling places] Persons by social levels	392.3602
392.36088	[Dwelling places] Persons by occupational groups		392.36004
392.360882	[Dwelling places] Religious groups		392.360088
392.3609	[Dwelling places] Historical, geographic, persons treatment		392.36009
394	**General Customs**		
394.26	Holidays	Carnivals	394.25
394.2612	Kwanzaa	New number	
394.2628	Mother's Day	New number	
394.88	Suicide	New number	
394.9	Cannibalism	New number	
398	**Folklore**		
398.36	[Scientific themes] Agriculture	[Technical themes] Agriculture	398.356

Exercises in the Use of Class 300

From the brief summaries that follow, develop classifications for each utilizing the Schedules, Tables, and Relative Index. When the notations are complete, check them against the Library of Congress's in the section called "Answers to the Exercises" found in the Appendix.

1. A work on multicultural or bilingual middle school education.
2. A work on the political situation in Iraq.
3. A work on counterterrorism in the United States.
4. A work about the history of the Canadian Air Force.
5. A work about the youth culture in India.
6. A work on the history of commerce between India and Central Asia.
7. A work on the history of slavery in Africa.
8. A work on British amphibious operations in the late 1940s.
9. A work about U.S. Marine assaults by sea.
10. A work on U.S. surveillance flights.

Literature Cited

Comaromi, John P. 1977. Decimal Classification Editorial Policy Committee Report. *Library Resources & Technical Services* 21 (1):94.

———. 1976. *The Eighteen Editions of the Dewey Decimal Classification.* Albany, NY: Forest Press Division, Lake Placid Education Foundation.

Dewey, Melvil. 2003. *Dewey Decimal Classification and Relative Index.* 22nd ed. Dublin, OH: OCLC Online Computer Library Center.

9

Class 400: Language

John Phillip Comaromi, among others, long felt that fundamental changes in the way that DDC views language should be reviewed. A proposal was forwarded to the editor from an Editorial Policy Committee member to greatly expand Grammar (–5). Moreover, Comaromi had long felt that the composition of a language, up to the stage at which the composition moves into the literary arena (808), belonged in the usage of a particular language. Indeed, the underlying structure of DDC—with languages and literature separated by a chasm of science, technology, and the arts—continues to perplex many.

Summary and Details of Class 400

400 Language

410 Linguistics

420 English and Old English (Anglo-Saxon)

430 Germanic Languages; German

440 Romance Languages; French

450 Italian, Sardinian, Dalmatian, Romanian, Rhaeto-Romanic Languages

460 Spanish and Portuguese Languages

470 Italic Languages; Latin

480 Hellenic Languages; Classical Greek

490 Other Languages

Division 400: The first Division is used only for the Standard Subdivisions (401–409). The Special Topics of the Class are bilingualism and multilingualism (404).

Division 410: The second Division is used for works on the structure of spoken and written language in general. The structure here is the same as in Table 4 and is followed by all of the succeeding languages: writing systems (–1 in Table 4, 411 in the Schedules); etymology (–2.412); dictionaries (–3.413); phonology and phonetics (–15.414); grammar (–5.415); slang, jargon, and the history or evolution of language (–7.417); standard usage of language (–8.418). The last Section is language other than that spoken and written, such as sign languages and finger spelling (419).

Divisions 420 –480: The rest of the Divisions are for specific languages, each of which is basically organized as is the 410 Division. These are English and Old English (420); Germanic languages (430); French, Occitan, Franco-Provençal, and Catalan (440); Italian, Sardinian, Dalmatian, Romanian, and Rhaeto-Romanian languages (450); Spanish and Portuguese (460); Latin and Italic (470); and Greek (480).

Division 490: The last Division encompasses all other languages that follow, to some degree, the numbering pattern of Table 2. The first Section, including East Indo-European and Celtic languages (491); Afro-Asiatic and Semitic languages (492); non-Semitic Afro-Asiatic languages (493), Altaic, Uralic, Hyperborean, Dravidian languages (494) have numbering outside this pattern. The last five Sections do mirror Table 2 notations and are languages of east and southeast Asia, Sino-Tibetan languages (495), African languages (496), North American native languages (497), South American native languages (498), and Non-Austronesian languages of Oceania, Austronesian languages, Esperanto, and Interlingua (499).

The Number Building Process

A book of English to Spanish phrases for medical personnel will provide a good example of number building in the 400 Class. The Spanish language is found at 46 with standard usage represented by **468.** Instructions under 468 indicate that numbers are built "according to instructions under 460.1–468." Under those add instructions for subdivisions of the Spanish language, are directions to "add to base number 46 notation 01–8 from Table 4" (Dewey 2003, 2:909, 911).

Reviewing Table 4, which represents Standard Usage, the number for bilingual phrase books is 834, which when added to the classification number being built is **468.34.**

Under 834 in Table 4 are instructions to add "notation 2–9 from Table 6" (Dewey 2003, 1:658). The number for English is 21, which is then added to the classification that is being built resulting in **468.3421.**

That notation would be sufficient for ordinary phrase books, but this work is specifically for medical personnel. At this point we go to Standard Subdivisions in Table 1 and find –024 is used for the subject meant for persons in specific occupations, resulting in the classification being built now **468.3421024.** All that needs to be done to finalize the classification is to add the number for medicine according to the instructions. Medicine and Health is found at 610. A final zero is never used, so the number to add is **61.**

LC Classification: **468.342102461**

Medical Spanish made incredibly easy.

DDC 22 Class 400 Revisions

After extensive revisions in Edition 20, Language has lain fallow through the 21st edition. Now, once again, attention has been directed upon the 400 Class with ninety-two new numbers being assigned. Many of these expansions are found under grammar and syntax (415), but most appear under 492 to 498 where previously numbers were built using Table 6 notations.

Danish, Swedish, and Norwegian (439) were revised, also as was the geographic variations of other languages. Detailed lists of Class 400 changes follow.

Table 9.1

Current Number	**Current Topic**	**Old Topic/ Comment**	**Old Number**
401	**Language**		
401.41	Discourse analysis	Semantics	
411.7	Paleography and epigraphy	Paleography	
415.0182	Generative grammar	New number	

Current Number	Current Topic	Old Topic/ Comment	Old Number
415.1084	Dependency grammar	New number	
415.5	Nouns, pronouns, adjectives, articles	New number	
415.54	Nouns	New number	
415.55	Pronouns	New number	
415.6	Verbs	New number	
415.62	Tense	New number	
415.63	Aspect	New number	
415.7	Miscellaneous word classes	New number	
415.76	Adverbs	New number	
415.9	Morphology	New number	
415.92	Word formation	New number	
415.95	Inflection	New number	
418	Standard usage (Prescriptive linguistics); Applied linguistics	General instruction in lipreading	371.9127
418		Comprehensive works on use of signs and fingerspelling for manual coding of multiple standard spoken languages	419
419	Sign languages		
[Discontinued]	[Sign languages] Treatment by specific continents, countries, and localities in modern world		[419.094 to .099]
419.1	Sign languages used primarily for purposes other than communication of deaf people	New number	

Current Number	Current Topic	Old Topic/ Comment	Old Number
419.4 to .9	Sign languages used primarily for communication among deaf persons or between hearing and deaf persons	New number	
427.02094 to .02099	Geographic variations of Middle English		427.1 to .9
437.01094 to .01099	Geographic variations of Old High German		437.1 to .9
437.02094 to .02099	Geographic variations of Middle High German and Early New High Germany		437.1 to .9
439.5	North Germanic languages (Nordic languages)	Comprehensive works on West Scandinavian languages	439.6
439.5	North Germanic languages (Nordic languages)	Comprehensive works on modern West Scandinavian languages	439.69
439.69	Icelandic and Faeroese	Modern West Scandinavian languages; Modern Icelandic	
439.77001	[Swedish] Standard subdivisions		439.7701
439.77001	[Old Danish to 1500] Philosophy and theory		
439.77002 to .77008	[Swedish] Standard subdivisions		439.7702 to .7708
439.77009	[Swedish] Historical geographic, persons treatment		439.7709

Current Number	Current Topic	Old Topic/ Comment	Old Number
439.7701	[Swedish] Old Swedish to 1526		439.770902
439.776 to .779	[Swedish] Treatment by specific continents, countries, and localities in modern world		439.77094 to .77099
439.817001	[Danish and Norwegian] Philosophy and theory		439.81701
439.817002 to .817008	[Danish and Norwegian] Standard subdivisions		439.81702 to .81708
439.817002 to .817008	[Old Danish to 1500] Standard subdivisions		
439.817009	[Danish and Norwegian] Historical, geographic, persons treatment		439.81709
439.817009	[Old Danish to 1500] Historical, geographic, persons treatment		
439.81701	Old Danish to 1500		439.8170902
439.8171	Treatment by specific continents, countries, and localities in modern world		439.817094 to .817099
439.82	Norwegian	New Norse, Landsmal	439.83
439.827001	[Norwegian] Philosophy and theory		439.82701

Current Number	Current Topic	Old Topic/ Comment	Old Number
439.827002	[Norwegian] Miscellany		439.82702
439.827002	[Middle Norwegian] Miscellany		
439.827003 to .827008	[Norwegian] Standard subdivisions		439.82703 to .82708
439.827003 to .827008	[Middle Norwegian] Standard subdivisions		
439.827009	[Norwegian] Historical, geographic, persons treatment		439.82709
439.827009	[Middle Norwegian] Historical, geographic, persons treatment		
439.82702	Middle Norwegian, 1350–1525		439.8270902
439.8272	[Middle Norwegian] Treatment by specific continents, countries, and localities in modern world		439.827094 to .827099
439.8272 to .8274	[Middle Norwegian] Geographic variations in Norway		
439.8279	[Middle Norwegian] Geographic variations in other places		
447.01094 to .01099	Geographic variations of Old French		447.1 to .9
447.02094 to .02099	Geographic variations of Middle French		447.1 to .9

Current Number	Current Topic	Old Topic/ Comment	Old Number
449	Occitan, Catalan, and Franco-Provinçal	Provençal (Langue d'oc) Franco-Provençal, Catalan	
457.01094 to .01099	Geographic variations in Old Italian		457.1 to .9
457.02094 to .02099	Geographic variations in Middle Italian		457.1 to .9
467.01094 to .01099	Geographic variations in Old Spanish		467.1 to .9
467.02094 to .02099	Geographic variations in Middle Spanish		467.1 to .9
469.701094 to .701099	Geographic variations in Old Portuguese		469.71 to .79
469.702094 to .702099	Geographic variations in Middle Portuguese		469.71 to 469.79
491.469	Konkani		491.467
491.7701094 to .7701099	Geographic variations in Old Russian		491.774 to .779
491.7702094 to .7702099	Geographic variations in Middle Russian		491.774 to .779
495.17094 to .17099	[Chinese] Treatment by specific continents, countries, and localities in modern world	New number	
495.171 to .178	Geographic variations in China	New number	
492.179	Geographic variations in other places	New number	

Current Number	Current Topic	Old Topic/ Comment	Old Number
496.3976	Venda (Tshivenda)	New number	
496.3989	Ndebele (South Africa)	New number	
497.256	Mescalero-Chiricahua Apache	New number	
497.26	Navajo	New number	
497.27	Tlingit	New number	
497.28	Haida	New number	
497.312	Kickapoo	New number	
497.313	Menomini	New number	
497.314	Mesquakie, Fox	New number	
497.315	Miami	New number	
497.316	Potawatomi	New number	
497.317	Shawnee	New number	
497.323	Cree	New number	
497.333	Ojibwa, Chippewa	New number	
497.336	Ottawa	New number	
497.343	Micmac	New number	
497.344	Mohegan, Narragansett	New number	
497.345	Unami (Delawae, Lenni Lenape)	New number	
497.347	Powhatan	New number	
497.348	Wampanoag	New number	
497.352	Blackfoot, Siksika	New number	
497.353	Cheyenne	New number	
497.354	Arapaho	New number	
497.385	Muskogee (Creek)	New number	
497.3859	Seminole	New number	
497.386	Chickasaw	New number	
497.387	Choctaw	New number	

Current Number	Current Topic	Old Topic/ Comment	Old Number
497.4122	Klamath, Modoc	New number	
497.4124	Nez Percé	New number	
497.4127	Yakama	New number	
497.4128	Tsimshian	New number	
497.4133	Miwok	New number	
497.422	Cakchikel	New number	
497.423	Quiché	New number	
497.427	Maya, Yucatec Maya	New number	
497.4287	Tzotzil	New number	
497.452	Nahuatl (Aztec)	New number	
497.4542	Yaqui	New number	
497.4544	Huichol	New number	
497.4546	Tarahummara	New number	
497.4552	Tohono O'Odham	New number	
497.522	Mandan	New number	
497.5243	Dakota	New number	
497.5244	Lakota	New number	
497.5253	Omaha	New number	
497.52539	Ponca	New number	
497.5254	Osage	New number	
497.526	Winnebago	New number	
497.5272	Crow	New number	
497.5274	Hidatsa	New number	
497.5542	Mohawk	New number	
497.5543	Oneida	New number	
497.5546	Seneca	New number	
497.555	Wyandot, Huron	New number	
497.557	Cherokee	New number	
497.5722	Mohave	New number	

Current Number	Current Topic	Old Topic/ Comment	Old Number
497.5724	Havasupai, Walapai, Yavapai	New number	
497.576	Washo	New number	
497.63	Mixtec	New number	
497.68	Zapotec	New number	
497.83	San Blas Kuna	New number	
497.882	Miskito	New number	
497.922	Taino	New number	
497.932	Arikara	New number	
497.933	Pawnee	New number	
497.9435	Kalispel, Pend d'Oreille	New number	
497.953	Kwakiutl	New number	
497.955	Nootka	New number	
497.96	Purépecha	New number	
497.992	Kutenai	New number	
497.994	Zuni	New number	
498.422	Carib (Galibi)	New number	
498.72	Mapudungun (Mapuche)	New number	
498.92	Yanomamo	New number	

Exercises in the Use of Class 400

Following are examples of books written about subjects found in the 400 Class. From the brief summaries, develop classifications for each and then check them against those assigned by the Library of Congress found in the section called "Answers to the Exercises" in the Appendix.

1. A work on French language grammar for English speakers.
2. A French language phrase book for English-speaking people.
3. A Spanish language phrase book for English-speaking people.

4. A work on grammar in the Chinese language.
5. An Arabic language phrase book for English-speaking people.
6. A dictionary in French and English languages.

Literature Cited

Dewey, Melvil. 2003. *Dewey Decimal Classification and Relative Index*. 22nd ed. Dublin, OH: OCLC Online Computer Library Center.

10

Class 500: Natural Sciences and Mathematics

The word "science" contains the root of the word that means "to know." Knowing goes on throughout the Schedules; however, the ways of knowing differ from mode to mode, from reason to imagination to memory. The 500 Class is nothing but a collection of topics that Western civilization has decided to call "science." The editors have correctly said that mathematics should not be a part of 500, thus it was renamed Natural Sciences and Mathematics in Edition 20.

The linear structure of the natural sciences in the DDC reflects the nature of the universe (from the broadest scale) to the nature of matter at the molecular level, which was the smallest known level in 1876, when the DDC was first created; the nature of organic life at its earliest level on the planet (paleontology and paleozoology in 560) to its most recent and most highly developed level in the 590s.

Criticisms of the life science Divisions have long been heard. More than forty years ago, we were told:

> The science sections in the Dewey Classification . . . with the emphasis on paleontology, fit American science in the later 19th century like a shoe. Unfortunately, the creature wearing the shoe turned out to be a millipede—a situation with which Dewey's successors were never able to cope. (Richmond 1963, 399)

Summary and Details of Class 500

500 Natural Sciences and Mathematics

510 Mathematics

520 Astronomy and Allied Sciences

530 Physics

540 Chemistry and Allied Sciences

550 Earth Sciences

560 Paleontology; Paleozoology

570 Life Sciences; Biology

580 Plants

590 Animals

Division 500: The first Division is used for general, physical, and space sciences (500.2, 500.5) and natural history (508). The Standard Subdivisions are also found here (501–507, 509), but history and description with respect to kinds of persons is separated from the rest in 500.8.

Division 510: Mathematics is found in this Division beginning with mathematical logic, graphs, combinatorial analysis, and mathematical models in the first Section (511). This is followed by the branches of mathematics in 512 to 516, for algebra, arithmetic, topology, calculus and other numerical analysis, and geometry. The last Section is for probabilities (519.2); general game theory (519.3), sampling and statistics (519.5); programming (519.7); queuing and other applications of mathematics (519.8).

Division 520: Astronomy is located in this Division in Sections 521 through 525. Gravitation, orbits, and similar topics are in the 521 Section and are followed in 522 by features usually found in the Standard Subdivision notation –028, which are techniques, procedures, apparatus, equipment, and materials (in this case, observatories, telescopes, and similar instruments). The next Section is used for the universe in total, including, Galaxies, and quasars (523.1); the solar system (523.2); our moon (523.3); the planets in our solar system (523.4); meteors and solar wind (523.5); comets (523.6); our sun (523.7); and the stars (523.8). The Sections end with natural satellites of other planets (523.9). Then in the usual egocentric way, our home, the Earth, is found in its own Section (525), which ends the astronomical part of this Division.

The next Section is used for cartography, surveying, geodetic surveying, and geographic positions (526). Then methods used for locating, both in time and place, with celestial navigation (527), astronomical and nautical almanacs (528), and calendars (529) ending the Division.

Division 530: This Division is reserved for physics, and the first Section contains the Standard Subdivisions (530.01–.09) plus general aspects of physics including relativity, quantum, and other theories (530.1); solid, liquid, gaseous states of matter in general (530.4); instruments (530.7); and measurement (530.8). The next three Sections are used for more detailed works on the states of matter, which are dynamics, mass and gravity of matter, aspects of solid states, as well as energy in general (531); fluids and their properties (532); and the properties of gases (533).

The next Sections are for specific forms of energy, which include sound (534), light (535), heat (536), electricity (537), and magnetism (538). The last Section is reserved for what is called "modern physics," which refers to the structure of matter (539.1); radiation (539.2); atoms and molecules (539.6); and atomic and nuclear physics (539.7).

Division 540: Chemistry is found in 541 to 547 of this Section. Standard Subdivisions of the Division are in 540, except –028 (techniques, procedures, apparatus, equipment, and materials), which are found in 542 and separates physical chemistry (541) from analytical chemistry (543). Inorganic chemistry (546) and organic chemistry (547) end the chemistry parts of this Division. Crystallography (548) and mineralogy (549) are the sciences allied with chemistry and conclude the Section. Sections 544 and 545 are not used in Edition 22.

Division 550: This Division is reserved for the earth sciences of geology, hydrology, and meteorology (551). Petrology, or the study of rocks, is next (552), followed by geologic materials with economic value (553). The rest of the Division (554–559) is used for geographic treatments of the earth sciences, utilizing the notations from Table 2 representing the localities.

Division 560: The seventh Division is used for what euphemistically could be called the "old life" sciences of paleontology and paleozoology, which lead to the life sciences in the next Division. The first Section has the Standard Subdivisions (560.1–.9), stratigraphic paleontology (560.17), and paleoecology (560.45). Paleobotany and fossil microorganisms are in the next Section (561), then fossil invertebrates (562), followed by the various fossils of marine and seashore invertebrates (563). Fossils of mollusks (564), arthropoda (565), and chordates (566) are found in Sections 564 to 566. Continuing to move up the evolutionary chain, we find the fossils of cold-blooded vertebrates and fishes (567), birds (568), and mammals (569). Prehistoric man is found at the end of the Division (569.9).

Division 570: This Division is used for the life sciences with the Standard Subdivisions in the first Section (570.1–.9) and microscopy (570.282) under the Standard Subdivision Miscellany. Sections 571–575 are internal biological processes and structures, with the first two Sections containing processes common to all organisms, which are physiology, diseases, reproduction, pathology (571), and biochemistry (572). Next are specific systems of animals and physiology (573) and the specific parts and systems of plants (575).

The rest of the Division is for more general aspects such as genetics and evolution (576); ecology (577); and adaptation, harmful or rare organisms, and organisms of specific environments (578). The last Section begins with topics devoted to the natural history of specific organisms, the first of which are microorganisms, fungi, and algae (579), which bridge into the last Divisions of the Class.

Division 580: This Division is used for topics on the study of plants, with Standard Subdivisions in the first Section (580.1 to 580.9), and genetics, evolution, adaptation, and plant ecology in the next Section (581), and ending with the geographic treatment of plants (581.9). Next are herbaceous and woody plants noted for their flowers (582) followed by flowering plants (583–584). Conifers (585), seedless plants (586), vascular seedless plants (587), mosses and liverworts (588) conclude the Division.

Division 590: The last Division of the Class is used for animals and is arranged like the previous Division. Standard Subdivisions (590.1–.9) are found in the first Section, followed by genetics, evolution and the young animals (591.3); adaptation (591.4); behavior (591.5); beneficial, harmful, rare, and endangered animals (591.6); animal ecology (591.7); and the geographic treatment of animals (591.9) ends the Section.

Specific groups of animals complete the Class beginning with invertebrates, such as various types of worms (592). Moving up the evolutionary ladder, saltwater invertebrates are in 593 and mollusks in 594. The next three Sections of the Division contain arthropods, chordates, and cold-blooded vertebrates, such as fish. Birds are found under 598 and lead to mammals in 599, with humans at the top in 599.9.

The Number Building Process

The number building example for the 500 Class is a work on groundwater quality in the Wichita region of Kansas. According to the Relative Index, the notation for groundwater is **553.79.** Looking up this number in the Schedules, no special instructions or notes are found that would alter the normal number building process. Thus the usual process of adding geographic notations by adding 09 from Table 1 is followed, resulting in **553.7909.** Kansas is found at notation 78 in Table 2, with Wichita at **78186.**

LC Classification: 553.790978186

Status of ground-water levels and storage volume in the Equus Beds aquifer near Wichita, Kansas, January 2000–January 2003, by Cristi V. Hansen and Walter R. Aucott; prepared in cooperation with the City of Wichita, Kansas.

DDC 22 Class 500 Revisions

Natural sciences and mathematics have long been the focus of attention by both the Editorial Policy Committee and the editors. The last four editions have seen extensive revisions, and these endeavors have continued in this edition with a total of 346 changes, more than half of which are new numbers.

510 Mathematics Revisions

One would think that because mathematics has been around for thousands of years—sophisticated computations being used to build the pyramids, project the existence of planetary bodies that were not seen with the naked eye, in navigation, and for many other endeavors in which humans were engaged—that this part of the Schedules should be rather stable. This is not the case. Mathematics (510) was completely revised in Edition 18, but the result was not totally satisfactory to users. Edition 19 included expansions, but again it was not found acceptable to all of the librarians using DDC. Edition 20 had some minor changes; the most effective were the relocations of Decimal Systems (to 513.55) and Business Arithmetic (to 650.01513). The 21st edition had sixteen changes including two new numbers. However, edition 22 has been given a lot of attention with 102 changes, almost 90 percent of which are new numbers.

Table 10.1

Current Number	Current Topic	Old Topic/Comment	Old Number
510	**Mathematics**		
511.1	Finite mathematics	New number	
[511.2]	Mathematical systems	Discontinued	
[511.24]	Deductive mathematics	Discontinued	
511.31	Nonclassical logic	New number	
511.312	Many-valued logic (Multiple-valued logic)	New number	
511.313	Fuzzy logic	New number	
511.3223	Fuzzy sets	New number	
511.326	Functions and relations	New number	511.33
511.332	Partially ordered sets		511.32
511.34	Model theory	New number	
511.352	Recursive functions	New number	
511.36	Proof theory and constructive mathematics	Intuitionistic mathematics	511.22
511.4	Approximations and expansions		513.24
511.422	Splines	New number	
511.54	Directed graphs (Digraphs)	New number	
511.56	Coloring of graphs	New number	
511.64	Permutations and combinations	Permutations	512.925, 513.25
511.64	Permutations and combinations	Combinations	512.72, 512.925, 513.25

Current Number	Current Topic	Old Topic/Comment	Old Number
511.66	Extremal combinatorics	Matching theory	511.5
512.21	Permutation groups	New number	
512.22	Representations of groups	New number	
512.23	Finite groups	New number	
512.25	Abelian groups (Commutative groups)	New number	
512.27	Semigroups	New number	
512.28	Groupoids	New number	
512.32	Galois theory	New number	
512.4	Rings	Free algebras, Algebras based on group properties, Flexible algebras	512.24
512.42	Modules and ideals	New number	
512.44	Commutative rings	New number	
512.44	Commutative rings	Commutative algebras	512.24
512.46	Associative rings	New number	
512.46	Associative rings	Brauer groups	512.2
512.46	Associative rings	Associative algebras	512.24
512.48	Nonassociative rings	New number	
512.48	Nonassociative rings	Jordan algebras, nonassociative algebras	512.24
512.482	Lie algebras and groups	New number	512.55
512.554	Banach algebras	New number	
512.556	Self-adjoint operator algebras	New number	
512.6	Category theory, homological algebra, K-theory	New number	

Current Number	Current Topic	Old Topic/Comment	Old Number
512.62	Category theory	New number	511.3, 512.55
512.64	Homological algebra	New number	512.55
512.66	K-theory	New number	512.55
512.72	Elementary number theory	Factorization	512.74
512.723	Prime numbers	New number	
512.73	Analytic number theory	Sieves	512.72
512.78	Specific fields of numbers	New number	
512.782	Rational numbers	New number	
512.784	Algebraic numbers	New number	
512.786	Real numbers	New number	
512.788	Complex numbers	New number	
[512.925]	Combinations, permutations, distributions	Discontinued	
512.9422	Polynomial equations	New number	
512.94222	Quadratic equations	New number	
512.9426	Simultaneous equations	New number	
512.9436	Eigenvalues and eigenvectors	New number	512.9434
[513.25]	Combinations, permutations, distributions	Discontinued	
513.5	Numeration systems		513.54
513.5	Numeration systems		513.56- .57
514.224	Structures and spaces	Fiber bundles, fiber spaces	516.362
514.32	Systems and spaces	Uniform spaces	514.3202

Current Number	Current Topic	Old Topic/Comment	Old Number
514.32	Systems and spaces	Derived spaces	514.3203
514.3201–.3209	[Systems and spaces] Standard Subdivisions		514.32001 to .32009
514.34	Topological manifolds	New number	
514.744	Catastrophes	New number	
515.22	Properties of functions	Uniformity and Multiformity	515.223
515.23	Operations on functions	Determination, expansion, evaluation of functions	515.232 to .235
515.24	Sequences and series	Algebraic, arithmetic, and geometric progressions	512.93, 513.4
515.25	Equations and functions by origin		515.254
515.3533	Elliptic equations	New number	
515.3534	Parabolic equations	New number	
515.3535	Hyperbolic equations	New number	
515.357	Inverse problems	New number	
515.39	Dynamical systems	New number	515.352
515.39	Dynamical systems	Hamiltonian systems	514.74
515.392	Stability theory	New number	515.35
515.42	Theory of measure and integration	Abstract measure theory	515.783
515.48	Ergodic theory	New number	515.42
515.642	Control theory	New number	
515.7	Functional analysis	Functionals	515.74
515.75	Functional equations	New number	
515.78	Valuation theory		515.784
515.942	Analytic spaces	New number	
515.946	Complex manifolds	New number	
515.96	Potential theory	New number	

Current Number	Current Topic	Old Topic/Comment	Old Number
516.1	General aspects of geometry	Geometry of inequalities	516.17
516.11	Finite geometry	New number	
516.12	Incidence geometry	New number	
516.132	Tilings	New number	
516.152	One-dimensional configurations	New number	
516.154	Two-dimensional configurations	New number	
516.154	Two-dimensional configurations	Planes	516.05
516.156	Three-dimensional configurations	New number	
516.156	Three-dimensional configurations	Solids	516.06
516.158	Four-dimensional and higher-dimensional configurations	New number	
516.158	Four-dimensional and higher-dimensional configurations	Polytopes	516.35
516.18	Nonpoint base geometries	Circle and modular geometries, Geometries over algebras, geometries over rings	516.184 to .186
516.246	Trigonometric functions	New number	
516.3601 to .3609	[Curves, etc.] Standard subdivisions		516.36001 to .36009
516.37	Metric differential geometries	Euclidean geometry	516.372
518	Numerical analysis	New number	515
518	Numerical analysis	Applied numerical analysis	519.4
518.1	Algorithms	New number	511.8

Current Number	**Current Topic**	**Old Topic/Comment**	**Old Number**
518.2	Specific numerical methods	New number	
518.23	Graphic methods	New number	
518.23	Graphic methods	Nomography	511.5
518.25	Finite element analysis	New number	
518.26	Iterative methods	New number	
518.28	Probabilistic methods	New number	
518.282	Monte Carlo	New number	519.282
518.4	Numerical methods in algebra, arithmetic, number theory	New number	
518.42	Numerical methods in algebra	New number	
518.42	Numerical methods in algebra	Numerical algebra	512
518.43	Numerical linear algebra	New number	
518.45	Numerical methods in arithmetic	New number	
518.47	Numerical methods in number theory	New number	
518.5	Numerical approximation	New number	
518.53	Numerical differentiation	New number	515.623
518.54	Numerical integration	New number	515.624
518.6	Numerical methods in analysis	New number	
518.63	Numerical solutions of ordinary differential equations	New number	
518.64	Numerical solutions of partial differential equations	New number	

Current Number	Current Topic	Old Topic/Comment	Old Number
518.66	Numerical solutions of integral equations	New number	
519.22	Stochastic analysis	New number	
519.236	Martingales	New number	519.287
519.27	Games of chance (Stochastic games)	New number	
519.32	Differential games	New number	
519.57	Design of experiments	New number	
519.6	Mathematical optimizations	New number	519.3
519.62	Stochastic optimization	New number	
519.64	Combinatorial optimization	New number	

520–530 Astronomy and Physics Revisions

Astronomy and Allied Sciences (520) and Physics (530) have a total of four minor changes in notations between them. However, throughout Physics "Infrared and ultraviolet" replaces "Paraphotic phenomena" in topic headings.

Table 10.2

New Number	New Topic	Old Topic/Comment	Old number
523	**Astronomy and Allied Sciences**		
523.015	Light and infrared and ultraviolet phenomena	Light and paraphotic phenomena	
523.24	Extrasolar systems	New number	
526	Mathematical geography	Map drawing	526.022 1
530	**Physics**		
530.143 3	Quantum electrodynamics	New number	537.67

540 Chemistry and Allied Sciences Revisions

Chemistry and Allied Sciences (540) have had an extensive "going over," with two entire Sections being moved and the numbers no longer used, these being Qualitative Analysis (544) and Quantitative Analysis (545), which are now located in various notations under General Topics in Analytical Chemistry (543.1). Qualitative and Quantitative Analysis in the Add Table under Inorganic Chemistry (546) have also been moved to –6 from –64 and –65. Besides these massive changes, there are five new numbers in this Division.

Table 10.3

Current Number	Current Topic	Old Topic/Comment	Old Number
540	**Chemistry and Allied Sciences**		
540.1	[Chemistry] Philosophy and theory	Phlogiston theory	540.118
540.11	Alchemy and Systems	Ancient and medieval theories	
540.113	Systems	New number	
541	Physical chemistry		541.3
541.01 to .03	[Physical chemistry] Standard subdivisions		541.301 to .303
541.05. to .09	[Physical chemistry] Standard subdivisions		541.305 to .309
541.220212	Formulas and specifications	Formulas	541.221
541.3	Miscellaneous topic in physical chemistry	Physical chemistry	
541.335	Absorption	New number	
541.382	Radiation chemistry	Radiolysis	
541 39	Chemical reactions	Specific reactions other than oxidation-reduction	541.393
541.393	Oxidation-reduction reaction (Redox reaction)	Specific reactions	

Current Number	Current Topic	Old Topic/Comment	Old Number
543	Analytical chemistry	Specific qualitative techniques	544
543	Analytical chemistry	Specific quantitative techniques	545
543	Analytical chemistry	Analytical organic chemistry	547.139
543	Analytical chemistry	Analytical chemistry of metals in general	546.3
543	Analytical chemistry	Specific techniques of analytic chemistry	547.3
543.01	Philosophy and theory		543.001
543.02	Miscellany		543.002
543.0284	Materials	Reagents	543.01
543.03 to .06	Standard subdivision		543.003 to .006
543.07	Education, research, related topics		543.007
543.08	History and description with respect to kinds of persons		543.008
543.17	Analytical organic chemistry	Comprehensive works on analytic organic chemistry	547.3
543.19	Techniques of general application	Sample preparation	543.02
543.19		Instrumentation	543.07
543.2 to .8		Specific methods	543.08
543.09	Historical, geographic, persons treatment		543.009
543.1	General topics in analytical chemistry	Qualitative analysis	544
543.1	General topics in analytical chemistry	Quantitative analysis	545
543.17	Analytical organic chemistry		547.3

Current Number	Current Topic	Old Topic/Comment	Old Number
543.19	Techniques of general application	Sample preparation	544.02, 544.07
543.19	Techniques of general application	Instrumentation	545.02, 545.07
543.2	Classical methods	Diffusion methods, Gravimetric analysis	544.5, 544.93, 545.1
543.22	Microchemistry (Microanalysis)		544.8, 545.84
543.24	Volumetric analysis		545.2
543.26	Thermal analysis		543.086, 544.2, 545.4
543.4	Electrochemical analysis		543.0874, 545.3
543.5	Optical spectroscopy (Spectrum analysis)		543.085, 544.6, 544.95, 545.81, 545.83
543.5	Spectroscopy	Spectroscopy in organic chemistry	543.5
543.52	Atomic emission spectroscopy		
543.54	Molecular spectroscopy		
543.55	Spectrophotometry		
543.56	Luminescence spectroscopy		543.08584
543.57	Infrared and Raman spectroscopy		543.08583, 543.08584
543.59	Methods based on refraction, interference, scattering		543.0853, 545.816
543.6	Nonoptical spectroscopy		

Current Number	Current Topic	Old Topic/Comment	Old Number
543.62	X-ray and electron spectroscopy		543.08586
543.63	Radiochemical analysis		543.088, 544.98
543.65	Mass spectrometry (Mass spectroscopy)		543.0873
543.66	Nuclear magnetic resonance spectroscopy		543.0877
543.67	Electron paramagnetic resonance spectroscopy		
543.8	Chromatography		543.0893, 544.92, 545.89
543.82	Ion-exchange chromatography		543.0893
543.84	Liquid chromatography		543.0894
543.85	Gas Chromatography		543.0896
543.86	Supercritical fluid chromatography		543.0896
546.224	Theoretical chemistry	Specific topics in theoretical chemistry	546.2242 to .2248
546.225	Physical chemistry	Specific topics in physical chemistry	546.2253 to 2259
546.25	Theoretical chemistry of hydrogen	Specific topics in theoretical chemistry	546.252 to .258
546.26	Physical chemistry of hydrogen	Specific topics in physical chemistry	546.263 to .269
546.34	Salts	Specific kinds of salts	546.342 to .345
546.51	Titanium group (Group 4)	Group 4B (IVB)	
546.52	Vanadium group (Group 5)	Group 5B (VB)	

Current Number	Current Topic	Old Topic/Comment	Old Number
546.53	Chromium group (Group 6)	Group 6B (VIB)	
546.54	Manganese group (Group 7)	Group 7B (VIIB)	
546.6	Groups 8, 9, 10, 11, 12, 13, 14	Group 8, 1B, 2B, 3A, 4A	
546.62	Iron, cobalt, nickel	Group 8 (VIII)	
546.65	Group 11	Group 1B (IB)	
546.66	Group 12	Group 2B (IIB)	
546.67	Group 13	Group 3A (IIIA)	
546.68	Group 14	Group 4A (IVA)	
546.7	Groups 15, 16, 17, 18	Groups 5A, 6A, 7A, O	
546.71	Group 15	Group 5A (VA)	
546.72	Group 16	Group 6A (VIA)	
546.73	Halogens (Group 17)	Group 7A (VIIA)	
546.75	Noble gases (Group 18)	Group O	
546.8	Periodic law and table	Periodic law and periodicity	541.24
547.046			547.0464 to .0465
547.07	Organophosphorus compounds	Specific Organophosphorus compounds	547.071 to .077
547.2	Organic chemical reactions	Chemical reaction (0464 to 0465) in 547 table	
547.2	Organic chemical reactions		547.139
547.2	Organic chemical reactions	Chemical reactions of compounds identified by component elements	547.01 to .08

Current Number	Current Topic	Old Topic/Comment	Old Number
547.2	Organic chemical reactions	Chemical reactions of compounds identified by structure and function	547.2, .4 to .8
547.2	Organic chemical reactions	Acylation and alkylation	547.21
547.2	Organic chemical reactions	Halogenation, Hydroxy addition and substitution	547.22
547.2	Organic chemical reactions	Hydrolysis	547.225
547.2	Organic chemical reactions	Comprehensive works on organic condensation	547.28
547.21	General topics in chemical reactions	Acylation, alkylation, aromatization	
547.212	Chemical equilibrium	New number	
547.214	Reaction kinetics	New number	
547.215	Catgalysis	New number	
547.27	Reactions producing specific kinds of organic compounds	Aromatization	547.21
547.27	Reactions producing specific kinds of organic compounds	Esterification	547.24
547.27	Reactions producing specific kinds of organic compounds	Halogenation	547.223
547.27	Reactions producing specific kinds of organic compounds	Saponification	547.225, 547.770 4593
547.27	Reactions producing specific kinds of organic compounds	Amination and diazotization	547.25
547.27	Reactions producing specific kinds of organic compounds	Nitration and nitrosation	547.26

Current Number	Current Topic	Old Topic/Comment	Old Number
547.7	Macromolecules and related compounds	Alkaloids, antibiotics, hormones, proteins, steroids, vitamins	547.72 to .76
547.7	Macromolecules and related compounds	Nucleic acids	547.79
547.78	Carbohydrates	Specific kinds of carbohydrates	547.781 to .783

550 Earth Sciences Revisions

Earth Sciences (550) have forty-three changes recorded in the following table, twelve of which are new numbers. Specific Oceans and Seas, and Coastal Saltwater Bodies that were located in notations 551.461 to 551.469 are now all located under 551.461 (.4613 to .4618).

Table 10.4

Current Number	Current Topic	Old Topic/ Comment	Old Number
550	**Earth Sciences**		
551.46	Hydrosphere and submarine geology; Oceanography	Hydrosphere; Oceanography	
551.46	Hydrosphere and submarine geology; Oceanography	Deep-sea surveys and explorations	551.4607
551.4601	Philosophy and theory		551.46001
551.4602 to .4606	Standard subdivisions		551.46002 to .46006
551.4607	Education, research, related topics		551.46007
551.4608	History and description with respect to kinds of persons		551.46008

Current Number	Current Topic	Old Topic/ Comment	Old Number
551.4609	Historical, geographic, persons treatment		551.46009
551.461	Specific oceans and seas, coastal saltwater bodies	Used for Atlantic Ocean	
551.4613	Atlantic Ocean		551.461
551.46132	Arctic Ocean (North Polar Sea)		551.468
551.46135	South Atlantic Ocean		551.464
551.46136	Southwest Atlantic Ocean		551.4646
551.461364	Gulf of Mexico		551.4634
551.461365	Caribbean Sea		551.4635
551.46137	Southeast Atlantic Ocean		551.4647
551.46138	Mediterranean Sea		551.462
551.4614	Pacific Ocean		551.465
551.46141	Southeast Pacific Ocean		551.4661
551.46142	East Pacific Ocean		551.466
551.46143	Northeast Pacific Ocean		551.4663
551.4615	Indian Ocean		551.467
551.4617	Antarctic waters		551.469
551.4618	Coastal saltwater bodies		551.4609
551.462	Ocean circulation	Dynamic oceanography	551.47
551.462	Ocean circulation	Ocean currents	551.4701
551.463	Waves		551.4702
551.4637	Tsunamis	New number	
551.464	Tides		551.4708

Current Number	Current Topic	Old Topic/ Comment	Old Number
551.465	Physical properties of seawater		551.4601
551.4653	Temperature	New number	
551.4654	Acoustical properties	New number	
551.4655	Optical properties	New number	
551.466	Chemical oceanography		551.4601
551.4664	Salinity	New number	
551.46643	Temperature-salinity relationships	New number	
551.468	Submarine geology		551.4608
551.4683	Submarine geomorphology	New number	
551.4686	Sediments	New number	
551.4829	Salt lakes and inland seas	New number	551.4609
551.55	Atmospheric disturbances and formations	Other storms	551.559
551.556	Ice storms	New number	551.559
551.559	Dust storms	Other storms	
551.5634	Ball lightning	New number	
551.793	Holocene epoch	Recent (Postglacial) epoch	

560–590 Life Sciences Revisions

Life sciences (560–590) were among those that had such extensive changes in Edition 21 that Comparative and Equivalence Tables were provided to DDC users. Changes in this edition are much less dramatic, most of which being new numbers, eighty-eight to be exact.

Table 10. 5

Current Number	Current Topic	Old Topic/Comment	Old Number
560	**Paleontology; Paleozoology**		
560.41	Fossilization (Taphonomy)	New number	
560.43	Trace fossils	New number	
560.47	Micropaleontology	New number	
561.11	Stratigraphic paleobotany	New number	
561.15	Fossil leaves	New number	
561.52 to .58	Pinophyta (Gymnosperms)	Coniferales (Conifers)	561.52 to .55
569.93	Australopithicus	New number	
569.97	Homo erectus	New number	
569.98	Homo sapiens	New number	
569.986	Neanderthals	New number	
570	**Life Sciences; Biology**		
571.8452	Plants	New number	
571.8452	Plants	Comprehensive works on palynology	561.13
571.91	Animal diseases	New number	
571.92	Plant diseases	New number	
571.975	Injuries and wounds	New number	
572.3	General topics of biochemistry	Ion transport	571.64
572.577	Membrane lipids	New number	
572.69	Bioactive proteins	Carrier proteins	

Current Number	Current Topic	Old Topic/Comment	Old Number
572.696	Carrier and transport proteins	New number	
572.838	Molecular evolution	Radiogenetics	576.542
573.154	Biochemistry	New number	
573.38379	Bile	New number	
576.58	Population genetics	Role of species in evolution	576.86
576.86	Speciation	Species in evolution	576.58
577	Fire ecology	New number	
577.79	Deep sea ecology	Ecology of abyssal zone	
577.799	Hydrothermal vent ecology	New number	
578.472	Camouflage		578.47
578.62	Nonnative species	New number	
579.171	Specific ecosystem processes of ecology	New number	
579.172	Specific factors affecting ecology	New number	
580	**Plants**		
581.62	Nonnative species	New number	
581.71	Specific ecosystem processes of ecology	New number	
581.72	Specific factors affecting ecology	New number	
590	**Animals**		
591.44	[Physical adaptation] Head	New number	

Current Number	Current Topic	Old Topic/Comment	Old Number
591.472	Camouflage		578.47
591.56	Behavior relating to life cycle	Comprehensive works on life cycle of animals	571.81
591.57	Locomotion	New number	
591.62	Nonnative animals	New number	
591.71	Specific ecosystem processes of ecology	New number	
591.72	Specific factors affecting ecology	New number	
597.33	Lamnidae	Isuridae	
597.858	Ambystomatidae (Mole salamanders)	New number	
597.859	Plethodontidae (Lungless salamanders)	New number	
597.8592	Plethodon	New number	
597.865	Pipoidea	New number	
597.8654	Xenopus	New number	
597.872	Bufo	New number	
597.875	Leptodactylidae	New number	
597.8754	Eleutherodactylus	New number	
597.877	Dendrobatidae (Poison arrow frogs)	New number	
597.878	Hylidae (Tree frogs)	New number	
597.8782	Hyla	New number	
597.892	Rana	New number	
597.922	Chelydridae (Snapping turtles)	New number	
597.923	Kinosternidae	New number	
597.924	Testudinidae	New number	
597.9246	Geochelone	New number	

Current Number	Current Topic	Old Topic/Comment	Old Number
597.925	Emydidae	New number	
597.9257	Clemmys	New number	
597.9259	Chrysemys, Pseudemys, Deirochelys, Graptemys, Malaclemys, Trachemys	New number	
597.92592	Chrysemys	New number	
597.92594	Pseudemys	New number	
597.926	Trionychidae, Carettochelyidae, Dermatemydidae, Platysternidae	New number	
597.928	Chelonioidea	New number	
597.928	Chelonioidea	Marine turtles	597.92177
597.9289	Dermochelyidae	New number	
597.929	Pleurodira	New number	
597.948	Amphisbaenia	New number	
597.952	Gekkonidea	New number	
597.954	Iguanidae	New number	
597.9542	Iguanas	New number	
597.9548	Anolis (Anoles)	New number	
597.955	Agamidae	New number	
597.956	Chamaeleontidae (Chameleons)	New number	
597.957	Scincidae	New number	
597.9573	Eumeces	New number	
597.958	Teiidae, Cordylidae, Lacertidae	New number	
597. 9582	Teiidae	New number	
597.95825	Cnemidophorus	New number	
597.959	Anguinomorphoidea	New number	

Current Number	Current Topic	Old Topic/Comment	Old Number
597.9592	Anguidae	New number	
597.9595	Helodermatidae (Beaded lizard)	New number	
597.95952	Heloderma suspectum (Gila monster)	New number	
597.9596	Monitor lizards and Earless monitor lizards	New number	
597.95968	Varanus komodoensis (Komodo dragon)	New number	
597.9598	Xantusiidae (Night lizards)	New number	
597.962	Colubridae	New number	
597.963	Viperidae (Vipers	New number	
597.9636	Vipera	New number	
597.9638	Crotalus (Rattlesnakes and Sistrurus (Pigmy rattlesnakes)	New number	
597.964	Elapidae	New number	
597.9642	Cobras	New number	
597.9644	Coral snakes	New number	
597.965	Hydrophiidae (Sea snakes)	New number	597.96177
597.967	Booidea (Henophidia)	New number	
597.9678	Pythoninae (Pythons)	New number	
597.969	Typhlopoidea (Scolecophidia)	New number	
597.982	Crocodilidac (Crocodiles)	New number	
597.984	Alligatoridae	New number	

Current Number	Current Topic	Old Topic/Comment	Old Number
598.74	Cuculiformes	Opisthocomidae (Hoatzin)	598.64
599.144	[Mammalia] Head	New number	
599.78	Ursidae (Bears)	Comprehensive works	599.784
599.785	Ursus americanus (American black bear)	Eurarctos (American black bear)	
599.786	Ursus maritimus (Polar bear)	Thalarctos (Polar bear)	

Exercises in the Use of Class 500

Following are seven brief statements about books in the subject areas of Class 500. Apply your skills and develop classification numbers for each then check your numbers against those assigned by the Library of Congress in the section "Answers to the Exercises" in the Appendix.

1. A work on amphibians and reptiles in Arkansas.
2. A work on abbreviation dictionaries in the subject of astronomy.
3. A work on debris avalanches in Yunnan Sheng, China.
4. A work on natural history in the state of Washington.
5. A work on paleontological biological diversity in the Ordovician period.
6. A work on forest ecology in Fiordland, New Zealand.
7. A work on fishes found in Mexico.

Literature Cited

Richmond, Phyllis A. 1963. The Future of Generalized Systems of Classification. *College and Research Libraries* 24 (5):399.

11

Class 600: Technology (Applied Sciences)

Although the 600 Class is one of the largest of the DDC Classes in number of entries, there is more of a consistency to its contents than the mega Class 300. It embodies the enormous growth of technology during the century since Dewey first developed his system. Classes 610 and 620 were targeted for revision on the Comaromi survey, but they ranked second and third in the order of urgency. A major readjustment would move both Human anatomy (611) and Human physiology (612) into Zoology (591), partially to liberate space in the 610s and to affirm their relationship to the anatomy and physiology of animals. However, the idea was withdrawn after receiving extensive criticism. What to do about these problems is less obvious. Recent questions from the field focus on increasing financial hazards attached to issuing new revisions:

> Is a new edition, on the lines with which we are familiar, probable? And if it is, do we want it? Well, I should think that on one plane (not the economic one, that is) we most certainly do. The classification has (as any classification will have) many areas where radical change is needed. Medical Sciences come at once to mind, and the Fine Arts. . . . In his recent review of DDC19 Peter Butcher has reminded us of the difficulties we experience with the 720/Architecture –624/Civil engineering –690/Building split (A huge task, this, to rectify and rationalize this field—but one which should give great satisfaction when done). Life Sciences, 560, 70, 80, and 90 plus 611 and 612, stand greatly in need of rewriting. (Jelinek 1980, 1–2)

Much like Class 300, the problems of illogical arrangement, disciplinary overlap, and overcrowding in this Class are widely recognized. According to one classifier, it is "an unpredictable disarray of 'disciplines' and/or subjects . . . an arbitrary arrangement of heterogeneous mass" (Kaltenbach 1968, 47). Until decisions are made to implement drastic changes, 600 will remain a strange amalgamation of parts that are shoehorned together under the caption of Technology and Applied sciences.

Summary and Details of Class 600

600	Technology (Applied Sciences)
610	Medicine and Health
620	Engineering and Allied Operations
630	Agriculture and Related Technologies
640	Home and Family Management
650	Management and Auxiliary Services
660	Chemical Engineering and Related Technologies
670	Manufacturing
680	Manufacture of Products for Specific Uses
690	Buildings

Division 600: The first section is used for Standard Subdivisions, which are found in 601–609. Special Topics (604) is used for Technical Drawing (604.2), and methods used with hazardous materials technology (604.7). History and Description with Respect to Kinds of Persons is found at 604.8 instead of its usual place at –08, thus freeing 608 to be used for Inventions and Patents.

Division 610: Medicine is found in this Division. Standard Subdivisions (610.1 to 610.9) are joined by nursing and other health professionals (610.73) and share the notation for education and research. Physicians are found under 610.6, or organizations in Table 1, the Standard Subdivisions. Human anatomy and cell and tissue biology are in the next Section (611) and are followed by Human Physiology (612). Health and Safety are found next to Forensic Medicine and Public Health in 613 and 614. Treatment and therapeutics including pharmacology are next in 615 and are followed by various diseases in 616. The various branches of medicine and surgery conclude the Division in 617 to 618. Section 619 is not used in this edition.

Division 620: If the Division for medicine seemed packed, the third Division, used for engineering is bulging. While 610 was used for Standard Subdivisions, this Division is loaded with engineering topics from sound to nanotechnology. It begins as usual with Standard Subdivisions (620.001 to 620.009) with the special topics of engineering in 620.004 being such aspects as design, testing, and measurement and quality. Other general features of engineering are also in this Section, such as engineering mechanics and materials (620.1), sound and similar vibrations (620.2), and mechanical vibration (620.3). Engineering for specific kinds of geographic environments, fine particle and remote control technology, and surface engineering all share 620.4. Nanotechnology is found in 620.5, with Human factors and safety engineering (620.8) ending this Section.

The next Section is used for engineering involving the principles of physics, such as energy (621.042), plasma (621.044), steam (621.1), and hydraulics (621.2). The notation 621.3 is used for aspects of electric power, such as power generation and transmission, various characteristic kinds of lighting and optical engineering, engineering of various kinds of electronics including computers (621.39).

Those forms of energy called "prime movers" are found in 621.4 with heat engineering. Topics found here include various types of engines, solar-based energy, and nuclear energy. Vacuums and low temperatures are next at 621.5, followed by Blowers, fans, and pumps in 621.6. Machine engineering (621.8) and Tools (621.9) complete this Section.

Mining and ores are in the third Section (622) followed by military and nautical engineering in 623. Civil (624), railroads and roads (625), hydraulic (627), sanitary and environmental engineering (628) complete the major Sections of engineering. The final Section of the Division continues with other branches of engineering including aerospace (629.1), all types of land vehicles (629.2), vehicles that ride on cushions of air (629.3), astronautics (629.4), and concludes with automatic control engineering (629.8).

Division 630: Most of the Division is reserved for agriculture (630–636) and begins with the usual Standard Subdivisions (630.1–.9), however, specific techniques, apparatus, equipment, and materials that would normally be at 630.28 are in the next Section (631) in order to provide sufficient room for the details required for agriculture. Plant damage by injury, disease, or pests are in the third Section (632) followed by large-scale plantings and crops (633), orchards, fruits (634.1–.8), and forestry (634.9). Gardening and vegetables is followed by the care of domestic animals in 635 to

636 and complete the topics of agriculture.

Processing dairy and poultry products are found in 637 and are followed by insect culture (638). The Division shifts from agriculture and agricultural products to activities that harvest the natural or wild environments, which are hunting and fishing (639.1 and .2). The culture of various marine and aquatic animals are found in 639.3 to 639.8. The Division ends with the conservation of biological resources in 639.9.

Division 640: This Division is for Home and Family Management. As usual, the Standard Subdivisions are in the first Section (640.1 to.9) including Specific Topics of household management in 640.4, such as management of finances and household employees.

Food and drink are in the next section (641) followed by their consumption at meals (642). Aspects of managing households continue the Division with housing and equipment (643), utilities (644), and furnishings (645).

Clothing, sewing, cleanliness, and guides to family living (646) begin a new group of subjects. Institutional housekeeping (647) is followed by housekeeping in the home (648). The Division concludes with child rearing (649.1–.7) and home care of the ill or disabled (649.8).

Division 650: This Division, Management and Auxiliary Services, is concerned with business office activities and seems far removed from plasma engineering or surgery, which are found in the same Class. But as usual, Standard Subdivisions are found first (650.01 to 650.09), with personal success in business (650.1) completing the short Section.

Office equipment, management, communication, and data processing are in the second Section (651) followed by methods used in written communication (652–653). Numbers 654 to 656 are unused in Edition 22. Aspects of business accounting are next (657) and are followed by management of the various activities of business in 658. The final aspects of business and its management are advertising and public relations which conclude the Division in 659.

Division 660: Chemical engineering, metallurgy, and similar subjects are found in this Division, which begins with Standard Subdivisions (660.01–.09), and includes biotechnology (660.6) and industrial stoichiometry (660.7). The production of chemicals used as raw materials or in the production of other materials is found in the second Section (661) and is followed by the technologies for explosives and fuels (662).

Commercial manufacture of beverages (663) and food (664) are next and are followed by the manufacture of waxes (665.1), fats and oils (665.2–.4), petroleum (665.5), and gases (665.7–.8).

The various ceramic, masonry, and building materials are in the next Section (666), then the cleaning and coating of materials in 667. Organic-based products, such as plastics and perfumes are in 668 and metallurgy concludes the Division in 669.

Division 670: Manufacturing is in this Division, with Standard Subdivisions in the first Section (670.1 to 670.9), which are accompanied by the engineering of factory operations as a Special Topic in 670.42. The manufacture of products from specific materials are covered in the rest of the division, which are metal (671), iron and steel (672), nonferrous metals (673), lumber (674), leather and fur (675), pulp and paper (676), textiles (677), rubber and similar materials (678), and other miscellaneous materials conclude the Division in 679.

Division 680: This Division is reserved for the manufacture of products for specific uses. There are no Standard Subdivisions for this Division, instead the first Section covers precision instruments (681.1–.4, .7) and printing, writing, and duplicating equipment (681.6) and ends with musical instruments (681.8).

Blacksmithing is the next Section (682), and is followed by the topics hardware and household appliances (683), furnishings and home workshops (684). Leather and fur products (685) are in the next Section, with printing, bookbinding and photocopying following in 686. The manufacture of various articles of clothing is found in 687, with the manufacture of miscellaneous items, such as models, costume jewelry, recreation equipment, concluding the Division in 688, 689 not being in this edition.

Division 690: Buildings are found in the last Division of the 600 Class. Standard Subdivisions are found in the first Section (690.01 to 690.09), with parts of the structure (690.1), general construction activities (690.2), and types of buildings (690.5–.8) sharing the Section. Building materials are in the next Section (691) and are logically followed by plans, drawings, and contracting activities in 692. Next in this logical progression of building are the types of materials used in construction (693–694), with the various building processes are found in the last Sections of the Class (695–698). Section 699 is not used in Edition 22.

The Number Building Process

An example of number building in the 600 Class is a handbook on first aid for boating injuries, or medicine in a naval environment. The base number for first aid according to the Relative Index is **616.0252.** However, this handbook is not for the generalist, but for use shipboard or in a boating environment. This type of subdivision would come from the Standard Subdivisions in Table 1. After checking the schedules and ascertaining that there are no special instructions, scanning the Standard Subdivisions reveals that 024 is used for "the subject for persons in specific occupations" (Dewey 2003, 1:190), which when added to the base number results in **616.0252024.**

The next step is to add the appropriate numbers to denote sailors. Going back to Table 1, instructions indicate: "Add to base number 024 notation 001–999" (Dewey 2003, 1:190). This instruction means that numbers from the schedules that represent the specific occupations should be added. In the Relative Index we find notations for merchant mariners, navy personnel, sports enthusiasts, and technologists. Again this handbook does not specify a type of environment so the last of these subgroups appears to be more appropriate. Going once more to the Schedules, seamanship is found with nautical engineering at 623.8, which seems to be the appropriate numbers to be added for our classification.

LC Classification: 616.02520246238

Advanced first aid afloat, by Peter F. Eastman.

DDC 22 Class 600 Revisions

Similar to Classes 300 and 500, the 600 Class, used for technology and applied sciences, is so diverse that six separate tables are being used to list the changes in *DDC* 22 in order that they will be less confusing to the classifiers reviewing them. There are significant revisions in the 22nd Edition 600 class, especially in Medicine (610), which is one of the largest of DDC divisions and supports what must be one of the largest bodies of literature available to libraries.

610 Medicine Revisions

In this country medicine is maybe the single most heavily research-invested of the applied sciences and, as befitting this distinction, has by far the largest numbers of changes—325 with almost half of the changes being new numbers also apt for a discipline in which new frontiers are constantly being explored. Three Add Tables in the division have significant revisions that effect number building.

Table 11.1

Current Number	Current Topic	Old Topic/ Comment	Old Number
Add Table 616.1 to .9	**Specific Diseases**		
014	Medical bacteriology	Added number	
014	Medical bacteriology	Specific kinds of bacteria	0142 to 0149
014	Medical bacteriology	Medical microbiology of rickettsiae	
015	Medical mycology	Added number	
016	Medical protozoology	Added number	
019	Medical virology	Added number	0194
0231	Nurses	Added number	610.7369
0233	Allied health personnel	Technicians and Assistants	
02332	Physician assistants	Added number	
029	Palliative and terminal care	Terminal care	
060724	[Therapy] Experimental research	Added number	
061 to 069	Specific therapies	Specific kinds of therapies used for prevention	05
0610724	[Drug therapy] Experimental research	Added number	
071	Etiology	Added number	
075 to 079	Diagnosis, prognosis, death, immunity	Added number	

Current Number	Current Topic	Old Topic/ Comment	Old Number
Add Table 617	**Miscellaneous Branches of Medicine; Surgery**		
01	Surgical complications, preoperative, intraoperative, postoperative care	Surgical complications and sequelae	
0231	Nurses	Added number	610.7369
0233	Allied health personnel	Technicians and Assistants	
02332	Physician assistants	Added number	
0421 to 0423	Surgical complications, preoperative, intra-operative,postoperative care, special topics, rehabilitation	Surgical complications and sequelae; special topics, rehabilitation	
0597	Endoscopic surgery	Added number	
0598	Laser surgery	Added number	
060724	Experimental research	Added number	
061 to 069	Specific therapies	Specific kinds of therapies used for prevention	052
0610724	[Drug therapy] Experimental research	Added number	
071	Etiology	Added number	
075 to 079	Diagnosis, prognosis, death, immunity	Added number	
Add Table 618.1 to .8	**Gynecology and Obstetrics**		
0597	Endoscopic surgery	Added number	
0598	Laser surgery	Added number	
060724	[Therapy] Experimental research	Added number	
061 to 069	Specific therapies	Specific kinds of therapies used for prevention	05

Current Number	Current Topic	Old Topic/Comment	Old Number
0610724	[Drug therapy] Experimental research	Added number	
071	Etiology	Added number	
075 to 079	Diagnosis, prognosis, death, immunity	Added number	

Other significant changes include "Medical aspects" of crime prevention being moved from Social Problems in 360 to Medicine. Experimental Medicine was moved from Section 619 to 616.027 under Diseases with seven new numbers assigned for this topic.

Table 11.2

Current Number	Current Topic	Old Topic/ Comment	Old Number
610	**Medicine and Health**		
610.69	Medical personnel and relationships	Specific kinds of medical personnel	610.695
610.695	Physicians		610.6952
610.737069	Comprehensive works on nature of duties, characteristics of the profession of allied health personnel		610.6953
610.7372069	Nature of duties, characteristics of the profession of physician assistants		610.6953
610.736	Long-term care nursing		610.7361
610.737	Services of allied health personnel	Services of medical technicians and assistants	
610.737069	Comprehensive works on nature of duties, characteristics of the profession of allied health personnel		610.6953

620–630 Engineering and Agriculture Revisions

Bowing to the reality that almost all computers now used are digital, the word "digital" has been removed from computer headings. For example, the 21st edition used the terms "digital supercomputers," "digital mainframe computers," and "digital microcomputers" (Dewey 1996, 3:174). These topics are now "supercomputers," "mainframe computers," and "microcomputers" (Dewey 2003, 3:205). Analog computers are still found with hybrid computers.

In Civil Engineering (624) bridges have been moved from the number range 624.3 to 624.8 and consolidated in 624.2 resulting in nine new numbers in the range 621.21 to .24.

Agriculture and Related Technologies (630), which includes hunting, fishing, and conservation, had only one minor change.

Table 11.3

Current Number	Current Topic	Old Topic/Comment	Old Number
621	**Applied Physics**		
621.31243	Thermoelectric generation	Radioisotope thermoelectric generation	621.3125
621.3191	Polycyclic current systems		621.31916
621.321	Principles of lighting	Direct, indirect, semi-indirect lighting	621.3212 to .3213
621.36	Optical engineering	Applied optics and paraphotic technology	
621.361	Spectroscopy	Infrared, light, ultraviolet, microwave, radiofrequency, gamma-ray, X-ray, magnetic resonance spectroscopy	621.3612 to .3617
621.3848	Radar	Special developments	621.38489
621.3848	Radar	Racon and shoran	621.384892 to .384893

Current Number	Current Topic	Old Topic/Comment	Old Number
621.38806	High-definition television (HDTV)	New number	
621.38807	Digital television	New number	
621.389	Security, sound recording, related systems	Language translators	621.3894
621.3993	Computer vision	New number	
621.3994	Computer pattern recognition	New number	
621.3996	Computer graphics	New number	
621.40223	Conduction	New number	
621.40225	Convection	New number	
621.40227	Radiation	New number	
621.46	Electric and related motors	Ion and plasma motors	621.465 to .466
621.83	Gears, ratchets, cams	Ratchets	621.837
621.865	Excavating machinery	Power shovels	
621.873	Cranes	Derricks	621.872
621.934	Saws	New number	
621.98	Pressing, impressing, molding equipment	Straightening tools	621.983
624	**Civil Engineering**		
624.1526	Blasting	New number	
624.17725	Columns	New number	
624.2	Bridges	Long-span bridges	624.3
624.2	Bridges	Compound bridges	624.7
624.20284	Materials		624.257
624.21	Girder and related kinds of bridges	New number	624.3

Current Number	Current Topic	Old Topic/Comment	Old Number
624.21	Girder and related kinds of bridges	Tubular bridges	624.4
624.215	Box-girder bridges	New number	624.4
624.217	Iron and steel truss bridges	New number	
624.218	Timber truss bridges	New number	
624.219	Cantilever bridges	New number	
624.22	Arch bridges	New number	624.6
624.225	Masonry arch bridges	New number	
624.23	Suspension and cable-stayed bridges	New number	624.5
624.24	Movable bridges	New number	624.8
624.283	Structural analysis and design of floor systems		624.253
624.284	Structural analysis and design of foundations		624.254
629	**Other Branches of Engineering**		
629.243	Suspension systems	Springs and shock absorbers	
629.893	Specific kinds of robots	New number	
629.8932	Mobile robots	New number	
629.8933	Manipulators	New number	

Current Number	Current Topic	Old Topic/Comment	Old Number
630	**Agriculture and Related Technologies**		
630	Interdisciplinary works on plants of agricultural importance		580
632.32	Bacterial diseases	Rickettsial diseases	632.8

640 Home and Family Management Revisions

A significant change in this division is its heading, which was changed from Home Economics and Family Living, reflecting the present attitudes in American society regarding the significance and complexity that is involved in running a household. Other major changes include Food and Drink (641) having been greatly expanded with twenty-six new numbers, some of which had previously been developed through Add notes. Topics for these new numbers range from pickling to afternoon teas.

Table 11.4

Current Number	Current Topic	Old Topic/ Comment	Old Number
640	**Home and Family Management**	Home Economics and Family Living	
641.2222	White wine	New number	
641.2223	Red wine	New number	
641.2224	Sparkling wine	New number	
641.308	Food additives	New number	
641.3565	[Food from plants] Field legumes		641.333
641.4	Food preservation and storage	Use of additives	641.47
641.462	Pickling	New number	
641.5024	Cooking for persons in specific occupations		641.51
641.532	Brunches	New number	

Current Number	Current Topic	Old Topic/ Comment	Old Number
641.534	Box and bag lunches	New number	
641.536	Afternoon teas	New number	
641.538	Suppers	New number	
641.539	Snacks	New number	
641.5611	Cooking for one	New number	
641.5612	Cooking for two	New number	
641.56222	Cooking for infants	New number	
641.563	Cooking for health, appearance, personal reasons	High-calorie cooking	641.5634
641.5631	Cooking for persons with medical conditions	Cooling for persons with illnesses	
641.56318	Cooking for persons with food allergies	New number	
641.56319	Cooking for pregnant women	New number	
641.56323	Low-salt cooking	New number	
641.56383	Low-carbohydrate cooking	New number	
641.563837	Sugar-free cooking	New number	
641.56384	Low-fat cooking	New number	
641.563847	Low-cholesterol cooking	New number	
641.5686	Christmas cooking	New number	
641.575	Travel cooking	Dining car cooking	641.576
641.5892	Food processors	New number	
641.5893	Blenders	New number	
641.625	Distilled liquor	Spirits	
641.6565	[Cooking] Field legumes		641.633
641.774	Stir frying	New number	
641.8157	Muffins	New number	
641.819	Garnishes	New number	

Current Number	Current Topic	Old Topic/ Comment	Old Number
641.8236	Chili	New number	
641.8248	Pizza	New number	
641.862	Frozen desserts	Ice cream	
641.8642	Gelatins	New number	
641.8644	Puddings	New number	
641.86539	Cake decorations	New number	
642.56	[Meals] Health care facilities	New number	
642.57	[Meals] Schools	New number	
642.79	Napkin folding	New number	
643.25	Vacation homes	New number	
643.27	Apartments	New number	
643.29	Mobile homes	New number	
643.3	Kitchens	Cooking apparatus, equipment, materials	641.50284
643.54	Living rooms, drawing rooms, parlors	Living rooms	
643.556	Swimming pools	New number	
644.6	Plumbing	New number	
645.029	Commercial miscellany	Evaluation and purchasing manuals	645.042
645.12	Rugs	New number	
645.32	Draperies	New number	
646.433	Suits, jackets, trousers, vests	Suits, trousers, jackets	
646.7247	Braiding hair	New number	
646.76	Social skills	Charm	
647.2	Employees	Outdoor employees	647.3
647.94	Lodging for temporary residents	Multiple dwellings for transient residents	

Current Number	Current Topic	Old Topic/Comment	Old Number
647.940253 to .940259	Directories of persons and organizations concerned with household management of lodging for temporary residents by specific continents, countries, localities		647.943 to .949
647.94093 to .94099	[Temporary lodging] Treatment by specific continents, countries, localities		647.943 to .949
647.942	Campsites	New number	
[647.4]	[Child health care] Clothing	Discontinued	
647.48	Substance abuse	New number	
649.6		Child training	649.1
649.68	Home preschool education	Home teaching of reading	649.58

650 Management and Auxiliary Services

This business-related Division has also received some attention in the 22nd edition, with seven-four changes but only fifteen new numbers. An interesting revision is the topics of resumes, cover letters, and job applications being moved from 808.066651, which was rhetoric of professional, technical, and expository literature to a new home in a new number under Success in Obtaining Jobs and Promotions, at 650.142, a very logical move. Most changes were less dramatic and involved relocations within the same number ranges, either reducing or increasing the lengths of the notations.

Table 11.5

Current Number	Current Topic	Old Topic/Comment	Old Number
650	**Management and Auxiliary Services**		
650.1	Personal success in business	Interdisciplinary works on success	646.7
650.11	Time management	New number	
650.142	Résumés, cover letters, job applications	New number	
650.142	Résumés, cover letters, job applications	Résumé writing	808.06665
650.142	Résumés, cover letters, job applications	Writing cover letters for job hunting	808.066651
650.144	Employment interviewing	New number	
651.59	Digitization of files	Computerization of files	
651.792	Intranets	New number	
652.3	Keyboarding	Typing	
652.32	Keyboarding for specific purposes	Keyboarding for personal use	652.325
652.4	Copying	Duplication of records and duplicating methods	
653.42	English-language systems	Early forms	653.421
653.42	English-language systems	Essentially nonphonetic systems	653.422
653.42	English-language systems	Geometric disjoined vowel systems	653.423
653.42	English-language systems	Geometric joined vowel systems	653.425

Current Number	Current Topic	Old Topic/Comment	Old Number
653.42	English-language systems	Semigeometric, script-geometric, semiscript system	653.426
653.424	Pittman systems		653.4242
653.427	Gregg systems	Conventional	653.4272
653.427	Gregg systems	Simplified systems	653.4273
657	Accounting	General works on financial accounting	657.48
657.48	Inflation accounting	Analytical (Financial) accounting	
657.7	Accounting for specific phases of business activity	Accounting for income, for profit	657.48
657.742	Payroll accounting	New number	
657.8322	[Accounting] Health care facilities	Hospitals	
657.8374	[Accounting] Hotels	New number	
657.8375	[Accounting] Restaurants	New number	
657.839	Commerce	Wholesale and retail trade	
657.9	Accounting for enterprises of specific sizes or specific kinds of legal or ownership form	Branches	657.99
657.904	Enterprises of specific sizes	[Accounting] Special topics	
658.0412	Home-based business	New number	
658.162	Mergers	New number	
658.164	Sales	New number	
658.166	Dissolution	New number	
658.3123	Telecommuting	New number	
658.31424	Promoting		658.3126
658.3144	Penalties	Demotion	658.3127

Current Number	Current Topic	Old Topic/Comment	Old Number
658.315	Employer-employee relationships	Labor relations counseling	658.3151
658.32	Compensation management	Wage and salary administration	
658.3225	Incentive compensation	Merit awards	658.3226
658.32259	Employee stock ownership plans	New number	
658.4022	Work teams		658.3128
658.4058	Contracting out	New number	
658.4083	Protection of environment	New number	
658.409 3	Time management	Personal efficiency	
658.56	Product control, packaging; waste control and utilization	Product analysis	658.566
658.57	Research and development	Product improvement research	658.576
658.788	Expediting and tracing		658.7886
658.8102	Organization of sales force	Organization by area	658.8103
658.8102	Organization of sales force	Organization of sales force by product	658.8104
658.8102	Organization of sales force	Organization of sales force by type of customer	658.8105
658.83	Market research	Market study	658.835
658.84	Export marketing		658.848
658.87	Marketing channels	Auctions, fairs, markets, comprehensive works on marketing channels	658.84
658.87	Marketing channels	Managing producers' cooperatives	334.6068

Current Number	Current Topic	Old Topic/Comment	Old Number
658.87	Marketing channels	Comprehensive works on marketing channels	658.84
658.87	Marketing channels	Marketing through specific wholesale channels	658.86
658.87	Marketing channels	[Marketing channels] Management	381.1068
658.87	Marketing channels	Independent retail stores	658.8701
658.87	Marketing channels	Sideline stores	658.8704
658.87	Marketing channels	Branch stores	658.8706
658.87	Marketing channels	Consumer cooperatives	658.8707
658.87	Marketing channels	Variety stores	658.873
658.87	Marketing channels	General stores	658.874
658.87	Marketing channels	Specialty shops	658.875
658.87	Marketing channels	Single-line outlets	658.876
658.8702	Chain stores	Voluntary retail chains	658.8703
658.8705	Outlet stores	Discount stores that are outlet stores	658.879
658.872	Telemarketing and direct marketing	Direct-mail marketing, direct marketing, direct selling, multilevel marketing, pyramid marketing, telemarketing, television selling.	658.84
658.879	Discount stores	Supermarkets that are not predominantly food stores	658.878
659.1315	Industrial advertising	Advertising directed to vocational uses	
659.14	Advertising in electronic media	Advertising by broadcast media	

Current Number	Current Topic	Old Topic/Comment	Old Number
659.144	Advertising in digital media	New number	
659.19	Advertising specific kinds of organizations, products, services	Class ere advertising of specific kinds of organizations, products, services in a specific kind of medium	659.13
659.19	Advertising specific kinds of organizations, products, services	Advertising of specific kinds of organizations, product, services by a specific kind of advertising	659.131
659.19	Advertising specific kinds of organizations, products, services	Advertising of specific kinds of organizations, products, services in a specific electronic medium	659.14

660 Chemical Engineering Revisions

This is the last of the Divisions of the 600 Class that had any revisions in the 22nd edition, all quite minor except for two new numbers in the Schedules that were previously developed using Add instructions. Manufacturing (670 and 680) and Buildings (690) are unchanged, although there were minor changes in these Divisions in the 21st edition.

Table 11.6

Current Number	Current Topic	Old Topic/Comment	Old Number
660	**Chemical Engineering and Related Technologies**		
660.2844	Unit processes	Acylation, alkylation, aromatization, halogenation, hydroxyl addition and substitution	660.28441 to .28442

Current Number	Current Topic	Old Topic/Comment	Old Number
660.2844	Unit processes	Esterification, animation, diazotization, nitration, nitrosation, sulfonation, condensation	660.28444 to .28448
660.28443	Oxidation-reduction reaction (redox reaction)	New number	Add table
660.28449	Fermentation	New number	Add table
664.58	[Flavoring] Complex condiments	Composites	
664.65	[Special purpose food] Complete dishes	Composites	
666.328	[Pottery] Auxiliary techniques and procedures		666.44
669.2	Precious and group 3 metals	Precious and group 3B metals	
669.29	Group 3 metals	Group 3B metals	

Exercises in the Use of Class 600

Following are eight brief statements about books with which you can test your skills. Utilizing the Schedules, Tables, and Relative Index build classification numbers for each then check your results from those assigned by the Library of Congress found in the Appendix.

1. A work on child psychotherapy using the Adlerian approach.
2. A work on women's mental disorders.
3. A work on drug therapy and drug prescriptions in the United States.
4. A work on business mathematics.
5. A work on *Apollo* flights to the moon.
6. A work on a space flight mission to Mars.
7. A work on cancer of the kidneys.
8. A work on cancer of the colon and rectum.

Literature Cited

Dewey, Melvil. 1996. *Dewey Decimal Classification and Relative Index*. 21st ed. Albany, NY: Forest Press.

———. 2003. *Dewey Decimal Classification and Relative Index*. 22nd ed. Dublin, OH: OCLC Online Computer Library Center.

Jelinek, Marjorie. 1980. Twentieth Dewey: An Exercise in Prophecy. *Catalogue & Index* 58:1–2.

Kaltenbach, Margaret. 1968. Problems Associated with Presenting and Teaching the Schedules: Science (500) and Technology (600). In *The Dewey Decimal Classification: Outlines and Papers Presented at a Workshop on the Teaching of Classification*. New York: School of Library Science, Columbia University.

12

Class 700: The Arts; Fine and Decorative Arts

The Dewey Decimal Classification is used successfully by several large art libraries, although it is designed primarily as a comprehensive scheme for general collections. A well-known art librarian says:

> While other approaches to classification systems have been pioneered by art librarians in the United States and abroad, e.g., the faceted classification for fine arts devised by Peter Broxis and special systems prepared by other English art librarians, most art libraries in the United States use the Dewey decimal classification system (DDC) or the Library of Congress system (LC), or systems modified from the Dewey or LC systems. For example, the systems used in the libraries of the Metropolitan Museum of Art and the Art Institute of Chicago are derived from the notation principles used in Dewey. . . .
>
> Dewey remains a popular system in American libraries, and may be satisfactory in smaller art library collections where close classification is not considered an important factor.
>
> Neither system may be as successful as faceted classification systems in analyzing complex works. However, as Wolfgang Freitag has observed: "A detailed enumerative system, in spite of all its errors and shortcomings, will meet the practical requirements of libraries far better than the few principles and guidelines provided in a system of faceted classification." (Walker 1975, 452, 469)

The entire 700 class has been faulted for its fragmentation and overlapping, but criticisms tend to focus on the final two divisions (Hickey 1968, 34).

Note that "arts" does not mean the medical arts, the engineering arts, the agricultural arts, the domestic arts, the management arts, the industrial arts, or the building arts. But landscaping arts, architectural (building) arts, carving arts, arts in two dimensions, the photographic arts (even if highly technical as in the making of motion pictures), and the athletic arts are meant. This recitation begs the question: Does "art" have any meaning in the DDC?

Summary and Details of Class 700

700 The Arts; Fine and Decorative Arts

710 Civil and Landscape Art

720 Architecture

730 Plastic Arts; Sculpture

740 Drawing and Decorative Arts

750 Painting and Paintings

760 Graphic Arts; Printmaking and Prints

770 Photography, Photographs, Computer Art

780 Music

790 Recreational and Performing Arts

Division 700: The first Division is used for two separate Standard Subdivisions: the first (700.1 to 700.9) is designated for the arts in general, or to use when more than one type of art is discussed, and the other (701–708) is for fine arts, decorative arts, and iconography. Unusual notations are History and Description with Respect to Kinds of Persons used in place of Special Topics (704), which leaves 708 for public, in galleries and museums, and private collections of fine and decorative arts, contrary to the usual DDC practice. Impermanent collections and exhibits are separate in notation 707.4 under education and research. Iconography is in 704.9.

Division 710: There are no Standard Subdivisions in the first Section of this second Division, which means, of course, that such facets are not used for Civil and Landscape Art in general. Instead, the Division begins with Area Planning in the second Section (711). The rest of the Sections are devoted to landscaping. Landscape design is first (712) and is followed by the landscaping of roads

(713). The next four Sections cover specific elements of landscape architecture, which are water, woody plants, herbaceous plants, and structures that are found in 714 through 717. The Division finishes with landscape design of cemeteries (718) and natural landscapes (719).

Division 720: The third Division is reserved for architecture, which begins with architectural structure (721) and historical examples (722 to 724). The next four Sections are used for buildings and are organized by their use, which are public (725), religious (726), education research (727), and residential (728). The last Section deals with the accessories or decorations of structures (729).

Division 730: Sculpture is in the next Division, which has its Standard Subdivisions alone in the first Section (730.1 to 730.9), then continues through 735 beginning with materials, equipment, techniques, and forms of sculpture (731), then historical styles of sculpture conclude the subject (732–735). Related arts are found in 736–739 with the Standard Subdivisions for them in the first Section (730.01 730.09). The first of these arts is carving (736), which is followed by numismatics and sigillography (737), ceramics (738), and ending with artistic metalwork (739).

Division 740: Drawing is in the first three Sections with various types of decorative art completing the Division. There are no Standard Subdivisions for the Division as a whole, but many subjects begin with their own distinctive Standard Subdivisions. The Division begins with the second Section, 741, which is used for drawing in general. Aspects of drawing follow, which are perspective (742) and drawings organized by subject (743).

Antiques, the design of mass-produced items, the design of objects arranged historically, handicrafts, calligraphy, the design of heralds, decorative coatings, dioramas and similar displays, and floral arrangements are in the 745 Section. These are followed by weaving, lacemaking, tapestries, needlework and embroideries, textile dyeing and printing, fashion design, rugs and other household furnishings made of textiles (746). Interior decorating (747), various decorative uses of glass (748), and furniture and picture frames conclude the Division (749).

Division 750: Painting is found in this Division, and its Standard Subdivisions are in the first Section (750.1 to 750.8). However, the Historical, Geographic, Persons Treatment, usually 09, and Techniques, Procedures, Apparatus, Equipment, and Materials, ordinarily 028, are found in their own independent Sections, 759 and 751, respectively. This change allows enough notations to cover complexities of their subjects.

Facets of painting include aspect of color that is found in the third Section (752) and is followed by iconography, found in the next six Sections beginning with symbolism and similar subjects (753), genre paintings (754), and religion (755). Subjects of paintings are in 757 and 758, and the Division is concluded with Historical, Geographic, and Persons Treatment of paintings as discussed earlier.

Division 760: Graphic arts and methods of making prints are in this Division with Standard Subdivisions and Special Topics of graphic arts in the first Section (760.01–760.09) and Standard Subdivisions for printmaking (760.1–.8). Sections 761–767 are used for various methods of printmaking, including block printing, lithographic, serigraphy, tinting processes, etching and drypoint. Prints conclude the Division in 769.

Division 770: This Division is used for photography with its Standard Subdivisions in the first Section (770.1–.9) except for Techniques, Procedures, Apparatus, Equipment, Materials, usually in 028, in their own section (771). These are followed by photographic processes in 772–775. Computer art is in 776, with special kinds of photography, cinematography, video production, and similar activities found next in 778. Photographs conclude the Division (779). Section 777 is not used in this edition.

Division 780: The Standard Subdivisions for Music (780.1 to 780.9), and its relation to other subjects (780.0001–.0999) are in the first Section. The general aspects of music and its forms, or kinds of music, are next (781), followed by vocal music (782), and music for single voices other aspects of the musical voice (783). Instrumental music concludes the Division in notations 784 through 788, including ensembles, keyboard instruments, stringed and wind instruments.

As an option, composers and traditions of music may be classed in 789 rather than their usual location in 780 through 788.

Division 790: Recreation and performing arts are covered in the last Division, beginning with Standard Subdivisions of recreation (790.01 to 790.09), with recreational activities (790.1) and the general aspects of performing arts (790.2) in the first Section. Public performances, such as traveling shows (791.1), circuses (791.2), motion pictures (791.43), radio (791.44), television (791.45), puppet shows (791.5), pageants (791.6), and animal shows (791.8) are in the second Section and are followed by stage presentations (792).

Games are in the next Sections, which are indoor amusements (793), indoor games of skill (794), games of chance (795), and athletic and outdoor sports (796–797). Recreation and the Division end with fishing, hunting, and shooting (799).

The Number Building Process

A work on an exhibition in San Francisco displaying the history of fashion, architectural, and industrial design in the twentieth century is the example of number building in the 700 class. Notations for design in the Relative Index were mostly found under topics of engineering in the 620s, but it is also included the topics of elementary education (372.52) and the philosophy of design (124). Close to our subject matter is the number for design in the arts, 745.4, which is used for pure and applied design and decoration, which still does not fit this book. Checking further in the Relative Index, Fashion Design is found at 746.92 and industrial design at 745.2. Architectural design is at 729 but the classifier is cautioned to check in the Manual where we find under that number, "Use 729 only for general works that focus specifically on architectural design.... Use 729 for works on decoration only when the subject is being treated as an aspect of architectural decoration rather than as an art object in itself" (Dewey 2003, 1:149).

Reviewing all these possible base numbers, it appears that **745.2** may be the best choice, especially when the Schedules indicate that it represents industrial art and design, which would cover all three aspects of the work being classified.

Noting that the book is concerned only with the twentieth century, the next step is to add the notation that limits the work to this era. Checking the Schedules, no special instructions are found that will effect number building, so going to Table 1 under historical periods, the twentieth century is found at –0904, which resulted in the classification now **745.20904.**

Beside the twentieth century, an asterisk leads to an instruction at the bottom of the page directing the classifier to "Add as instructed under 0901–0905" (Dewey 2003, 1:211), where an Add Table indicates that –074 is the notation for exhibitions, which is added resulting in the number **745.20904074.**

Following the 074 notation are additional instructions to "add to 074 notation 4–9 from Table 2" (Dewey 2003, 1:210). Looking up San Francisco in Table 2 we find San Francisco at **79461.**

LC Classification: **745.2090407479461**

Glamour: fashion, industrial design, architecture, edited by Joseph Rosa and others.

DDC 22 Class 700 Revisions

The arts have been part of humankind's existence since people clothed themselves in furs and became hunters and gatherers. They etched pictures representing their world on the walls of caves and probably sang of their prowess and fears around the campfire. So one would think that there could be little new in these topics, but humankind does not stand still, even in the arts.

700–776 Fine and Decorative Arts Revisions

Out of thirty-seven changes in the Fine and Decorative Arts, seventeen, which is almost half, are new numbers. These include Japanese paper cutting and folding, sand sculpture, and drawing flowers and trees, none of which is new. But there is also new technology, such as digital cameras and photography, computer or digital art, and multimedia computer art. Following art details of the changes in 700 to 779.

Table 12.1

Current Number	Current Topic	Old Topic/ Comment	Old Number
700	**The Arts; Fine and Decorative Arts**		
704.085	History and description with respect to kinds of persons by kinship characteristics		704.043 to .046
704.083 to .084	History and description with respect to kinds of persons by age		704.05
704.086	History and description with respect to kinds of persons by miscellaneous social characteristics		704.06

Current Number	Current Topic	Old Topic/ Comment	Old Number
704.088	History and description with respect to kinds of persons by various occupational characteristics		704.09 to .87
704.943	Nature and still life		704.94963
704.943 43	[Still life] Flowers	New number	
725.13	Local government buildings	County and city government buildings	
726.5	Buildings associated with Christianity	Christian chapels	726.4
736.69	Schrimshaws	New number	
736.96	Sand sculpture	New number	
736.980 952	Paper cutting and folding of Japan	New number	
739.220 9	Historical, geographic, persons treatment		739.227
739.309	[Clocks] Historical, geographic, persons treatment		739.37
739.409	[Ironwork] Historical, geographic, persons treatment		739.47
741.924 3	[Drawing collections] 2000–2099	New number	
743.4	Drawing human figures	Draped figures	743.5
743.73	Drawing flowers	New number	
743.76	Drawing trees	New number	
745.409	[Design and decoration] Historical, geographic, persons treatment		745.44

Current Number	Current Topic	Old Topic/ Comment	Old Number
745.514	Woodburning (Pyrography)	New number	
745.594 16	[Handicrafts] Holidays	New number	
745.922 4	Western flower arrangements	Occidental compositions	
745.922 5	Asian flower arrangements	Oriental compositions	
746.447	Silk ribbon embroidery	New number	
747.09	[Interior decoration] Historical, geographic, persons treatment		747.2
748.209	[Glass] Historical, geographic, persons treatment		747.29
748.509	[Stained glass] Historical, geographic, persons treatment		747. 59
749.09	[Furniture] Historical, geographic, persons treatment		749.2
758.5	Plants	Agriculture	758.963
771.31	Specific makes of cameras that use file	Specific makes (brands) of cameras	
771.32	Specific types of cameras that use film	Specific types of cameras	
771.33	Digital cameras	New number	
775	Digital photography	New number	
776	Computer (Digital) art	New number	709.04
776.2	Graphics displayed on computer display devices	New number	

Current Number	Current Topic	Old Topic/ Comment	Old Number
776.4	Prints of computer graphics	New number	
776.6	Animation and video	New number	709.04
776.7	Multimedia computer art	New number	

780 Music Revisions

All but one of the changes in Music result from the elimination of Table 7. These revisions under Sacred Music (781.7) result when schedule notations replace those formerly drawn from Table 7, which had been used for adding subdivisions representing groups of persons.

Table 12.2

Current Number	Current Topic	Old Topic/Comment	Old Number
780	**Music**		
780.8	[Education, etc.] History and description of music with respect to kinds of persons		306.484208
781.711 to .719	Christian sacred music of specific denomination and sects	Notation 281–289 replaces notation 21–28 from Table 7 with the result that many numbers have been reused with new meanings	
781.74 to .79	Sacred music of other religions and sects	Notation 294–299 replaces notation 294–299 from Table 7 with the result that many numbers have been reused with new meanings	

Current Number	Current Topic	Old Topic/Comment	Old Number
782.322 1 to .322 9	Services of specific denominations	Notation 281–289 replaces notation 21–28 from Table 7 with the result that many numbers have been reused with new meanings	
782.34 to .39	Services of other specific religions and sects	Notation 294–299 replaces notation 294–299 from Table 7 with the result that many numbers have been reused with new meanings	

790 Recreation and Performing Arts Revisions

The major of changes under Recreational and Performing Arts (790) are new numbers, many for innovations in the sporting world, such as extreme sports and snowboarding. Other interesting revisions include the relocations of crossword-puzzle dictionaries from the language class (400), and weightlifting for bodybuilding contests has been separated from the care of the physique under the Management of Personal and Family Life (646.7)

Table 12.3

Current Number	Current Topic	Old Topic/Comment	Old Number
790	**Recreational and Performing Arts**		
790.019	Psychological principles		790.0132
790.1	General kinds of recreational activities	Recreational activities	
790.1	General kinds of recreational activities	Leisure	790.0135
790.18	Travel and tourism	New number	
791.4334	Animated films	New number	
792.38	Panto	New number	

Current Number	Current Topic	Old Topic/Comment	Old Number
793.73203	Crossword-puzzle dictionaries		413.1 and 420–490 + –31 in Table 4
794.733	Pool (American pocket billiards)	New number	
796.046	Extreme sports	New number	
796.41	Weight lifting	Body building for contests	646.75
796.5224	Sport climbing	New number	
796.67	Street luge racing	New number	
796.815	Oriental martial arts forms	Jujitsu and related martial arts forms	
796.939	Snowboarding	New number	
799.16	Saltwater fishing	In specific bodies of water	799.166
799.1609163 to .1609167	Saltwater fishing in specific bodies of water		799.166

Exercises in the Use of Class 700

Utilizing the brief descriptions of the following works, build classifications for each title, applying all of the number building tools discussed in this manual. Verify your results by checking against the classifications assigned by the Library of Congress found in "Answers to the Exercises" in the Appendix.

1. A work on the philosophy of dance.
2. A work on instruction and study of the bass guitar.
3. A work on American baseball players and teams.
4. A work on twentieth-century art deco architecture in New York.
5. A work on depression era art deco decorative arts.

6. A work on an exhibition of German expressionist prints in Milwaukee, Wisconsin.
7. Biographies of television comedians.
8. A work on drawing techniques of Italian art.

Literature Cited

Dewey, Melvil. 2003. *Dewey Decimal Classification and Relative Index.* 22nd ed. Dublin, OH: OCLC Online Computer Library Center.

Hickey, Doralyn J. 1968. Problems Associated with Presenting and Teaching the Schedules: Philosophy (100); Religion (200); and the Fine Arts (700). In *The Dewey Decimal Classification: Outlines and Papers Presented at a Workshop on the Teaching of Classification.* New York: School of Library Science, Columbia University.

Walker, William B. 1975. Art Books and Periodicals: Dewey and LC. *Library Trends* 23 (3):452, 469.

13

Class 800: Literature (Belles-Lettres) and Rhetoric

We have been told that Dewey's early contributions to the principle of faceting were evident in language (the 400s), literature (the 800s), and history and geography (the 900s) (Batty 1976, 212). Class 800 intricacies multiplied through the years, showing substantive changes, particularly in its auxiliary tables, and instructional changes in the Schedules. Most criticisms address its formal presentation rather than its content. However, a critique of its assumptions concerning literary forms appeared at the time *DDC* 18 was published.

The most common problems are the following:

1. Problems encountered by the catalogers:
   - (a) the difficulty in application caused by the lack of clear, workable definitions of the forms;
   - (b) the problems of treating works of mixed forms or uncertain forms; and
   - (c) some of the forms that are questionable in their nature as literary forms.
2. Problems encountered by the users:
   - (a) inconvenience resulting from the separation and scattering of works written by and about single authors and
   - (b) confusion caused by the seemingly arbitrary decisions made by the catalogers as regards the forms of certain literary works. (Chan 1971, 458)

Bloomberg and Weber give special attention to the analysis of long DDC class 800 numbers.

> This approach is most appropriate in this class because of the many different possible subdivisions and elements represented in each number. These elements include the base number for the language, a possible number for literary form (poetry or drama, for example), a possible number for the time or period of the work, a number for collections or history and criticism, and, finally, a number for specific themes. (Bloomberg and Weber 1976, 151)

Table 3 (Subdivisions of Individual Literatures) made its first appearance in *DDC* 18 (1971). Not surprisingly, it proved hard to apply, although it was a move toward synthetic faceting.

> In theory, synthesizing a literature number was quite simple. The classifier found a base number for a literature form the Schedules, turned to Table 3 and found the appropriate number there. If necessary, the Schedules could be checked again for a period number for the literature in question. In practice, steps one and three were not difficult, but the second step was. The classifier had to choose from a variety of citation orders, depending, of course, upon work being classified.. . . Directions were correspondingly complex, and all of the above considerations had to be kept in mind as one solved the puzzle. (Comaromi 1976, 587–588)

Still, the Comaromi survey showed that 89 percent of the classifiers claimed to handle literature according to the prescribed method (Michael 1976, 54). *DDC* 19 polished up its instructions. As one reviewer says:

> Table 3 has comprehensible instructions at last, and has sprouted a sub-table which appears to provide even more scope for synthesis than in *DDC* 18. It is intriguing to reflect that DDC still goes overboard for far more synthesis in the horribly named "belle-lettristic arts" than in any other area: is it really logical to be able to say "criticism of the treatment of gardens in 19th century French drama written in Belgium" but to be unable to say "employment services for the mentally ill"? (Butcher 1979, 7)

By "logical" we take the critic to mean reasonable. And, of course, it is not reasonable that intense analysis of works of the imagination—works that reveal an unreal world, do not forget—is done when intense analysis of the real world is not.

It is important that the classifiers using DDC remember the application of the Tables: 3-A is for individual authors, 3-B for more than one author, and 3-C for a topic in literature or literature focused on specific persons. The Manual provides guidance to novices still learning how to handle literature.

Summary and Details of Class 800

800 Literature (Belles-Lettres) and Rhetoric

810 American Literature in English

820 English and Old English (Anglo-Saxon) Literatures

830 Literatures of Germanic Languages; German Literature

840 Literatures of Romance Languages; French Literature

850 Literatures of Italian, Sardinian, Dalmatian, Romanian, Rhaeto-Romanic Languages; Italian Literature

860 Literatures of Spanish and Portuguese Languages; Spanish Literature

870 Literatures of Italic Languages; Latin Literature

880 Literatures of Hellenic Languages; Classical Greek Literature

890 Literatures of other Specific Languages and Language Families

Division 800: The first Section is used for the Standard Subdivisions of literature in general (801–807). Also included in this "neutral" location are literary texts from more than two literatures in 808, replacing History and Description with Respect to Kinds of Persons usually found in that notation, but which has been relocated to 808.008. Also found in this Section are the History, Description, and Critical Appraisal of More than Two Literatures found in 809.

Divisions 810–880: The remaining Sections are for literature in the various languages, with American literature in English (810), English and Old English (820) leading the groups of literatures. German literature in its specific forms (831–838) and other Germanic literatures (839) in the fourth Section. Then specific forms of French literature are in 841 to 848, and Occitan, Catalan, Franco-Provençal conclude the next Section (849). Specific forms of Italian literature are found in 851–858, with Romanian and Rhaeto-Romanic literatures in 859 concluding the Section. Spanish literature's specific forms are in 861 to 868 followed by Portuguese literature (869) concluding the Section.

The ancient languages are in the next two Sections. These are Latin and Italic literatures in the 870s, classical Greek or Hellenic literatures in 881–888. Modern Greek literature is added to the mixture and concludes the Section (889).

Division 890: The last Division covers all other literatures of the world. These include East Indo-European and Celtic literatures (891); Afro-Asiatic literatures (892); Non-Semitic Afro-Asiatic literatures (893); Altaic, Uralic, Hyberborean, and Dravidian literatures (894); East and Southeast Asian and Sino-Tibetan literatures (895); African literatures (896); literatures in the North American (897) and South American native languages (898). The Division is concluded with non-Austronesian literatures of Oceania, Austronesian, and any other literatures of specific languages (899).

The Number Building Process

A work that is a historical look at crime fiction in English is the example of number building in the 800 Class. Being a work in English, but not American, the base number for this classification would be **82.** Instructions direct the classifier to consult Table 3, in this case of multiple authors, Table 3B. History, description, and critical appraisal of works is found at 09, which when added to our base number results in **820.9.**

Instructions in Table 3B direct the classifier to Table 3C when the work be classified is about a particular subject. This work focuses on crime, which is found under Social Problems and Services at **3556.**

LC Classification: **820.93556**

Victorian crime, madness, and sensation, edited by Andrew Maunder and Grace Moore.

DDC 22 Class 800 Revisions

Out of the thirty-nine changes in the 800 Class, twenty-seven are new numbers, all but two of which are in the 890 Section, with the majority expanding the native American literatures (897), which is similar to expansions in the 400 Class (Language).

A less dramatic but significant change is found in the second Period Table for 810.1 to 818, Subdivisions of American literature in English which is now "for countries of North, Middle, and South America other than Canada, for comprehensive works on American literature in English" (Dewey 2003, 3:774). Previously this Table was used for the United States alone.

There have also been several revisions in Class 839, Other Germanic Literatures. Details of these and other changes follow.

Table 13.1

Current Number	Current Topic	Old Topic/Comment	Old Number
800	**Literature (Belles-Lettres and Rhetoric)**		
808.0428	Rhetoric in English for those whose native language is different	New number	
808.805 to .879	Literature for and by persons of general and larger western ethnic, and national groups	Literature for and by persons of general and larger western racial, ethnic, and national groups	808.803. to .879
839.5	North Germanic literatures (Nordic literatures)	Scandinavian (North Germanic) literatures	
839.5	North Germanic literatures (Nordic literatures)	Comprehensive works on West Scandinavian literatures	839.6
839.5	North Germanic literatures (Nordic literatures)	Comprehensive works on modern West Scandinavian literatures	839.69
839.6	Old Norse (Old Icelandic), Icelandic, Faeroese literatures	West Scandinavian literatures; Old Norse (Old Icelandic)	
839.82	Norwegian literature	Norwegian (Bokmal, Riksmal) literature	
839.82	Norwegian literature	New Norwegian, Landsmal literature	839.83
849	Occitan, Catalan, Franco-Provençal literatures	Provençal (Langue d'oc), Franco-Provençal, Catalan literatures	
891.469	Konkani literature	New number	
894.347	Kyrgyz	Kirghiz	
895.634	Bunka-Bunsei period (1804–1829)		895.64

Current Number	Current Topic	Old Topic/Comment	Old Number
896.3976	Venda (Tshivenda)	New number	
896.3989	Ndebele (South Africa)	New number	
897.26	Navajo	New number	
897.28	Haida	New number	
897.323	Cree	New number	
897.333	Ojibwa, Chippewa	New number	
897.422	Cakchikel	New number	
897.423	Quiché	New number	
897.4287	Tzotzil	New number	
897.4542	Yaqui	New number	
897.4544	Huichol	New number	
897.4552	Tohono O'Odham	New number	
897.45529	Akimel O'Odham	New number	
897.4574	Shoshoni	New number	
897.458	Hopi	New number	
897.492	Kiowa	New number	
897.494	Tewa	New number	
897.5243	Dakota	New number	
897.557	Cherokee	New number	
897.68	Zapotec	New number	
897.83	San Blas Kuna	New number	
897.933	Pawnee	New number	
897.9435	Kalispel, Pend d'Oreille	New number	
897.994	Zuni	New number	
898.372	Shuar	Jivaroa proper	
898.72	Maqudungun (Mapuche)	New number	

Exercises in the Use of Class 800

Utilizing the Schedules, Tables, and Relative Index, assign classification numbers for the following books. Check your work against the classifications assigned by the Library of Congress found in "Answers to the Exercises" in the Appendix.

1. A late-twentieth-century American work of fiction.
2. A work of African fiction in English.
3. A critical work on twentieth-century American poetry.
4. A work of criticism on classical Greek poetry.
5. A translated work of rhetoric by Aristotle.
6. A work of French composition.
7. A twenty-first-century work of English fiction.

Literature Cited

Batty, David C. 1976. Library Classification One Hundred Years after Dewey. In *Major Classification Systems: The Dewey Centennial.* Urbana-Champaign: University of Illinois Graduate School of Library Science.

Bloomberg, Marty, and Hans Weber. 1976. *An Introduction to Classification and Number Building in Dewey.* Edited by John Philip Immroth. Littleton, CO: Libraries Unlimited.

Butcher, Peter. 1979. Dewey? We Sure do! *Catalogue & Index* 55:7.

Chan, Lois Mai. 1971. "The Form Distinction in the 800 Class of the Dewey Decimal Scheme." *Library Resources & Technical Services* 15 (4):458.

Comaromi, John Phillip. 1976. *The Eighteen Editions of the Dewey Decimal Classification.* Albany, NY: Lake Placid Education Foundation.

Dewey, Melvil. 2003. *Dewey Decimal Classification and Relative Index.* 22nd ed. Dublin, OH: OCLC Online Computer Library Center.

Michael, Mary Ellen. 1976. Summary of a Survey of the Use of the Dewey Decimal Classification in the United State and Canada. In *Major Classification Systems: The Dewey Centennial.* Urbana-Champaign: University of Illinois Graduate School of Library Science.

14

Class 900: History, Geography, and Auxiliary Disciplines

One might think that because history cannot change there would not be much change in this Class besides those updates required by the constant evolution (sometimes revolution) of governments as leaders are replaced and wars started and halted. But history can be transformed to the extent that changing philosophies can interpret the past differently. Differences also occur because the existence of governments is at the whim of humankind's aggressions and desires. Thus, a country can emerge from another (as with the former Soviet states); others can be merged into one following a war. Consequently, the 900 Class will always change and evolve and drive classifiers mad from their constant need to revise their collections.

Summary and Details of Class 900

900 History, Geography, and Auxiliary Disciplines

910 Geography and Travel

920 Biography, Genealogy, Insignia

930 History of Ancient World to ca. 499

940 History of Europe; Western Europe

950 History of Asia; Orient; Far East

960 History of Africa

970 History of North America

980 History of South America

990 History of Other Parts of World, of Extraterrestrial Worlds; Pacific Ocean Islands

Division 900: In the mnemonic manner found in the Schedules, the last Class is used for geography and history of places, as the Standard Subdivision for the history of topics is always found in 09. The Standard Subdivisions for the Class, as usual, are found in the first Section (900.1–900.9) The Standard Subdivisions of history alone are found in 901, 903, and 905–908. The customary locations for Special Topics (904) is used for adventure and collected of accounts of events. The notation for history of a topic, normally 09 and in this Section 909, is used for World History.

Division 910: Geography and travel are in the second Division, with physical geography in 910.02. Standard Subdivisions are next (910.2 to 910.9) with the Special Topics of Accounts of Travel and Facilities for Travelers in 910.4. The next Section is used for Historical Geography (911) and is followed by atlases, maps, and charts of the earth and extraterrestrial areas (912). Geography and travel in specific places are arranged like Table 2 and conclude the Division (913–919).

Division 920: Like the entire 900 Class, this Division, used for biographies, mirrors the Standard Subdivisions, in this example, the 092 or persons treatment. The Standard Subdivisions of the discipline of biography are found at the top of the Division in double zeros 001–009, and the single zero slots 01–09 are reserved for collections of biographies.

Biographies of certain types of people extend from 920.1 through 928 using Table 2 notations to distinguish the types of persons. The last Section is devoted to genealogies, awards, seals, and identifications (929) and concludes the Division.

Divisions 930–990: The rest of the Class is used for history and, as is predictable, follows the country numbers found in Table 2. The ancient world is found in 930, and the modern world and extraterrestrial worlds in 940–990, which are Europe (940), Asia (950), Africa (960), North America (970), and South America (980). The 990s are the notations for the rest of the world and extraterrestrial areas, which are as follows: New Zealand (993), Australia (994), Pacific and Atlantic islands (995–997), polar areas (998), and extraterrestrial worlds (999).

The Number Building Process

A work on society and culture in French-speaking countries is the number building example for the 900 Class. Because this book does not focus only on the culture in France but the French culture found throughout the world, civilization in the general sense is the correct classification to use, which is **909** for the base number.

The next step is to add the notation restricting the subject to only the French-speaking cultures, which is a Standard Subdivision of the topic. "Specific Areas, Regions, Places in General" is found at .091 to .099. Instructions indicate, "Add to base number 909.09 the numbers following –1 in notation 11–19 from Table 2" (Dewey 2003, 3:834).

The Summary in this part of Table 2 indicates that seventeen Socioeconomic regions, and eighteen other kinds of terrestrial regions are the most likely places to find the notations that are required. Regions Where Specific Languages Predominate is found at 175, the very subdivision that is needed. As instructed, only the numbers following the "1" are added to the classification, resulting in **909.0975.**

Instructions found at 175 direct the classifier to "Add to base number –175 notation 05-99 from Table 6" (Dewey 2003, 1:227). Referring to Table 5, French is found at **–41**, which are the final numbers added.

LC Classification: 909.097541

Contemporary French cultures and societies, edited by Frédéric Royall.

DDC 22 Class 900 Revisions

The expression "nothing is new in the world" is very applicable to this Class of history and geography. Although the physical world has been in its current existence for eons, the political changes, or what man has wrought, are constant because it is the nature of humankind to want change, whether for good or bad. Of the 439 changes in Edition 22, 316 are new numbers, which is more than 70 percent.

Another change is that under wars, "Operations" has become "Military operations," and "Naval history" has become "Naval operations."

910–920 Geography, Travel, and Biography Revisions

There have been a number of modifications of the Add Table for 913 to 919. This Table is more than three pages long and is the method for adding all facets to geography and travel organized by place.

Table 14.1

Current Number	Current Topic	Old Topic/Comment	Old Number
913–919 Add Table			
–06	Facilities for travelers	New number	
–06	Facilities for travelers	Interdisciplinary and descriptive works on lodging for temporary residents, hotels, motels, inns in specific locations	647.943 to .949
–062	Resorts	New number	
–062	Resorts	Interdisciplinary and descriptive works on lodging for resorts in specific locations	647.943 to .949
–064	Bed and breakfast accommodations	New number	
–064	Bed and breakfast accommodations	Interdisciplinary and descriptive works on lodging for Bed and breakfast accommodations in specific locations	647.943 to .949
–066	Hostels	New number	
–066	Hostels	Interdisciplinary and descriptive works on lodging for Hostels in specific locations	647.943 to .949
–068	Campsites	New number	
–068	Campsites	Interdisciplinary and descriptive works on lodging for Campsites in specific locations	647.943 to .949

A major change under geography and travel, and one requested by DDC users, is the facilities for travelers being moved from 647.94 under home economics to 910.4 under the notations for Special Topics. Road maps were also moved from transportation by road (388.102 23) to 912 under the heading Graphic Representations of Surface of Earth and of Extraterrestrial Worlds.

There was only one change under the topics of biography, heraldry, and genealogy.

Table 14.2

New Number	New Topic	Old Topic/Comment	Old Number
900	**History, Geography and Auxiliary Disciplines**		
910.4	Accounts of travel and facilities for travelers	Account of travel	
910.46	Facilities for travelers	New number	
910.46	Facilities for travelers	Interdisciplinary and descriptive works on lodging for temporary residents, hotels, inns, motels	647.94
910.46	Facilities for travelers	Directories of lodging for temporary residents	647.94025
910.4609	[Facilities for travelers] Historical and persons treatment	New number	
910.462	Resorts	New number	647.94
910.46209	[Resorts] Historical and persons treatment	New number	
910.464	Bed and Breakfast accommodations	New number	647.94
910.46409	[Bed and Breakfast accommodations] Historical and persons treatment	New number	
910.466	Hostels	New number	647.94
910.46609	[Hostels] Historical and persons treatment	New number	

New Number	New Topic	Old Topic/Comment	Old Number
910.468	Campsites	New number	647.94
910.46809	[Campsites] Historical and persons treatment	New number	
912	Graphic representations of surface of earth and of extraterrestrial worlds	Road maps	388.10223
920.009	Historical, geographic, persons treatment of biography; general collections of biography by period, region, group	General collections of biography by period, region, group	

930 History of Ancient World

General early history to ca. 499 A.D., the Middle East to 640 A.D., and North Africa have new numbers for very old periods. Also, the dates under the ancient history of Italy have been modified, and dates have been added to the Black Sea area. Finally, Ethiopia to 500 has been changed to Nubia to 500.

Table 14.3

Current Number	Current Topic	Old Topic/Comment	Old Number
930	**History of Ancient World**		
930.1	Archaeology	Early history to 4000 B.C.	930.2
930.15	Copper and Bronze Age	3999–1000 B.D.	930.3
930.16	Iron Age	999–1 B.C.	930.4
936.01	Early history to ca. 1000 B.C.	New number	
936.02	Ca. 1000–ca. 200 B.C.	New number	
936.03	Ca. 200 B.C.–ca. 499 A.D.	New number	

Current Number	Current Topic	Old Topic/Comment	Old Number
937	**Italy, Ancient History**		
937.01	Early history to 510 B.C.	Earliest period and Roman Kingdom, to ca. 500 B.C.	
937.02	Roman Republic, 51–31 B.C.	Roman Republic, ca. 500–31 B.C.	
937.03	Unification, 510–264 B.C.	Unification, ca. 500–264 B.C.	
939.4	**Middle East to 640**		
939.401	Early to ca. 1900 B.C.	New number	
939.402	Babylonian and Assyrian Empires, ca. 1900–539 B.C.	New number	
939.403	Persian Empire, 539–332 B.C.	New number	
939.404	Hellenistic period, 332–30 B.C.	New number	
939.405	Roman period, 30 B.C.–ca. 640 A.D.	New number	
939.5	**Black Sea and Caucasus Regions to 640**		
939.51	Scythia to 640	Scythia	
939.55	Armenia to 640	Armenia	
939.7	**North Africa to ca. 640**		
939.701	Early history to ca. 800 B.C.	New number	
939.702	Carthaginian period, ca. 800–146 B.C.	New number	
939.703	Roman period, 146 B.C–ca. 640 A.D.	New number	
939.78	Nubia to 500	Ethiopia to 500	

940 History of Europe

Edition 22 has major revisions in the Division for Europe, more than 40 percent of the changes for the entire 400 Class. A large number of those changes were new numbers for various aspects of WWI and WWII, many of which are used for the subdivisions by place, and notations for the Holocaust under WWII were greatly expanded.

Seventeenth- and eighteenth-century Europe were expanded with new numbers, as were the early history to 1880 notations for areas in Ireland. Germany has new numbers for historic periods, as do Austria and Lichtenstein.

Table 14.4

Current Number	Current Topic	Old Topic/Comment	Old Number
940	**History of Europe**		
940.2523	1648–1688	New number	
940.2526	1701–1715	War of Spanish Succession, 1701–1714	
940.2531	1715–1740	New number	
940.2533	1748–1756	New number	
940.2535	1763–1789	New number	
940.2714	Congress of Vienna	New number	
940.3 to .4	**World War I, 1914–1918**		
940.3224 to .3229	[Allies]Treatment by continent, country, locality	New number	
940.3244 to .3249	[Central Powers] Treatment by continent, country, locality	New number	
940.3254 to .3259	[Neutrals] Treatment by continent, country, locality	New number	
940.4124 to .4129	[Allies military] Treatment by continent, country, locality	New number	

Current Number	Current Topic	Old Topic/Comment	Old Number
940.4134 to .4139	[Central Powers Military] Treatment by continent, country, locality	New number	
940.4144	Western front		940.4143
940.4147	Eastern front		940.4143
940.425	1915, Eastern front	1915, Eastern Europe	
940.45134 to .45139	[Submarine warfare, Allied] Treatment by continent, country, locality	New number	
940.53	**World War II, 1939–1945**		
940.531	Social, political, economic history; Holocaust	Social, political, economic history	
940.5318	Holocaust	With respect to Jews	940. 531808 9924
940.53181	General topics of Holocaust	New number	
940.531811	Causes	New number	
940.531813	Economic history	New number	
940.5318132	Actions against business and property	New number	
940.5318134	Forced labor	New number	
940.531814	Consequences	New number	
940.5318142	Emigration of Jews	New number	
940.5318144	Indemnification, restitution of confiscated /stolen property	New number	
940.531818	Holocaust denial	New number	

Current Number	Current Topic	Old Topic/Comment	Old Number
940.53183	Resistance movements and rescue operations	New number	
940.531832	Resistance movements	New number	
940.531835	Rescue operations	New number	
940.53184	Specific events	New number	
940.531842	Events of 1933–1938	New number	
940.531844	Events of 1939–1945	New number	
940.5318445	Babi Yar Massacre	New number	
940.531846	Events of 1945	New number	
940.53185	Ghettos and extermination camps by Axis Powers	New number	940.531 7094
940.531853 to .531859	Specific ghettos and extermination camps	New number	940.531743 to .531749
940.53186	Commemorations and memorials	New number	
940.531862	Commemorations	New number	
940.531864	Memorials	New number	
940.53187	Welfare services to Holocaust victims	New number	362.87
940.5322	Diplomatic history, Allies	New number	
940.53224 to .53229	Treatment by continent, country, locality	New number	
940.53244 to .53249	[Diplomatic history, Axis] Treatment by continent, country, locality	New number	
940.53254 to .53259	[Diplomatic history, Neutrals] Treatment by continent, country, locality	New number	
940.5332	Allies	United Nations	

Current Number	Current Topic	Old Topic/Comment	Old Number
940.5338	Countries occupied by Allies	Occupied by United Nations	
940.5404	Ethnic minorities in troops	Racial minorities as troops	
940.5412	Military units of Allies	Units of United Nations	
940.54124 to .54129	[Allies military] Treatment by continent, country, locality	New number	
940.54134 to .54139	[Axis military] Treatment by continent, country, locality	New number	
940.5423	African theater	Middle East and African theaters	
940.5424	Middle East theater	New number	940.5423
940.5425	East and South Asian theaters	New number	
940.54251 to .54252	Battles in China, Korea, Japan, adjacent areas	New number	
940.54259	Southeast Asian theater	New number	
940.54293	Atlantic Ocean	New number	
940.54434 to .544349	[Air bases] Treatment by continent, country, locality	New number	
940.54654 to .54659	[Monuments and Cemeteries] Treatment by continent, country, locality	New number	
940.54674 to .54679	Rolls/lists of honor, dead	New number	

Current Number	Current Topic	Old Topic/Comment	Old Number
940.54724 to .54729	[POWs; Medical and social services] Treatment by continent, country, locality	New number	
940.54814 to .54819	[Personal narratives, Allies] Treatment by continent, country, locality	New number	
940.54824 to .54829	[Personal narratives, Axis] Treatment by continent, country, locality	New number	
940.54834 to .54839	[Military life, Allies] Treatment by continent, country, locality	New number	
940.54844 to .54849	[Military life, Axis] Treatment by continent, country, locality	New number	
940.5094 to .5099	[Unconventional warfare] Treatment by continent, country, locality	New number	
940.54864 to .54869	[Unconventional warfare, Allies] Treatment by continent, country, locality	New number	
940.54874 to .54879	[Unconventional warfare, Axis] Treatment by continent, country, locality	New number	
940.548864 to .548869	[Propaganda, Allies] Treatment by continent, country, locality	New number	

Current Number	Current Topic	Old Topic/Comment	Old Number
940.548874 to .548879	[Propaganda, Axis] Treatment by continent, country, locality	New number	
941	**British Isles**		
941.701-.707	[Republic of Ireland] Early history to 1800	New number	
941.801 to .807	[Leinster] Early history to 1800	New number	
941.901 to .907	[Munster] Early history to 1800	New number	
943	**Central Europe: Germany**		
943.024	1138–1198	Period of Hohenstaufen dynasty, 1138–1254	
943.026	1273–1346	1273–1378	
943.027	1346–1438	Reign of Charles IV, 1346–1378	943.026
943.054	Period of 1st and 2nd Silesian Wars, 1740–1745	1st Silesian War, 1740–1742	943.053
943.074	Revolution of 1848–1849	New number	943.076
943.083	Reign of William I, 1871–1888	Comprehensive works on admin. of Otto von Bismarck, 1862–1890	932.081
943.0849	Period of WWI, 1914–1918	New number	
943.0851	Revolution of 1918	New number	
943.0862	1933–1939	New number	
943.0864	Period of WWII, 1939–1945	New number	
943.087	1945–1990	1945–1999	

Current Number	Current Topic	Old Topic/Comment	Old Number
943.0875	Administration of Konrad Adenauer, 1949–1962	1950–1959	
943.0875	Administration of Konrad Adenauer, 1949–1962	1960–1962	943.0876
943.0876	1962–1969	1960–1969	
943.0877	1969–1982	1970–1979	
943.0877	1969–1982	1980–1982	943.0878
943.0878	1982–1990	1980–1989	
943.0881	Later half of admin. of Helmut Kohl, 1990–1998	New number	943.0879
943.0882	Admin. of Gerhard Schroder	New number	
943.0882	Admin. of Gerhard Schroder	1998–1999	943.0879
943.1	**NE Germany**		
943.101 to .107	Early history to 1866	New number	
943.108	1866–	New number	
943.1081 to .1086	1866–1945	New number	
943.1087	Period of East Germany, 1945–1990	1945–1999	
943.10874	1945–1949	New number	
943.10875	Admin. of Walter Ulbricht, 1949–1971	New number	
943.10875	Admin. of Walter Ulbricht, 1949–1971	1960–1969	943.10876
943.10875	Admin. of Walter Ulbricht, 1949–1971	1970–1971	943.10877
943.10877	Admin. of Erich Honecker, 1971–1989	New number	

Current Number	Current Topic	Old Topic/Comment	Old Number
943.10877	Admin. of Erich Honecker, 1971–1989	1980–1989	943.10878
943.10879	1989–1990	New number	
943.1088	Period as part of Fed. Republic, 1990–	New number	
943.10881	1990–1998	New number	943.10879
943.10882	1998–	New number	
943.10882	1998–	1998–1999	943.10879
943.6	**Austria and Lichtenstein**		
943.602	Medieval period, 476–1526	Medieval period, 481–1500	
943.6022	476–976	476–481	936.3
943.6025	1273–1526	1500–1526	943.603
943.6031	1526–1740	New number	
943.6032	1740–1815	New number	
943.604	1815–1918	1815–1919	
943.6044	Austro–Hungarian Monarchy, 1867–1918	Austro–Hungarian Monarchy, 1867–1919	
943.60441	1867–1914	New number	
943.60442	WWI, 1914–1918	New number	
943.605	1918–	1919–	
943.6051	1st Republic, 1918–1938	Period of Republic, 1919–1938	
943.60511	1918–1933	New number	
943.60511	1918–1933	1918–1919	943.6044
943.60512	1933–1938	New number	
943.60532	1955–1970	New number	
943.60533	1970–1983	New number	
943.60534	1983–1999	New number	

Current Number	Current Topic	Old Topic/Comment	Old Number
943.60535	2000–	New number	
943.648	Liechtenstein	Period 476–481	936.3
943.7	**Czech Republic and Slovakia**		
943.7102	Czech Republic	Kingdom of Bohemia	943.702
944	**France and Monaco**		
944.0142	Reign of Charlemagne, 768–814	New number	
944.9	Provence–Côte d'Azur, Monaco, Corsica	Southeastern France and Monaco; Provence region	
945	**Italy and Adjacent areas**		
945.8501	Malta, early to 1530	New number	
945.8502	Knights of Malta, 1530–1798	New number	
945.8503	1798–1964	New number	
945.8504	1964–	New number	
948	**Scandinavia**		
948.02	Medieval period, ca. 800–1523	Period of migration and conquest, 800–1387	
948.022	Viking period, ca. 800–ca. 1050	Viking period, ca. 800–ca. 1066	
948.023	Ca. 1050–1387	1050–1066	948.022
948.04	1523–1814	1648–1792	948.05
948.04	1523–1814	1792–1814	948.06
948.05	1814–1905		948.07
948.06	1905–1999		948.08
948.061	1905–1939	New number	

Current Number	Current Topic	Old Topic/Comment	Old Number
948.062	1940–1945	New number	
948.063	1945–1969	New number	
948.064	1970–1999	New number	
948.07	2000–		948.09
948.1	**Norway**		
948.101	Early to 1536	1387–1536; Union of Kalmar, 1397–1523	948.102
948.102	Union with Denmark, 1536–1814	Union with Denmark, 1387–1814	
948.1043	1945–1969	New number	
948.1043	1945–1969	1945–1959	948.1045
948.1043	1945–1969	1960–1969	948.1046
948.1044	1970–1999	New number	
948.1044	1970–1999	1970–1979	948.1047
948.1044	1970–1999	1980–1989	948.1048
948.1044	1970–1999	1990–1999	948.1049
948.5	**Sweden**		
948.5014	Viking period, ca. 800–ca. 1050	Viking period, ca. 800–ca. 1060	
948.5018	Ca. 1050–1523	Ca. 1050–1060	948.5014
948.503	1523–1809	1654–1818	
948.5032	Period of Vasa, 1523–1611	New number	948.502
948.5034	Age of greatness, 1611–1718	New number	
948.5036	Age of Freedom, 1718–1772	New number	
948.5038	Gustavian Period, 1772–1809	New number	
948.504	1809–1905	1809–1818	948.503
948.5053	1945–1969	New number	

Current Number	Current Topic	Old Topic/Comment	Old Number
948.5053	1945–1969	1945–1959	948.5055
948.5053	1945–1969	1960–1969	948–5056
948.5054	1970–1999	New number	
948.5054	1970–1999	1970–1979	948.5057
948.5054	1970–1999	1980–1989	948.5058
948.5054	1970–1999	1990–1999	948.5059
948.9	**Denmark and Finland**		
948.9014	Vikings, ca. 800–ca. 1050	1047–ca. 1050	948.9015
948.9015	Ca. 1050–1387	1047–1387	
948.902	Union with Norway and Sweden, 1387–1536	1523–1536	948.903
948.903	Union with Norway, 1536–1814	Union with Norway, 1523–1814	
948.9053	1945–1969	1945–1959	948.9055
948.9053	1945–1969	1960–1969	948.9056
948.9054	1970–1999	1970–1979	948.9057
948.9054	1970–1999	1980–1989	948.9058
948.9054	1970–1999	1990–1999	948.9059
949.12	**Iceland**		
949.1203	1550–1874	1848–1874	949.1204
949.1204	Period of Governors, 1874–1904	Modern period, 1848–1940	
949.1205	1904–1999	1904–1940	949.1204
949.1206	2000–	New number	
949.1206	2000–	Period of Republic, 1944–	949.1205

Current Number	Current Topic	Old Topic/Comment	Old Number
949.7	**Serbia, Montenegro, Croatia, Slovenia, Bosnia and Hercegovina, Macedonia**		
949.702	Yugoslavia, 1918–1991		949.7103

950 History of Asia

All but six of the seventy changes in the history of Asia are new numbers. However, two major parts of this area, China and Japan, do not include any changes. Hong Kong and Macau have new numbers for historic periods, and Cambodia's numbers for historic periods have been modified and four new numbers added.

Table 14.5

Current Number	Current Topic	Old Topic/Comment	Old Number
950	**History of Asia; Orient; Far East**		
950.21	1162–1227	New number	
950.22	1227–1294	New number	
950.23	1294–1336	New number	
950.24	1336–1405	New number	
950.25	1405–1480	New number	
951.25	**Hong Kong**		
951.2504	Period as a British dependency, 1843–1997	Period as a British dependency, 1843–	
951.2505	1945–1997	1945–	
951.2506	Period as part of People's Republic, 1997–	New number	

Current Number	Current Topic	Old Topic/Comment	Old Number
951.26	**Macau**		
951.2601 to .2603	Chinese period to 1849	New number	
951.2604	Period as an overseas territory of Portugal, 1849–1999	New number	
951.2606	Period as part of People's Republic, 1999–	New number	
951.9	**Korea**		
951.9301 to .9304	[N. Korea] Historical periods	New number	
951.9501 to .9504	[S. Korea] Historical periods	New number	
953.3	**Yemen**		
953.302	622–1517	New number	
953.303	Period of Ottoman Empire, 1517–1740	New number	
953.304	1740–1918	New number	
953.3202 to .3204	622–1918	New number	
953.32052	1918–1990	New number	
953.3502	622–1517	New number	
953.3503	1517–1839	New number	
953.3504	British period, 1839–1967	New number	
953.35052	1967–1990	New number	
953.8	**Saudi Arabia**		
953.802 to .805	622–	New number	

Current Number	Current Topic	Old Topic/Comment	Old Number
954	**South Asia; India**		
954.052	1977–1999	1977–	
954.053	1999–	New number	
954.91	**Pakistan**		
954.9102 to .9103	647–1947	New number	
954.9104	1947–1971	New number	
954.9105	1971–	New number	
954.91051	1971–1988	New number	
954.91052	1988–1999	New number	
954.91053	1999–	New number	
954.92	**Bangladesh**		
954.9202 to .9203	647–1947	New number	
954.9204	1947–1971	New number	
955	**Iran**		
955.022	Period of Arab domination, 637–1055	New number	
955.024	Period of Turkish domination, 1055–1219	New number	
955.026	Period of Mongol Domination, 1219–1335	New number	
955.028	1335–1499	New number	
955.0542	Period of Khomeini, 1979–1989	Iraqi–Iranian Conflict, 1980–1988	
955.0544	Admin. of Muhammad Khatami, 1997–	New number	

Current Number	Current Topic	Old Topic/Comment	Old Number
956.1	**Turkey**		
956.10151	1300–1451	New number	
956.10152	1451–1566	New number	
956.10153	1566–1774	New number	
956.10154	1774–1918	New number	
956.9	**Syria, Lebanon, Cyprus, Israel, Jordan**		
956.901 to .905	Early history to present	New number	
956.94	**Palestine; Israel**		
956.94031	640–1096	New number	
956.94032	Period of Crusades, 1096–1291	New number	
956.94033	Mameluke period, 1291–1517	New number	
956.94034	Period of Ottoman Empire, 1517–1917	New number	
958	**Central Asia**		
958.507	[Turkmenistan] Pre–Russian period to 1855	New number	Add Note
958.508	[Turkmenistan] 1855–	New number	Add Note
958.607	[Tajikistan] Pre–Russian period to 1855	New number	Add Note
958.608	[Tajikistan] 1855–	New number	Add Note
958.707	[Uzbekistan] Pre–Russian period to 1855	New number	Add Note
958.708	[Uzbekistan] 1855–	New number	Add Note

Current Number	Current Topic	Old Topic/Comment	Old Number
959.1	**Myanmar**		
959.1051	1948–1962	New number	
959.1052	1962–1989	New number	
959.1053	1989–	New number	
959.57	**Singapore**		
959.5705	1963–	Periods of confederation with Malaysia, 1963–1965, and separate nationhood, 1965–	
959.6	**Cambodia**		
959.601	Early history to 802	New number	959.603
959.602	Period of Khmer Empire, 802–1431	New number	959.603
959.6042	1970–1993	1970–	
959.6043	1993–	New number	
959.8	**Indonesia and East Timor**		
959.86	Lesser Sunda Islands	New number	
959.87	East Timor	New number	959.86
959.8701	Early history to 1520	New number	
959.8702	1520–1945	New number	
959.8703	1945–1999	New number	
959.87031	1945–1975	New number	
959.87032	1975–1999	New number	
959.8704	1999–	New number	

960 History of Africa

As in the previous Division, the changes of history of Africa are mostly new numbers, seventy-eight out of eighty-seven. Many of these new numbers are to accommodate the passage of time, such as in South Africa, Edition 22 had the administration of Nelson Mandela 1994–, and this has been changed to 1994 to 1999 and the administration of Thabo Mbeki 1999– added as a new number. Also, many new numbers were formerly achieved through number building additions.

Table 14.6

Current Number	Current Topic	Old Topic/Comment	Old Number
960	**History of Africa**	General History of Africa	
961.2	**Libya**		
961.2022	Period of Arab rule, 644–1551	New number	
961.2024	Period of Ottoman Empire, 1551–1911	New number	
962	**Egypt**		
962.024	Mameluke period, 1250–1517	New number	
962.052	1936–1953	Reign of Fauk I, 1936–1952; Regency, 1952–1953	
962.4	**Sudan**		
962.4041	1956–1969	New number	
962.4042	Admin. of Ja'far Muhammad Numayri, 1969–1985	New number	
962.4043	1985–	New number	
963	**Ethiopia**		
963.4	Northern provinces	New number	

Current Number	Current Topic	Old Topic/Comment	Old Number
963.5	**Eritrea**		
963.501	Early history to 640	New number	
963.502	640–1543	New number	
963.503	1543–1855	New number	
963.504	1855–1889	New number	
963.5041	Reign of Theodore II, 1855–1868	New number	
963.5042	1868–1889	New number	
963.505	Period of Italian control, 1889–1941	New number	
963.506	Period of British control, 1941–1952	New number	
963.507	1952–	New number	
963.5071	Period of union with Ethiopia, 1952–1993	New number	
963.5071	Period of union with Ethiopia, 1952–1993	1952–1974	963.506
963.5072	1993–	New number	
964	**Morocco**		
964.021	647–ca. 1050	New number	
964.023	Ca. 1050–ca.1550	New number	
964.025	Ca. 1550–1830	New number	
964.051	Later portion of reign of Muhammad V, 1956–1961	New number	
964.052	Reign of Hassan II, 1961–1999	New number	
964.053	1999–	New number	
964.8	**Western Sahara**		
964.801	Early history to 1888	New number	

Current Number	Current Topic	Old Topic/Comment	Old Number
964.802	Spanish period, 1888–1976	New number	
964.803	Moroccan period, 1976–	New number	
965	**Algeria**		
965.022	Periods of Arab and Berber rule, 647–1516	New number	
965.024	Period of Ottoman Empire, 1516–1830	New number	
966.25	**Burkina Faso**		
966.25051	1960–1983	New number	
966.25052	Admin. of Thomas Sankara, 1983–1987	New number	
966.25053	1987–	New number	
966.3	**Senegal**		
966.3051	1960–2000	New number	
966.3052	2000–	New number	
966.51	**Gambia**		
966.51031	Admin. of Dawda Kairaba Jawara, 1965–1994	Admin. of Dawda Kairaba Jawara, 1965–	
966.51032	1994–	New number	
966.52	**Guinea**		
966.52051	Admin. of Ahmed Sékou Touré 1958–1984	New number	
966.52052	1984–	New number	

Current Number	Current Topic	Old Topic/Comment	Old Number
966.62	**Liberia**		
966.62031	1945–1980	New number	
966.62032	Admin. of Samuel K. Doe, 1980–1990	New number	
966.62033	1990–	New number	
966.68	**Côte d'Ivoire**		
966.68051	Admin. of Félix Houphouet–Boigny, 1960–1993	Admin. of Felix Houphouet–Boigny, 1960–	
966.68052	1993–	New number	
966.7	**Ghana**		
966.7051	1957–1979	New number	
966.7052	1979–2001	New number	
966.7053	2001–	New number	
966.9	**Nigeria**		
966.9053	1970–1999	1970–	
966.9054	1999–	New number	
967.1	**Cameroon**		
967.11041	Admin. of Ahmadou Ahidjo, 1960–1982	New number	
967.11042	Admin. of Paul Biya, 1982–	New number	
967.24	**Republic of the Congo**		
967.24053	1992–1997	1992–	
967.24054	2nd admin. of Denis Sassou Nguesso, 1997–	New number	

Current Number	Current Topic	Old Topic/Comment	Old Number
967.5	Democratic Republic of the Congo		
967.51033	Admin. of Mobutu Sese Seko, 1965–1997	Admin. of Mobutu Sese Seko, 1965–	
967.51034	1997–	New number	
967.571	**Rwanda**		
967.57101	Early history to 1899	New number	
967.57102	German period, 1899–1917	New number	
967.57103	Belgian period, 1917–1962	New number	
967.571041	1962–1973	New number	
967.571042	Admin. of Juvénal Habyarimana, 1973–1994	New number	
967.571043	1994–	New number	
967.5710431	Civil War of 1994	New number	
967.572	**Burundi**		
967.57201	Early history to 1899	New number	
967.57202	German period, 1899–1917	New number	
967.57203	Belgian period, 1917–1962	New number	
967.62	**Kenya**		
967.62042	Admin. of Daniel Arap Moi, 1978–2002	Admin. of Daniel Arap Moi, 1978–	
967.62043	Admin. of Mwai Kibaki, 2002–	New number	

Current Number	Current Topic	Old Topic/Comment	Old Number
967.8	**Tanzania**		
967.801	Early history to 1884	New number	
967.802	German period, 1884–1916	New number	
967.803	1916–1964	New number	
967.81	**Zanzibar and Pemba Regions**		
967.81041	1963–1985	New number	
967.81042	1985–	New number	
967.82	**Mainland Regions**	**Tanganyika**	
967.82041	1961–1985	New number	
967.82042	1985–	New number	
968	**South Africa**	**Southern Africa; Republic of South Africa**	
968.065	Admin. of Nelson Mandela, 1994–1999	Admin. of Nelson Mandela, 1994–	
968.066	Admin. of Thabo Mbeki, 1999–	New number	
968.2	**Gauteng, North–West, Limpopo, Mpumalanga, Former Homelands of Republic of S. Africa**	**Transvaal**	
968.205	Period of Union, 1910–1961	New number	
968.206	Period of Republic, 1961–	New number	
968.29	Former homelands	New number	

Current Number	Current Topic	Old Topic/Comment	Old Number
968.4	**KawZulu–Natal**	**Natal**	
968.405	Period of Union, 1910–1961	New number	
968,406	Period of Republic, 1961–	New number	
968.5	**Free State**	**Orange Free State**	
968.505	Period of Union, 1910–1961	New number	
968.506	Period of Republic, 1961–	New number	
968.7	**Northern, Western, Eastern Cape**	**Cape of Good Hope**	
968.705	Period of Union, 1910–1961	New number	
968.706	Period of Republic, 1961–	New number	
968.81	**Namibia**		
968.81041	Admin. of Sam Nujoma, 1990–	New number	

970 History of North America

More than three-fourths of the sixty-one modifications in this Division were new numbers. Many of them were added to reflect the passage of time, such as numbers added for 2000–. Other alterations were changes in the notations for the United States involved with the War of 1812, the Civil and Spanish-American Wars, and the Northern Territories of Canada have new numbers, which were formerly built using “adds.”

Table 14.7

Current Number	Current Topic	Old Topic/Comment	Old Number
970	**History of North America**		
971	Canada		
971.06	1911–1999	1911–	
971.064	1957–1999	1957–	
971.0648	1993–1999	1993–	
971.07	2000–	New number	
971.071	Later portion of Prime Minister Jean Chrétien, 2000–	New number	
971.104	1945–1999	1945–	
971.105	2000–	New number	
971.2	Prairie Provinces		
971.203	1945–1999	1945–	
971.204	2000–	New number	
971.3	**Ontario**		
971.304	1945–1999	1945–	
971.305	2000–	New number	
971.4	**Quebec**		
971.404	1945–1999	1945–	
971.405	2000–	New number	
971.5	**Atlantic Provinces; Maritime Provinces**		
971.504	1945–1999	1945–	
971.505	2000–	New number	

Current Number	Current Topic	Old Topic/Comment	Old Number
971.51	**New Brunswick**		
971.5104	1945–1999	1945–	
971.5105	2000–	New number	
971.6	**Nova Scotia**		
971.604	1945–1999	1945–	
971.605	2000–	New number	
971.7	**Prince Edward Island**		
971.704	1945–1999	1945–	
971.705	2000–	New number	
971.8	**Newfoundland and Labrador, Saint Pierre and Miquelon**		
971.805	2001–	New number	
971.82	**Labrador**		
971.8205	2001–	New number	
971.9	**Northern Territories**		
971.901	Early history to 1870	New number	
971.902	1870–1945	New number	
971.903	1945–1999	New number	
971.904	1999–	New number	
971.91	**Yukon Territory**		
971.9101	Early history to 1898	New number	
971.9101	Early history to 1898	1870–1898	971.9102
971.9102	1898–1945	New number	

Current Number	Current Topic	Old Topic/Comment	Old Number
971.9103	1945–1999	New number	
971.9104	1999–	New number	
971.92	**Northwest Territories (1870–1999)**	New number	
971.93	Northwest Territories (1999–)	New number	
971.95	Nunavut	New number	
972	**Middle American; Mexico**		
972.083	[Mexico] 1964–2000	1964–	
972.084	[Mexico] 2000–	New number	
972.0841	[Mexico] Admin. of Vicente Fox Quesada, 2000–	New number	972.0837
972.84	**El Salvador**		
972.84053	1979–1994	1979–	
972.84054	1994–	New number	
972.86	**Costa Rica**		
972.86051	1948–1986	New number	
972.86052	1986–	New number	
972.87	**Panama**		
972.87053	1977–1999	1977–	
972.87054	1999–	New number	
972.93	**Dominican Republic**		
972.93054	1961–2000	1961–	
972.93055	2000–	New number	

Current Number	Current Topic	Old Topic/Comment	Old Number
973	**United States**		
973.523	[War of 1812] Military operations	Operations	
973.525	[War of 1812] Naval operations	Naval history	
[973.526]	Not used	Celebrations, commem–orations, memorials	
973.527	[War of 1812] Prisoners of war, medical and social services	Medical services	973.5275
973.528	Other topics of War of 1812	Secret service and spies	973.5285
973.624	[Mexican War] Military operations	Operations	973.623
973.6242	[Mexican War] Land operations	New number	973.623
973.6245	[Mexican War] Naval operations	Naval history	973.625
[973.626]	Not used	Celebrations, commemorations, memorials	
973.627	[Mexican War] Prisoners of war, medical and social services	Medical services	973.6275
973.7415	[Civil War] African American troops	Black troops	
973.893	[Spanish–American War] Military operations	Operations	
973.895	[Spanish–American War] Naval operations	Naval history	

Current Number	Current Topic	Old Topic/Comment	Old Number
973.897	[Spanish–American War] Prisoners of war, medical and social services	Medical services	973.8975
973.92	1953–2001	1953–	
973.929	Admin. of Bill Clinton, 1993–2001	Admin. of Bill Clinton, 1993–	
973.93	2001–	New number	
973.931	Admin. of George. W. Bush, 2001–	New number	

980 History of South America

The changes in this Division are similar to those in the previous Divisions, which are mostly new numbers that reflect changes due to time. There are also modifications adjusting time periods in Peru and Venezuela.

Table 14.8

Current Number	Current Topic	Old Topic/Comment	Old Number
980	**History of South America**	**General History of South America**	
981	Brazil		
981.064	1985–2002	1985–	
981.065	Admin. of Luiz Inácio Lula da Silva, 2003–	New number	
982	**Argentina**		
982.06	1910–1999	1910–	
982.064	1973–1989	1973–	
982.065	Admin. of Carlos Saul Menem, 1989–1999	New number	
982.07	1999–	New number	

Current Number	Current Topic	Old Topic/Comment	Old Number
985	**Peru**		
985.031	1555–1599	New number	
985.032	1600–1699	New number	
985.033	1700–1808	New number	
985.063	1895–1980	1895–	
985.0631	1895–1930	1895–1933	
985.0632	1930–1968	1930–1933	985.0631
985.0633	Period of the Revolutionary Government, 1968–1980	1968–	
985.064	1980–	New number	
985.0643	Admin. of Alberto Fujimori, 1990–2000	New number	
985.0644	2000–	New number	
985.065	2000–	New number	
986.6	**Ecuador**		
986.6074	1960–2000	1960–	
986.6075	2000–	New number	
987	Venezuela		
987.062	1848–1899	1848–1864	987.061
987.0628	1870–1899	New number	
987.063	1899–1989	1899–	
987.0631	1899–1945	1899–1935	
987.06314	Admin. of Eleazar Lopez Contreras, 1935–1941	New number	987.0632
987.06315	Admin. of Isaias Medina Angarita, 1941–1945		987.0632
987.0632	1945–1958	1935–1959	

Current Number	Current Topic	Old Topic/Comment	Old Number
987.0633	1958–1989	Revolution of 1958	987.0632
987.0633	1958–1989	1959–	
987.064	1989–	New number	
987.0642	Admin. of Hugo Chavez Frias, 1998–	New number	

990 History of Other Parts of Our and Other Worlds

There are just eight revisions in this last Division of the DDC, which are in Australia, New Zealand, New Guinea, and Samoa. The latter two changes are minor modifications to the heading.

Table 14.9

Current Number	Current Topic	Old Topic/Comment	Old Number
990	**History of Other Parts of the World, of Extraterrestrial Worlds; Pacific Ocean Islands**	**General History of Other Parts of World, of Extraterrestrial Worlds; Pacific Ocean Islands**	
993	**New Zealand**		
993.03	1908–1999	Dominion period, 1908–	
993.037	1970–1984	1970–	
993.038	1984–1999	New number	
993.04	2000–	New number	
994	**Australia**		
994.065	1991–1996	1991–1999	
994.066	1996–1999	New number	994.065
995	**Melanesia; New Guinea**		
995.1	Papua	Irian Jaya	

Current Number	Current Topic	Old Topic/Comment	Old Number
996	**Other parts of Pacific; Polynesia**		
996.14	Samoa	Western Samoa	

Exercises in the Use of Class 900

Following are eleven brief descriptions of books with subjects that fall within those of the 900 Class. Utilizing all of the number building tools that have been discussed in this manual, assign classifications to each, then compare your results with those assigned by the Library of Congress found in "Answers to the Exercises" in the Appendix.

1. Biographies of immigrants to California from Central American.
2. A work on nineteenth-century travel in the Sahara.
3. A work on an American aerial reconnaissance incident in Iraq in 1994.
4. A person's experience of an avalanche in twentieth-century British Colombia.
5. An atlas of the medieval world.
6. A work on Jewish life in the Middle Ages.
7. A work on a Russian Empress of the late eighteenth century.
8. A biography of a German soldier during World War I.
9. A work on the leadership concepts of Alexander the Great.
10. An encyclopedia about T. E. Lawrence.
11. A work on spies and espionage during World War I.

Literature Cited

Dewey, Melvil. 2003. *Dewey Decimal Classification and Relative Index.* 22nd Dublin, OH: OCLC Online Computer Library Center.

15

Book Numbers

Now that the DDC classification number is assigned, the next step is to establish a book or author number. In this chapter, two book number schemes are described with examples illustrating them. The two types are Cutter-Sanborn numbers and Library of Congress author numbers. Besides these two approaches, many local or homemade systems of book number codification are often used. It should be remembered that any system of book numbers and work marks will have to be adjusted to fit into an individual library's shelf list to maintain the desired shelf order.

The Functions of Book Numbers

The DDC number by itself is not sufficient to identify a work from others in the same class. The book number is a notation used to create a shelf location for each work in a library. This unique number is a *call number*, which contains a *classification number* (if classified) and an *author notation*, which also may be called a book number or cutter number. It is possible, or even likely, that several books in a library will be classified in the same DDC number. So it is necessary to use the author number to create this unique call number. The initial letter in the book number is usually the first letter of the author's surname or the first letter of the main entry.

The most obvious function of a book number is to create a unique call number for each work in a library; however, other purposes have been pointed out by Bertha Barden in her manual *Book Numbers* (1937, 9):

1. To arrange books in order on the shelves
2. To provide a brief and accurate call number for each book

3. To locate a particular book on the shelves
4. To provide a symbol for charging books to borrowers
5. To facilitate the return of books to the shelves
6. To assist in quick identification of a book when inventories are taken

Book Number Schemes

Although the two most frequently used schemes for assigning books numbers are generally used with the classification with which they are mostly closely associated, that is not always the case. The Cutter-Sanborn method is frequently used with the DDC but has often been substituted for the LC scheme in Library of Congress call numbers. The reverse is also true, and, in addition, individual libraries may create a system to suit their collections by varying call numbers, even though the classifications for the book will nearly always be the ones assigned by LC.

Cutter Tables

The most popular book number scheme used with the DDC was devised by Charles Ammi Cutter. The notations are called cutter numbers and assigning them is referred to as "cuttering" or "to cutter." The most commonly used version of the Cutter scheme is the *Cutter-Sanborn Three-Figure Author Table,* by Kate E. Sanborn, in which the cutter scheme is altered to have three figures. The original Cutter Table had only two figures.

The Cutter Table consists of three or more initial letters from a surname, or a surname and a three-digit number. Letters E, I, J, K, O, U, Y, and Z are followed by two-digit numbers. The table is arranged as follows:

Bem	455	Chandl
Ben	456	Chandler, M.
Benc	457	Chanl
Bend	458	Chann
Bendo	459	Chant

The numbers in the center apply to the letters in each adjoining column. The cutter number includes the initial letter of the author's name and then the corresponding number. To assign a cutter number, find the letter group nearest the author's surname and combine the initial letter with the numbers. If the author's name "fits" between two cutter numbers, use the first listed in the Schedule: Bendix is B458, *not* B459. Because it falls between Bend and Bendo, the first of these is used. Thus:

Bemis	B455
Benat	B456
Bendix	B458
Chandler, L.	C455
Chandler, M.	C456
Channing	C458

Work marks or work letters are commonly used with cutter numbers to help maintain alphabetical order on the shelves and to create a unique call number for each work. The work mark is usually the first letter of the title of the work, including articles. The work mark comes *after* the book or cutter number. Thus, the call number for James Michener's *Hawaii* would be as follows:

813.5

M623h

To maintain alphabetical order, it is sometimes necessary to use two letters from the title. Thus, Michener's *Caravans* and *Centennial* would have these work marks:

813.5	813.5
M623c	M623ce

or

M623ca

In many libraries, it is a policy to classify the literary works of authors with books *about* the author and his works. The books *by* an author are generally placed before the works *about* the author and his works. Usually a letter from the end of the alphabet is placed after the cutter or book number, followed by the initial of the author of the biography or criticism. Thus, Arthur Day's *James A. Michener*, which is a critical study of Michener's work, could be classified as follows:

813.5

M623zD

Using the "z" ensures that the criticism will stand after all other works by Michener.

Another commonly used work mark identifies different editions of a work. For this purpose, either the date can be placed in the call number or a number can be placed after the work mark. Thus, if a library happened to have three editions of Michener's *Hawaii,* the editions would be distinguished as follows:

813.5	813.5	813.5
M623h	M623h2	M623h3

or

813.5	813.5	813.5
M623h	M623h	M623h
1970		1972

The use of work marks is a matter of cataloging policy in each library. Their use and application vary from library to library depending on the size of the collection and on the patrons. In all cases, work marks should be kept simple and should not be confusing.

Library of Congress Author Numbers

The author notations used with the Library of Congress classification can also be used with the DDC. The author number consists of the initial letter of the author's name or main entry followed by a number derived according to the directions given in the tables that follow. The numbers are used decimally.

1. After the initial letter **S,**

for the second letter:	a	ch	e	hi	mop	t	u
use number:	2	3	4	5	6	7–8	9

2. After the initial letters **Qu,**

for the third letter:	a	e	i	o	r	y
use number:	3	4	5	6	7	9

3. After other initial consonants, for the

second letter:	a	e	i	o	r	u	y
use number	3	4	5	6	7	8	9

4. After initial vowels,

for the second letter:	b	d	lm	n	p	r	s	tu–y
use number:	2	3	4	5	6	7	8	9

If the letters in a name do not appear in the tables, use the letter closest to it. Using this system, which is only a general outline, it is possible that an author could have different author numbers for works classified in different DDC numbers. The following examples illustrate the application of these rules:

1. Names beginning with the letter **S:**

Sabine .S2	Seaton .S4	Steel .S7
Saint .S2	Shank .S5	Storch .S7
Schaefer .S3	Shipley .S5	Sturges .S8
Schwedel .S3	Smith .S6	Sullivan .S9

2. Names beginning with the letters **Qu:**

Quabbe .Q3	Quick .Q5	Qureshi .Q7
Queener .Q4	Quoist .Q6	Quynn .Q9

3. Names beginning with other consonants:

Carter .C3	Cinelli .C5	Crocket .C7
Cecil .C4	Corbett .C6	Croft .C7
Childs .C5	Cox .C6	Cullen .C8
		Cyprus .C9

4. Names beginning with vowels:

Abernathy .A2	Ames .A4	Arundel .A7
Adams .A3	Appleby .A6	Atwater .A8
Aldrich .A4	Archer .A7	Austin .A9

Practical Use of Book Numbers

Each library will decide which book number system is the most appropriate for their collection and their users. Whether it is LC's, the Cutter Tables, or another established or homegrown system, the method chosen must be carefully followed for each call number assigned so that a logical arrangement of unique call numbers is achieved.

It should be noted that, as in other things, rules are made to be broken. Many libraries must sacrifice "unique" call numbers for various reasons and, because of a lack of staff or to expedite the process, they decide to simplify the assignment of book numbers despite the fact that all copies of a work, and even works by different authors, will have the same shelf location. In a recent tour of libraries, the author found that a public school library added just the first three letters of the main entry, which is the author's surname or the title if there is no author.

For example, for an entire series called "Power of Algebra," the following call number was used:

512

POW

Two libraries that were part of two large public library systems with centralized cataloging and processing use similar methods. One library used

364.106

FR

for books on crime with authors' name starting with Fre, Fra, and Fri. The other library used

690 690

C C

1989 1993

for the title beginning with "Complete," and the other with an author named Case.

What is appropriate for one library may not be for another, so the cataloger of classifier should use the method of creating call numbers that is most suitable for the library's collection, patrons, or even the staff.

Literature Cited

Barden, Bertha R. 1937. *Book Numbers: A Manual for Students with a Basic Code of Rules.* Chicago: American Library Association.

Cutter-Sanborn Three-Figure Author Table. Swanson-Swift Revision, 1969. Distributed by Libraries Unlimited.

Select Bibliography

Berman, Sanford. 1980. DDC 19: An Indictment. *Library Journal* 105 (5):585–89.

———. 1989. DDC 20: The Scam Continues. *Library Journal* 114 (Sept. 15):45–48.

Campbell, N., B. Murphy, and D. A. Mundie. 1994. OCLC Forest Press and the Dewey Decimal Classification. *OCLC Newsletter* 207:12–20.

Chan, Lois M. 1972. Dewey 18: Another Step in the Evolutionary Process. *Library Resources & Technical Services* 16 (3):383–99.

———. 1971. The Form Distinction in the 800 Class of the Dewey Decimal Scheme. *Library Resources & Technical Services* 15 (4):458–71.

Coates, E. J. 1995. BC2 and BSO: Presentation at the Thirty-Sixth Allerton Institute, 1994 Session on Preparing Traditional Classifications for the Future. *Cataloging & Classification Quarterly* Conference 21 (2):59–67.

Cochrane, Pauline A., and Karen Markey. 1985. Preparing for the Use of Classification in Online Cataloging Systems and in Online Catalogs. *Information Technology and Libraries* 4:91–111.

Collins, W. P. 1993. Classification for Materials on the Baha'i Religion: A "B200" Schedule Based on the Dewey Decimal Classification—Part 1. *Cataloging & Classification Quarterly* 16 (4):103–21.

———. 1993. Classification for Materials on the Baha'i Religion: A "B200" Schedule Based on the Dewey Decimal Classification—Part 2. *Cataloging & Classification Quarterly* 18 (2):71–86.

Comaromi, John P. 1976. *The Eighteen Editions of Dewey Decimal Classification.* Albany, NY: Forest Press.

———. 1981. *Book Numbers: A Historical Study and Practical Guide to Their Use.* Littleton, CO: Libraries Unlimited.

Comaromi, John P., and Mohinder Satija. 1983. *Brevity of Notation in Dewey Decimal Classification.* New Delhi: Metropolitan.

DeHart, Florence E., and Marylouise D. Meder. 1987. Structure in Computer Science: DDC Reflections. *Technical Services Quarterly* 4 (3):41–54.

Dewey, Melvil. 1985. *Dewey Decimal Classification: 004-006 Data Processing and Computer Sciences and Changes in Related Disciplines, Revision of Edition 19.* Prepared by Julianne Beal. Albany, NY: Forest Press.

Donovan, Peter W. 1975. Mathematics in a Major Library Using the Dewey Decimal Classification. *Australian Academic and Research Libraries* 6 (2):87–91.

Duncan, E. E. 1990. Using the DDC in Online Catalogs. In *Annual Review of OCLC Research,* July 1989–June 1990. Dublin, OH: OCLC.

Finni, John J., and Peter J. Paulson. 1987. The Dewey Decimal Classification Enters the Computer Age: Developing the DDC Database and Editorial Support System. *International Cataloguing* 16 (4):46–48.

Gray, R. 1982. Disasters: Natural, Nuclear, and Classificatory. *RQ* 44:42–47.

———. 1986. Are There Serendipitous Rewards in Browsing in Dewey-Classified Libraries? *Journal of Educational Media and Library Science* 24 (1):22–37.

Humphry, John A., and J. Kramer-Greene. 1984. The DDC and Its Users: Current Policies. In *Reference Services and Technical Services: Interactions in Library Practice.* New York: Haworth Press.

Jelinek, Marjorie. 1980. Twentieth Dewey: An Exercise in Prophecy. *Catalogue & Index* 58:1–2.

Library of Congress. *Cataloging Service Bulletin.* Washington, D.C.: Library of Congress.

Liu, Songqiao, and Elaine Svenonius. 1991. DORS: DDC Online Retrieval System. *Library Resources & Technical Services* 35 (4):359–75.

Markey, K. 1985. Subject-Searching Experiences and Needs of Online Catalog Users: Implications for Library Classification. *Library Resources & Technical Services* 29:34–51.

———. 1987. Searching and Browsing the Dewey Decimal Classification in an Online Catalog. *Cataloging & Classification Quarterly.* 7 (3):37–68.

Markey, K., and A. N. Demeyer. 1986. *Dewey Decimal Classification Online Project: Evaluation of a Library Schedule and Index Integrated into the Subject-Searching Capabilities of an Online Catalog.* Dublin, OH: OCLC.

Markey, K., Ann, N. Demeyer, Jeffrey Gerckens, and Daryl T. Poe. 1990. Analysis of a Bibliographic Database Enhanced with a Library Classification. *Library Resources & Technical Services* 34 (2):179–98.

McKinlay, John. 1973. Dewey and mathematics. *Australian Academic and Research Libraries* 4 (3):105–11.

Micco, M., and Xiangyu Ju. 1993. Improving Intellectual Access to Material: An Online Browser for the Dewey Decimal Classification System. In *Proceedings of 3rd ASIS SIG/CR Classification Research.* Medford, NJ: Learned Information.

Miksa, F. 1998. *The DDC, the Universe of Knowledge, and the Post-Modern Library.* Albany, NY: Forest Press.

Mitchell, J. S. 1995. DDC 21 and Beyond: The Dewey Decimal Classification Prepares for the Future. *Cataloging & Classification Quarterly* Conference 21 (2):37–47.

———. 1995. Options in the Dewey Decimal Classification System: The Current Perspective. *Cataloging & Classification Quarterly*

19 (3/4):89–103.

Olson, Hope A. 2001. Sameness and Difference: A Cultural Foundation of Classification. *Library Resources & Technical Services* 45 (3):115–22.

O'Neill, E. T., M. Dillon, and D. Vizine-Goetz. 1987. Class Dispersion Between the Library of Congress Classification and the Dewey Decimal Classification. *Journal of the American Society for Information Science* 38 (3):197–205.

Rooke, S. 1987. From 001–006: Implementing the New Dewey Schedules. *Catalogue & Index.* 86:6–8.

Schultz, Lois. 1989. Designing an Expert System to Assign Dewey Classification Numbers to Scores. In *National Online Meeting. Proceedings 1989,* New York, May 9–11, 1989. Medford, NJ: Learned Information.

Soudek, Miluse. 1980. On the Classification of Psychology in General Library Classification Schemes. *Library Resources & Technical Services* 24 (2):114–28.

Svenonius, Elaine. 1983. Use of Classification in Online Retrieval. *Library Resources & Technical Services* 27:76–80.

Tait, James A. 1972. Dewey Decimal Classification: A Vigorous Nonagenarian. *Library Review* 23 (6):227–29.

van der Merwe, M.S. 1989. Adaptation of the Dewey Decimal Classification System in South African Libraries. *South African Journal of Library and Information Science* 57 (1):34–44.

———. 1990. Comments on Dewey 20. *Mousaion* 8 (1): 22–31.

Wiegand, W. 1996. Dewey Declassified: A Revelatory Look at the "Irrepressible Reformer." *American Libraries* 27 (1):54–60.

———. 1996. *Irrepressible Reformer: A Biography of Melvil Dewey*. Chicago: American Library Association.

Appendix: Answers to the Exercises

Chapter 5—Class 000: Generalities

1. *Interactive Storytelling: Techniques for 21st Century Fiction*, by Andrew Glassner (006.7).
2. *Linux on IBM Eserver zSeries and S/390: Performance Measurement and Tuning*, by Gregory Geiselhart, et al. (005.432).
3. *Dewey Decimal Classification: A Study Manual and Number Building Guide*, by Mona L. Scott (025.431).
4. *Owning Memory: How a Caribbean Community Lost Its Archives and Found Its History*, by Jeannette Allis Bastian (027.07297).
5. *Teen Genreflecting: A Guide to Reading Interests*, by Diana Tixier Herald (016.81300809283).
6. *Host Access Client Package V4 Update*, by Byron Braswell et al. (004.678).
7. *Parallel Scientific Computation: A Structured Approach Using BSP and MPI*, by Rob H. Bisseling (004.35).
8. *Microsoft Windows Command-Line Administrator's Pocket Consultant*, by William R. Stanek (005.44682).
9. *Linux Clustering with CSM and GPFS*, by Stephen Hochstetler and Bob Beringer (005.447682).

Chapter 6—Class 100: Philosophy, Parapsychology and Ocultism, Psychology

1. *American Naturalism and Greek Philosophy*, by John P. Anton (146.0973).
2. *The Essential Edgar Cayce*, edited and introduced by Mark Thurston (133.8092).

3. *Technology in Counseling and Psychotherapy: A Practitioner's Guide*, edited by Stephen Goss and Kate Anthony (158.3028).

4. *Mesopotamian Cosmic Geography*, by Wayne Horowitz (113.0935).

5. *The Ethics of Ontology: Rethinking an Aristotelian Legacy*, by Christopher P. Long (111.092).

6. *The Greek Concept of Nature*, by Gerard Naddaf (113.0938).

7. *African-Centered Psychology: Culture-Focusing for Multicultural Competence*, edited by Daudi Ajani ya Azibo (155.8496).

8. *Imagination in the Later Middle Ages and Early Modern Times*, edited by Lodi Nauta and others (153.309).

9. *Myths of Renaissance Individualism*, by John Jeffries Martin (141.409031).

10. *Intelligence Testing and Minority Students: Foundations, Performance Factors, and Assessment Issues*, by Richard R. Valencia and Lisa A. Suzuki (153.93086930973).

Chapter 7—Class 200: Religion

1. *Journey to the Father: New Perspectives on Gender and the Bahai Revelation*, by Joell Ann Vanderwagen (297.93082).

2. *Luomisesta Jurnalan Valtakuntaan* (English): *From the Creation to the Kingdom of God: The Concept of God's Revelation by the Reform Jew Schalom Ben-Chorin in Dialogues with Christianity and Islam*, by Timo Vasko (296.3092).

3. *When the Great Abyss Opened: Classic and Contemporary Readings of Noah's Flood*, by J. David Pleins (222.1106).

4. *The Ordination of Women in the Catholic Church: Unmasking a Cuckoo's Egg Tradition*, by John Wijngaards (262.142082).

5. *Radical Religion from Shakespeare to Milton: Figures of Nonconformity in Early Modern England*, by Kristen Poole (285.90942).

6. *The Erotic Word: Sexuality, Spirituality, and the Bible*, by David Carr (220.83067).

7. *Evangelical Revivals in New Zealand: A History of Evangelical Revivals in New Zealand, and an Outline of Some Basic Principles of Revivals*, by Robert Evans and Roy McKenzi (269.0993).

8. *Cosmos and Community: The Ethical Dimension of Daoism*, by Livia Kohn (299.5145).

Chapter 8—Class 300: Social Sciences

1. *Making Allies, Making Friends: A Curriculum for Making the Peace in Middle School*, by Hugh Vasquez and others (373.0117).
2. *Iraq: Axis of Evil? Saddam Hussein and the USA*, by Kamil Mahdi (320.9567).
3. *Toxic Terror: Assessing Terrorist Use of Chemical and Biological Weapons*, edited by Jonathan B. Tucker (363.320973).
4. *Canada's Air Force: At War and Peace*, by Larry Milberry (358.400971).
5. *Transnational Television, Cultural Identity and Change: When STAR Came to India*, by Melissa Butcher (305.230954).
6. *The Indian Diaspora in Central Asia and Its Trade, 1550–1900*, by Scott C. Levi (382.0954058).
7. *Slavery and Colonial Rule in Africa*, edited by Suzanne Miers and Martin Klein (306.362096).
8. *The Role of Amphibious Warfare in British Defence Policy, 1945–56*, by Ian Speller (355.46094109044).
9. *Air Assault from the Sea*, by Patrick Allen (359.9646).
10. *The Price of Vigilance: Attacks on American Surveillance Flights*, by Larry Tart and Robert Keefe (358.450973).

Chapter 9—Class 400: Language

1. *French Grammar in Context: Analysis and Practice*, by Margaret Jubb, Annie Rouxeville (448.2421).
2. *French* [Phrasebook] (448.3421).
3. *Subliminal Spanish: The Effortless Way to Absorb 1,000 Key Words and Phrases*, by Louis Aarons (468.3421).
4. *L'Emploi adverbial des verbes de qualité et des homonymes en Chinois moderne*, by Feng Li (495.15).

5. *Conversational Arabic in 7 Days: Master Language Survival Skills in Just One Week!* by Samy Abu-Taleb (492.783421).

6. *Harrap's French and English Pocket Dictionary*, edited by Isabelle Elkaim and Stuart Fortey (443.21).

Chapter 10—Class 500: Natural Sciences and Mathematics

1. *The Amphibians and Reptiles of Arkansas*, by Stanley E. Trauth, Henry W. Robison, and Michael V. Plummer (597.909767).

2. *StarBriefs Plus: A Dictionary of Abbreviations, Acronyms, and Symbols in Astronomy and Related Space Sciences*, edited by André Heck (520.148).

3. *Debris Flows: Geologic Process and Hazard, Illustrated by a Surge Sequence at Jiangjia Ravine, Yunnan, China*, by Kevin M. Scott and Wang Yuyi (551.307095135).

4. *Natural Wonders: The Flora, Fauna & Formations of Washington,* edited by Mark Higgins (508.9797).

5. *The Great Ordovician Biodiversification Event,* edited by Barry D. Webby and others (560.1731).

6. *Establishing Long-Term Changes in Takahe Winter Feeding Grounds in Fiordland Using Pollen Analysis,* by Janet M. Wilmshurst (581.73099396).

7. *Freshwater Fishes of México*, by Robert Rush Miller (597.1760972).

Chapter 11—Class 600: Technology and Applied Sciences

1. *Partners in Play: An Adlerian Approach to Play Therapy*, by Terry Kottman (618.92891653).

2. *Women and Borderline Personality Disorder: Symptoms and Stories*, by Janet Wirth-Cauchon (616.850082).

3. *CRC Directory of Outpatient Prescribed Medications: Demographics Data Analysis 2003/2004*, by Alan B. Fleischer, Jr. and others (615.580973).

4. *Mathematics: An Applied Approach*, by Michael Sullivan and Abe Mizrahi (650.01513).
5. *Apollo 11 Rockets to Moon Landing*, by Carl R. Green (629.4540973).
6. *Sojourner: An Insider's View of the Mars Pathfinder Mission*, by Andrew Mishkin (629.43543).
7. *Focus on Kidney Cancer Research*, edited by Kelvin R. Nuñez (616.99461).
8. *Positive Options for Colorectal Cancer: Self-Help and Treatment*, by Carol Ann Larson (616.994347).

Chapter 12—Class 700: The Arts; Fine and Decorative Arts

1. *Dancing Identity: Metaphysic in Motion* (792.801).
2. *Bass Grooves: Develop Your Groove & Play Like the Pros in Any Style*, by Ed Friedland (787.5193).
3. *A Team for the Ages: Baseball's All-Time All-Star Team*, by Robert W. Cohen (796.357).
4. *Art Deco New York*, by David Garrard Lowe (720.9747109041).
5. *Popular Art Deco: Depression Era Style and Design*, by Robert Heide and John Gilman (709.7309041).
6. G*erman Expressionist Prints: The Specks Collection at the Milwaukee Museum of Art*, by Stephanie D'Alessandro and others. (769.94309041074775595).
7. *Why You Crying? My Long, Hard Look at Life, Love, and Laughter*, by George Lopez (792.7028092).
8. *How to Draw Italy's Sights and Symbols*, by Betsy Dru Tecco (743.89945).

Chapter 13—Class 800: Literature (Belles-Lettres) and Rhetoric

1. *The Goddess Rules*, by Clare Naylor (813.54).

2. *A Prescience of African Cultural Studies: The Future of Literature in Africa Is Not What It Was*, by Handel Kashope Wright (820.99607).

3. *The Way Things Look Each Day: How Poets See the World*, by Willard Spiegelman (811.00922).

4. *Poetics before Plato: Interpretation and Authority in Early Greek Theories of Poetry*, by Grace M. Ledbetter (881.0109).

5. *Rhetoric*, by Aristotle; translated by W. Rhys Roberts (808.00938).

6. *Developing Writing Skills in French*, by Graham Bishop and Bernard Haezewindt (808.0441).

7. *Hunting Unicorns*, by Bella Pollin (823.92).

Chapter 14—Class 900: Geography, History, and Auxiliary Disciplines

1. *Migra me Hizo los Mandados: The Border Patrol Ate My Dust*, compiled by Alicia Alarcon (979.400468728).

2. *Skeletons on the Zahara: A True Story of Survival*, by Dean King (916.48041).

3. *A Chain of Events: The Government Cover-up of the Black Hawk Incident and the Friendly Fire Death of Lt. Laura Piper*, by Joan L. Piper (956.70444).

4. *In the Path of an Avalanche: A True Story*, by Vivien Bowers (971.168).

5. *Atlas of the Medieval World*, by Rosamond McKitterick (909.070223).

6. *Jewish Life in the Middle Ages*, by Israel Abrahams (940.04924).

7. *Catherine the Great and the Enlightenment in Russia*, by Nancy Whitelaw (947.063092).

8. *Corporal Hitler and the Great War 1914–1918, The List Regiment*, by John F. Williams (940.413433092).

9. *The Wisdom of Alexander the Great: Enduring Leadership Lessons from the Man Who Created an Empire*, by Lance B. Kurke (938.07092).

10. *Lawrence of Arabia: An Encyclopedia*, by Stephen E. Tabachnick (940.415092).

11. *Super Spies of World War I*, by Kate Walker and Elaine Argaet (940.4850922).

Index

004–006 Data Processing and Computer Science and Changes in Related Disciplines, 106

Adaptability, 19, 323–24
"Add area notation," 5
Add from notes, 31
Add notes, 6, 30
Add to notes, 30–31
Aesthetics (111.85), 121
Africa, history of (960)
  revisions, 304–10
  summary and details, 281, 282
Agriculture and Related Technologies (630)
  revisions, 249
  summary and details, 238, 239–40
Alaska, geographic areas, historical periods, persons (Table 2), revisions, 81
Algeria, history of (965), revisions, 306
American Library Association, 8
  International Relations Office, 10
American Literature in English (810), 275
American native peoples and languages (Tables 5 and 6), 26
Ancient World, history of (930)
  revisions, 286–87
  summary and details, 281, 282
Animals (590)
  revisions, 231–35
  summary and details, 210, 212
Anthropology, 121
Applied Sciences. *See* Technology and Applied Sciences (Class 600)
Architecture (720)
  revisions, 267
  summary and details, 262, 263
Argentina, history of (982), revisions, 315
Arts: Fine and Decorative Arts (700)
  revisions, 266–67
  summary and details, 262
Arts: Fine and Decorative Arts (Class 700)
  exercises, 271–72
  number building, 265
  revisions, 266–71
  summary and details, 262–65
Asia, history of (950)
  revisions, 299–303
  summary and details, 281, 282
Asia Foundation, 10
Associations (360)
  revisions, 187
  summary and details, 147, 148, 151
Astronomy and Allied Sciences (520)
  revisions, 220
  summary and details, 210
Atlantic islands, history of (990), 282
Atlantic Provinces, history of (971.5), revisions, 311
Australia, history of (994)
  revisions, 317
  summary and details, 282
Austria, history of (943.6), revisions, 295–96
Author notations, 319
Author numbers, 319, 322–23
Author's intent, 29
Autobiographies, 28
Auxiliary Tables, 27

Bangladesh, history of (954.92), revisions, 301
Barden, Bertha, 319
Base numbers, 27, 29
Beall, Julianne, 106
Bible (220)
  revisions, 139
  summary and details, 130–31

Bibliographies (010)
revisions, 113–14
summary and details, 108, 109
Biographies, 28
Biography (920)
revisions, 286
summary and details, 281, 282
Biology (570)
revisions, 230–31
summary and details, 210
Black Sea and Caucasus Regions to 640, history of (939.5), revisions, 287
Bloomberg, Marty, 19, 105, 129, 273–74
Book number schemes, 320–23
Book numbers
Cutter tables, 320–22
functions of, 319–20
Library of Congress author numbers, 322–23
practical use of, 323–24
schemes, 320–23
Book Numbers, 319
Bosnia, revisions
geographic areas, historical periods, persons (Table 2), 57
history of (949.7), 299
British Isles, history of (941), revisions, 293
Broad classification, 19
Broxis, Peters, 261
Buildings (690), 238, 241
Burkina Faso, history of (966.25), revisions, 306
Burundi, history of (967.572), revisions, 308
Butcher, Peter, 237

Call numbers, 319
Cambodia, history of (959.6), revisions, 303
Cameroon, history of (967.1), revisions, 307
Canada, geographic areas, historical periods, persons (Table 2), revisions, 70–79
Carnegie Corporation, 8
Catalogs (010), revisions, 114
Catalogue & Index, 11
Causation (120), 122
Centered entries, 18–19
Central Asia, history of (958), revisions, 302
Chemical Engineering and Related Technologies (660)
revisions, 257–58
summary and details, 238, 240–41
Chemistry and Allied Sciences (540)
revisions, 26, 221–27
summary and details, 201, 211
Christian Church, Denominations and Sects of (280)
revisions, 139
summary and details, 130, 132
Christian Church, Local (250), 130, 131
Christian Moral and Devotional Theology (240)
revisions, 139
summary and details, 130, 131
Christian Religious Orders (250), 130, 131
Christian Social and Ecclesiastical Theology (260)
revisions, 139
summary and details, 130, 131–32
Christian Theology (230), 130, 131
Christianity, Historical, Geographic, Persons Treatment of (270)
revisions, 139
summary and details, 130
Christianity (230), 130, 131
Church History (270), 130, 132
Citation order, 27
Civil and Landscape Art (710), 262
Civil engineering (624), revisions, 247–48
Class elsewhere notes, 30
Class here notes, 30
Class numbers, 21
Classical Greek Languages (480), 197
Classification, book, 27–29
Classification numbers, 319
Close classification, 19
Collections (080)
revisions, 119
summary and details, 108, 110

Colombia, geographic areas, historical periods, persons (Table 2), revisions, 82
Colorado, geographic areas, historical periods, persons (Table 2), revisions, 80–81
Comaromi, John Phillip, 8, 24, 177, 197
Commerce (380)
  revisions, 188, 190–92
  summary and details, 147, 148, 151
Communications (380)
  revisions, 188, 192
  summary and details, 148, 151
Communities (307), revisions, 162
Comprehensive works, 25
Computer Art (770)
  revisions, 268–69
  summary and details, 262, 264
Computer sciences (004–006)
  revisions, 26, 105–8, 111–13
  summary and details, 108–9
Congo, Republic of the, history of (967.24), revisions, 307–8
Corsica, geographic areas, historical periods, persons (Table 2), revisions, 56
Costa Rica, history of (972.86), revisions, 313
Côte d 'Ivoire, history of (966.68), revisions, 307
Council on Library Resources, 10
Croatia, revisions
  geographic areas, historical periods, persons (Table 2), 57
  history of (949.7), 299
Culture and Institutions (306), revisions, 26, 158–61
Cultures, 2, 7, 133
Custer, Benjamin A., 4, 5, 8, 11, 24, 147–48
Customs (390)
  classification of, 147
  revisions, 192–94
  summary and details, 148, 151–52
Cutter, Charles Ammi, 320
Cutter-Sanborn Three-Figure Author Table, 320
Cutter tables, 320–22
Cutter's Expansive Classification, 8
Cyprus, history of (956.9), revisions, 302
Czech Republic, revisions
  geographic areas, historical periods, persons (Table 2), 52–53
  history of (943.7), 296

Dalmatian Language (450), 197
Dalmatian Languages, Literatures of (850), 275
Data processing. *See* Computer sciences (004–006)
DDC
  hierarchical order, 17–19
  structure (schedules), 17
  theory of knowledge, 15–16
"De-slot-ification," 8
Decimal Classification Division, 8
Decimal Classification Editorial Policy Committee (EPC), 8
Denmark, history of (948.9), revisions, 298
Dewey, Melvil, 1, 8, 11, 21
Diaries, 28
Disciplines, 20, 21
Discontinuations, 24
"Divide like," 5, 6
Divisions, 18
Documentary media (070), 108
Dominican Republic, revisions
  geographic areas, historical periods, persons (Table 2), 80
  history of (972.93), 313
Drawing and Decorative Arts (740)
  revisions, 267–68
  summary and details, 262, 263

Earth Sciences (550)
  revisions, 26, 227–29
  summary and details, 201, 211
East Timor, revisions
  geographic areas, historical periods, persons (Table 2), revisions, 60
  history of (959.8), 303
Economics (330)
  revisions, 147, 166–76
  summary and details, 148, 149

Ecuador, revisions,
  geographic areas, historical periods, persons (Table 2), 83
  history of (986.6), 316
Editorial Policy Committee, 8, 12
Education (370)
  revisions, 188, 189–90
  summary and details, 148, 151
Educational media (070), 108
Egypt, revisions
  geographic areas, historical periods, persons (Table 2), 60
  history of (962), 304
El Salvador, history of (972.84), revisions, 313
Elementary education (372), revisions, 189–90
Encyclopedic works (030)
  revisions, 116
  summary and details, 108, 109
Engineering and Allied Operations (620)
  revisions, 246–48
  summary and details, 238, 239
England, geographic areas, historical periods, persons (Table 2), revisions, 48–49
English and Old English (Anglo-Saxon) Literatures (820), 275
English and Old English Language (420), 197
Epistemology (120), 121, 122
Eritrea, history of (963.5), revisions, 305
Ethics (170)
  revisions, 126–27
  summary and details, 121, 122, 123–24
Ethiopia, revisions
  geographic areas, historical periods, persons (Table 2), 61
  history of (963), 304
Etiquette (390)
  classification of, 147
  revisions, 192–93
  summary and details, 148, 152
Europe, history of (940)
  revisions, 288–99
  summary and details, 281, 282
Exercises
  answers to, 329–35
  Arts: Fine and Decorative Arts (Class 700), 271–72
  Generalities (Class 000), 119
  History, Geography, and Auxiliary Disciplines (Class 900), 318
  Language (Class 400), 207–8
  Literature (Belles-Lettres) and Rhetoric (Class 800), 279
  Natural Sciences (Class 500), 235
  Philosophy, Parapsychology and Occultism, Psychology (Class 100), 127–28
  Religion (Class 200), 144–45
  Social Sciences (Class 300), 194–95
  Technology and Applied Sciences (Class 600), 258
Expansions, 23
Extraterrestrial Worlds, History of (990)
  revisions, 317
  summary and details, 282

Faceted classification, 261
Facets, 18–19, 27, 30–31
Far East, history of (950)
  revisions, 299
  summary and details, 281, 282
Fédération Internationale d'Information et de Documentation (FID), 11
Fellows, Dorkas, 11
Ferguson, Milton, 11
Finland, history of (948.9), revisions, 298
Folklore (390)
  classification of, 147
  revisions, 147, 192–93
  summary and details, 148, 152
Forest Press, 3, 4, 6, 8, 10
Form, 28
Form Divisions, 35
France, revisions
  geographic areas, historical periods, persons (Table 2), 53–56
  history of (944), 296
Freitag, Wolfgang, 261

French Language (440)
revisions, 203
summary and details, 197
French Literature (840), 275

Gambia, history of (966.51), revisions, 306
Genealogy (920), 281, 282
General subjects, 28
Generalia, 15
Generalities (Class 000)
exercises, 119
number building, 110
revisions, 111–19
summary and details, 108–10
Geographical Divisions, 35
Geographical locations, 28
Geography, (900)
revisions, 283–86
summary and details, 281, 282
Geography (Class 900)
exercises, 318
number building, 283
revisions, 283–318
summary and details, 281–82
German Languages (430), revisions, 201
German Literature (830)
revisions, 277
summary and details, 275
Germanic Languages, Literatures of (830)
revisions, 277
summary and details, 275
Germanic Languages (430)
revisions, 201–3
summary and details, 197
Germany, NE, History of (943.1), revisions, 294–95
Germany, revisions
geographic areas, historical periods, persons (Table 2), 51–52
history of (943), 293–94
Ghana, history of (966.7), revisions, 307
Graphic Arts (760), 262, 264
Greek Literature, Classical (880), 275
Guinea, history of (966.52), revisions, 306
Guyana, geographic areas, historical periods, persons (Table 2), revisions, 83

Haykin, David, 11
Health (610)
revisions, 26, 242–45
summary and details, 238
Hellenic Languages, Literatures of (880), 275
Hellenic Languages (480), 197
Hercegovina, revisions
geographic areas, historical periods, persons (Table 2), 57
history of (949.7), 299
Hierarchical order, 17–19
Higher education (378), revisions, 190
Historical Periods (930–990), 26
History, realm of, 15, 16
History (900)
revisions, 283–86
summary and details, 281, 282
History, Geography, and Auxiliary Disciplines (Class 900)
exercises, 318
number building, 283
revisions, 283–318
summary and details, 281–82
Home and Family Management (640)
revisions, 249–52
summary and details, 238, 240
Hong Kong, history of (951.25), revisions, 299
Humankind (120), 122

Iceland, history of (949.12), revisions, 298
Illinois, geographic areas, historical periods, persons (Table 2), revisions, 80
Imagination, realm of, 15, 16
India, revisions
geographic areas, historical periods, persons (Table 2), 58
history of (954), 301
Indonesia, history of (959.8), revisions, 303

Inland waterway and ferry transportation (386), revisions, 192
Insignia (920), 281, 282
International Classification, 11
International commerce (382), revisions, 192
Internet, 7
Iran, revisions
  geographic areas, historical periods, persons (Table 2), 58–59
  history of (955), 301
Israel, history of (956.9), revisions, 302
Italian Language (450)
  revisions, 204
  summary and details, 197
Italian Languages and Literatures of (850), 275
Italic Languages and Literatures of (870), 275
Italic Languages (470), 197
Italy, 56–57
Italy, ancient history of (937), revisions, 287
Italy and Adjacent Areas, history of (945), revisions, 296

Jordan, revisions
  geographic areas, historical periods, persons (Table 2), 59
  history of (956.9), 302
Journalism (070)
  revisions, 117–18
  summary and details, 108, 109
Jurisdiction. *See* Law (340)

Knowledge, theory of, 15–16
Korea, history of (951.9), revisions, 300

Labrador, history of (971.82), revisions, 312
Lake Placid Club Education Foundation, 3
Landscape Art (710), 262–63
Language, classifying by, 28
Language (400)
  revisions, 199
  summary and details, 197
Language (Class 400)
  exercises, 207–8
  number building, 198–99
  revisions, 199–207
  summary and details, 197–98
Languages, Other (490)
  revisions, 204–7
  summary and details, 197
Latin Languages (470), 197
Latin Literature (870), 275
Law (340)
  revisions, 26, 147, 176–86
  summary and details, 148, 149–50
Lebanon, history of (956.9), revisions, 302
Liberia, history of (966.62), revisions, 307
Library and Information Sciences (020)
  revisions, 114–16
  summary and details, 108, 109
Library Association, 10
Library of Congress
  author numbers, 322–23
  cards, 8–9
  Decimal Classification Division, 8, 12
  and Dewey Decimal System, 8–10
Libya, history of (961.2), revisions, 304
Lichtenstein, history of (943.6), revisions, 295–96
Life Sciences (570)
  revisions, 230–31
  summary and details, 210, 212
Linguistics (410)
  revisions, 199–201
  summary and details, 197, 198
Literature, classifying, 28
Literature (Belles-Lettres) and Rhetoric (800)
  revisions, 277
  summary and details, 275
Literature (Belles-Lettres) and Rhetoric (Class 800)
  exercises, 279
  number building, 276
  precedence of, 15
  revisions, 276–78
  summary and details, 275–76

Literatures of other Specific Languages and Language Families (890)
  revisions, 277–78
  summary and details, 275, 276
Logic (160), 121, 122, 123

Macau, history of (951.26), revisions, 300
Macedonia, history of (949.7), revisions, 299
Madedonia, geographic areas, historical periods, persons (Table 2), revisions, 57
Main classes, 18
Malta, history of (945), revisions, 296
Management and Auxiliary Services (650)
  revisions, 252–57
  summary and details, 238, 240
Manual (DDC), 22–23, 26, 227, 274
Manual on the Use of the Dewey Decimal Classification: Edition 19, 6
Manufacture of Products for Specific Uses (680), 238, 241
Manufacturing (670), 238, 241
Manuscripts (090), 108, 110
Maritime Provinces, history of (971.5), revisions, 311
Mathematics (510)
  revisions, 26, 213–20
  summary and details, 209, 210
Mazney, Constantin, 9
Medicine and Health (610)
  revisions, 26, 242–45
  summary and details, 238
Melanesia, history of (995), revisions, 317
Memory, realm of, 15, 16
Mental faculties, 121
Metaphysics (110), 121, 122
Mexico, history of (972), revisions, 313
Middle East, history of (939.4), revisions, 287
Middle English (420), revisions, 201
Military Science (350)
  revisions, 186
  summary and details, 148, 150
Mind and body, 121
Mitchell, Joan S., 8
Monaco, revisions
  geographic areas, historical periods, persons (Table 2), 56
  history of (944), revisions, 296
Montenegro, revisions
  geographic areas, historical periods, persons (Table 2), 57
  history of (949.7), 299
Morocco, revisions
  geographic areas, historical periods, persons (Table 2), 61–62
  history of (964), 305
Museology (060), 108, 109
Music (780)
  revisions, 269–70
  summary and details, 262, 264
Myanmar, history of (959.1), revisions, 303

Namibia, history of (968.81), revisions, 310
Natural Sciences (Class 500)
  exercises, 235
  number building, 213
  revisions, 213–35
  summary and details, 209–12
New Brunswick, history of (971.51), revisions, 312
New Guinea, revisions
  geographic areas, historical periods, persons (Table 2), 84
  history of (995), 317
New York, 80
New Zealand, history of (993)
  revisions, 317
  summary and details, 282
Newfoundland, history of (971.8), revisions, 312
News media (070), 108, 109
Nicaragua, geographic areas, historical periods, persons (Table 2), revisions, 79
Nigeria, revisions
  geographic areas, historical periods, persons (Table 2), 62
  history of (966.9), 307

North Africa, history of to ca. 640
(939.7), revisions, 287
North America, history of (970)
revisions, 310–15
summary and details, 282
Northern Territories, history of (971.9),
revisions, 312
Northwest Territories, history of
(971.92), revisions, 313
Norway, revisions
geographic areas, historical periods,
persons (Table 2), 57
history of (948.1), 297
Notes, 29–31
Nova Scotia, history of (971.6),
revisions, 312
Number building
Arts: Fine and Decorative Arts (Class
700), 265
Generalities (Class 000), 110
History, Geography, and Auxiliary
Disciplines (Class 900), 283
Language (Class 400), 198–99
Literature (Belles-Lettres) and
Rhetoric (Class 800), 276
Natural Sciences (Class 500), 213
Philosophy, Parapsychology and
Occultism, Psychology (Class
100), 124–25
principles of, 27–34
Religion (Class 200), 132
Social Sciences (Class 300), 152
Technology and Applied Sciences
(Class 600), 241–42
theory of, 29–33

Occultism (100, 130), 122
Ontario, history of (971.3), revisions,
311
Options, 33
Oregon, 81
Organizations (060), 108, 109
Orient, history of (950)
revisions, 299
summary and details, 281, 282

Pacific Ocean islands, History of (990)
revisions, 317–18
summary and details, 282
Painting and Paintings (750)
revisions, 268
summary and details, 262, 263–64
Pakistan, history of (954.91), revisions,
301
Paleontology (560)
revisions, 230
summary and details, 210, 211–12
Paleozoology (560)
revisions, 230
summary and details, 210, 211–12
Palestine, history of (956.94), revisions,
302
Panama, revisions
geographic areas, historical periods,
persons (Table 2), 79
history of (972.87), 313
Paraguay, geographic areas, historical
periods, persons (Table 2),
revisions, 84
Paranormal phenomena (130), 121
Parapsychology (100, 130)
revisions, 125
summary and details, 122–23
Partial relocations, 25
Performing Arts (790), 262, 264
Persons, new numbers for, 44
Peru, revisions
geographic areas, historical periods,
persons (Table 2), 81–82
history of (985), 316
Philosophy, Ancient, Medieval, Eastern
(180), 122, 124
Philosophy, Modern Western and other
Non-Eastern (190)
revisions, 126, 127
summary and details, 122, 124
Philosophy, Parapsychology and
Occultism, Psychology (Class
100)
exercises, 127–28
number building, 124–25
revisions, 125–27
summary and details, 122–24
Philosophy, specific schools and
viewpoints (140), 122, 123

Philosophy and theory of religion (210), 130
Photography (770)
revisions, 268
summary and details, 262, 264
Physics, applied (621), revisions, 246–47
Physics (530)
revisions, 220
summary and details, 210, 211
Plants (580)
revisions, 231
summary and details, 210, 212
Plastic Arts (730)
revisions, 267
summary and details, 262
Poland, geographic areas, historical periods, persons (Table 2), revisions, 53
Polar areas, history of (998), 282
Political Science (320)
revisions, 147, 162–65
summary and details, 148, 149
Polynesia, history of (996), revisions, 318
Portuguese Language (460)
revisions, 204
summary and details, 197
Portuguese Languages, Literatures of (860), 275
Preference Notes, 27
Preference Order, 27
Prince Edward Island, history of (971.7), revisions, 312
Printmaking and Prints (760), 262, 264
Provence-Côte d'Azur, geographic areas, historical periods, persons (Table 2), revisions, 56
Psychology (100), 122
Psychology (150)
revisions, 121, 125–26
summary and details, 122, 123
Public Administration (350)
revisions, 186–87
summary and details, 148, 150
Public Administration and Military Science (350), 147
Publishing (070), 108, 109
Quebec, history of (971.4), revisions, 311

Race, 7
Rare materials (090), 108, 110
Reason, realm of, 15, 16
Recreation (790)
revisions, 270–71
summary and details, 262, 264–65
Reductions, 24
Relative Index, 19–21, 33, 106
Religion, philosophy and theory of (210)
revisions, 138
summary and details, 130
Religion (200), revisions, 133—38
Religion (Class 200)
exercises, 144–45
number building, 132
revisions, 26, 133–44
summary and details, 130–32
Religions, Non-Christian (290)
revisions, 140–44
summary and details, 130, 132
Religious bias, 2, 6, 26, 129, 133
Relocations, 24–25
Reminiscences, 28
Revisions in *DDC 22*
Arts: Fine and Decorative Arts (Class 700), 266–71
Ethnic and National Groups (Table 5), 93–95
Generalities (Class 000), 111–19
Geographic Areas, Historical Periods, Persons (Table 2), 43–84
History, Geography, and Auxiliary Disciplines (Class 900), 283–318
Language (Class 400), 199–207
Languages (Table 6), 96–103
Literature (Belles-Lettres) and Rhetoric (Class 800), 276–78
Mathematics (510), 213–20
Natural Sciences (Class 500), 213, 220–35

Revisions in *DDC 22* (*Cont.*)
Philosophy, Parapsychology and Occultism, Psychology (Class 100), 125–27
Religion (Class 200), 133–44
Social Sciences (Class 300), 152–94
Standard Subdivisions (Table 1), 39–40
Subdivisions for the Arts, for Individual Literatures, for Specific Literary Forms (Table 3), 87–88
Subdivisions of Individual Languages and Language Families (Table 4), 89–91
Technology and Applied Sciences (Class 600), 242–58
Rhaeto-Romanic Languages, Literatures of (850), 275
Rhaeto-Romanic Languages (450), 197
Romance Languages, Literatures of (840)
revisions, 277
summary and details, 275
Romance Languages (440)
revisions, 204
summary and details, 197
Romanian Language (450), 197
Romanian Languages, Literatures of (850), 275
Rwanda, history of (967.571), revisions, 308

Sahara, Western, history of (964.8), revisions, 305–6
Sanborn, Kate E., 320
Sardinian Language (450), 197
Sardinian Languages, Literatures of (850), 275
Saudi Arabia, history of (953.8), revisions, 300
Scandinavia, history of (948), revisions, 296–98
Scatter relocations, 25
Schedules
and DDC structure, 17
instructions, 27, 30, 33
and number building, 27
and Tables, 31–32
Scope notes, 29
Scotland, geographic areas, historical periods, persons (Table 2), revisions, 44–48
Sculpture (730)
revisions, 267
summary and details, 262, 263
Secondary education (373), revisions, 190
Sections, 18
Segmenting, 33
Senegal, history of (966.3), revisions, 306
Serbia, revisions
geographic areas, historical periods, persons (Table 2), 57
history of (949.7), 299
Serial publications (050)
revisions, 117
summary and details, 108, 109
Seymour, Evelyn (May), 11
Shelflist, 10
Singapore, history of (959.57), revisions, 303
"Slot-ification," 3, 4, 17
Slovakia, revisions
geographic areas, historical periods, persons (Table 2), 52–53
history of (943.7), 296
Slovenia, revisions
geographic areas, historical periods, persons (Table 2), 57
history of (949.7), 299
Social Groups (305), revisions, 26, 154–58
Social Problems and Services (360)
revisions, 187–88
summary and details, 148, 150
Social Sciences (300), revisions, 153—54
Social Sciences (Class 300)
exercises, 194–95
number building, 152
revisions, 152–94
summary and details, 148–52
South Africa, history of (968), revisions, 309–10

South Africa, Republic of, geographic areas, historical periods, persons (Table 2), revisions, 63–70
South America, history of (980)
revisions, 315–17
summary and details, 282
South Asia, history of (954), revisions, 301
Spain, autonomous communities of, 61
Spanish Language (460)
revisions, 204
summary and details, 197
Spanish Languages, Literatures of (860), 275
Spanish Literature (860), 275
Specific numbers, 28
Split relocations, 25
Standard Subdivisions. *See* Table 1. Standard Subdivisions
Statistics, Collections of General (310)
revisions, 153
summary and details, 148, 149
Subjects, 20, 21, 28
Sudan, revisions
geographic areas, historical periods, persons (Table 2), 60
history of (962.4), 304
Suriname, geographic areas, historical periods, persons (Table 2), revisions, 84
Sweden, history of (948.5), revisions, 297–98
Switzerland, geographic areas, historical periods, persons (Table 2), revisions, 57
Syria, history of (956.9), revisions, 302

Table 1. Standard Subdivisions, 32, 36–40
citation order, 37–39
and facets, 19
instructions, 27
revisions, 39–40
summary and applications, 37
and Table 7, 26
Table 2. Geographic Areas, Historical Periods, Persons, 32, 41–84
and Divisions 420–480, 198
revisions, 26, 43–84
summary and applications, 41–43
Table 3. Subdivisions for the Arts, for Individual Literatures, for Specific Literary Forms, 32, 85–88
and Class 800, 274
revisions, 87–88
Table 3A, 85
Table 3B, 86
Table 3C, 86
Table 4. Subdivisions of Individual Languages and Language Families, 32, 88–91
and Class 400, 198–99
revisions, 89–91
summary and applications, 89
Table 5. Ethnic and National Groups, 32, 92–95
revisions, 93–95
summary and applications, 92
Table 6. Languages, 32–33, 95–103
revisions, 96–103
summary and applications, 95–96
Table 7, 26
Tables of Precedence, 5–6
Tanzania, history of (967.8), revisions, 309
Tanzania, mainland regions of, geographic areas, historical periods, persons (Table 2), revisions, 63
Technology and Applied Sciences (600), 238
Technology and Applied Sciences (Class 600)
exercises, 258
number building, 241–42
revisions, 242–58
summary and details, 238–41
Theology. *See* Religion (Class 200)
Topics, 20, 21
Transportation (380)
revisions, 188, 192
summary and details, 148, 151
Travel (910)
revisions, 285–86
summary and details, 281

Turkey, revisions
geographic areas, historical periods, persons (Table 2), 59
history of (956.1), 302

United States, history of (973), revisions, 314–15
Universal Decimal Classification (UDC), 11, 36

Venezuela, history of (987), revisions, 316–17
Virginia, geographic areas, historical periods, persons (Table 2), revisions, 80

Wales, geographic areas, historical periods, persons (Table 2), revisions, 49–51
Washington, geographic areas, historical periods, persons (Table 2), revisions, 81
Weber, Hans, 19, 105, 129, 273–74
West Bank, geographic areas, historical periods, persons (Table 2), revisions, 59
Western Europe, history of (940), 281, 282
Work marks, 321–22
World War I, 1914–1918 (940.3-.4), revisions, 288–89
World War II, 1939–1945 (940.53–.54), revisions, 289–93
World Wide Web, 7

Yemen, history of (953.3), revisions, 300
Yugoslavia, history of (949.7), revisions, 299
Yukon Territory, history of (971.91), revisions, 312–13

About the Author

MONA L. SCOTT is currently Head of the Joint Personnel Recovery Library at Ft. Belvoir, Virginia. She was previously Head of Technical Services at the Bureau of the Census Library and NASA/Goddard Space Flight Center Library. This is the second edition of this book to be published, and soon the third edition of Conversion Tables: LC-Dewey, Dewey-LC will be in print.

Lightning Source UK Ltd.
Milton Keynes UK
172631UK00017B/4/P